Praise for *On the Hunt for Great Companies*

"Simon Kold is a clear and rational thinker in the mold of Charlie Munger. And he has a clear grasp of the many fallacies of thinking that are rife in the investment world. Armed with these, he dives deep into the critical factors that define business quality.

Unlike my book - which addresses the inner game of investing, Kold's book carefully examines all the factors that contribute to business quality. Any reader will come away with a better set of mental frameworks to use in searching for and evaluating business quality.

Kold's book is a must read for all serious investors and will certainly take its place along side other greats – especially other practically oriented books – like the Outsiders by Thorndike and Margin of Safety by Seth Klarman."

—**Guy Spier**, Author of *The Education of a Value Investor*

"Kold provides an excellent framework to help investors navigate the treacherous path toward investment success. This book will help both sophisticated professional investors and beginners achieve their investment objectives."

—**Brian C. Rogers**, Retired Chairman and CIO of T. Rowe Price

"Long-term fundamental value investing in high quality companies is the best way to generate consistent returns. Simon Kold has the track record to shed light on the key elements of this strategy."

—**Kasim Kutay**, CEO of Novo Holdings

"Having personally worked with Simon Kold, I can attest to his investment acumen and the analytical rigor displayed in this sophisticated yet entertaining investment book."

—**Bjarne Graven Larsen**, Founder of Qblue Balanced and former CIO of ATP and Ontario Teachers' Pension Plan

"I've read (and written) my fair share of dry, technical tomes on finance. *On the Hunt for Great Companies* is an inspiring, very practical and wonderful written book on identifying 'alpha return' companies."

—**Thomas Plenborg**, Professor at Copenhagen
Business School & Chairman of DSV

"*On the Hunt for Great Companies* is not only a thoughprovoking and refreshing take on the arduous journey of the true value investor, it is a reflection of what I have seen Simon Kold practice throughout the years I've known him."

—**Salah Saabneh**, Partner at Manikay Partners and former
Chairman of Tel Aviv Stock Exchange

On the Hunt for Great Companies

On the Hunt for Great Companies

An Investor's Guide to Evaluating Business Quality and Durability

Simon Kold

WILEY

Published by John Wiley & Sons, Inc., Hoboken, New Jersey.
Published simultaneously in Canada.

For general information on our other products and services or for technical support, please
contact our Customer Care Department within the United States at (800) 762-2974, outside
the United States at (317) 572-3993 or fax (317) 572-4002.

Wiley also publishes its books in a variety of electronic formats. Some content that appears
in print may not be available in electronic formats. For more information about Wiley
products, visit our web site at www.wiley.com.

Library of Congress Cataloging-in-Publication Data is Available:

ISBN 9781394285747 (Cloth)
ISBN 9781394285761 (ePDF)
ISBN 9781394285754 (ePub)

Cover Design: Thomas Nery
Cover Image: © Elymas/Shutterstock
Author Photo: Courtesy of Simon Kold
SKY10083885_090524

Contents

Acknowledgments

A t first I was afraid, I was petrified. Kept thinking I could never write this book without you by my side. But then I spent so many nights thinking about our editorial ping-pong. And I grew strong. And I learned how to get along. . . All jokes aside, I declare, without your help, this book would be absolutely nowhere. So thank you, for your golden touch, your feedback, and suggestions, meant so much. Thank you Alexander Pichler, Alex Petrin, Amir Saabneh, Anders Morgenstierne, Andrew Burns, Ashwin Aravindhan, Beeneet Kothari, Brian Rogers, Christopher Kjær Hansen, Claudine Innes, Daniel Ong Jia Qiang, Helen Gaffney, Henrik Kjær Hansen, Jakob B. Møller, Joachim Fogh, Johan Brønnum-Schou, Johannes Brenner, Jonathan Macklin, Josh Shores, Kasim Kutay, Kristian Korsgaard, Kaare Danielsen, Leo Zhong Li, Lil Oliefyr, Mads Horsted, Matthew Brown, Morten Kristiansen, Nataly Vukubrat, Niklas Landin Olsen, Dr. Nikolaus Werhahn, Nima Shayegh, Ole Søeberg, Per la Cour, Pieter Verrecas, Salah Saabneh, Sizi Chen, Sofia Hou, Stefan Culibrk, Steffen Jørgensen, Søren Funch Adamsen, Thomas Plenborg, Tiantian Lee, Tilman Versch, Victor Berg, Yash Bhatnagar, and Zi Hao Tan. Special thanks to those who helped me review multiple iterations or read the agonizing early versions.

Special thanks to Thomas Plenborg for encouraging me to use my humor in the book. I apologize to everyone for my bad execution of this idea.

Clearly, I must have ignored any sensible feedback I got on this, and none of the persons listed above should be held responsible. Thanks to my agent John Willig for good content feedback and for getting me an incredible publisher. Thanks to my wonderful editor Judith Newlin, managing editor Richard Samson, and all their colleagues at Wiley for believing in the book and for excellent support. Thanks to Sunnye Collins and Sheryl Nelson for great editorial inputs.

Thanks to all my former colleagues at Novo Holdings, especially to Morten Beck Jørgensen and Johan Brønnum-Schou for enduring a decade of my drollery.

Finally, thanks to my dear family. Thanks to my wife for tolerating this book spoiling so many mornings, weekends, and holidays. Thanks to my parents, especially my mom, for helping out so much with the kids and for the immense supply of frozen meatballs.

List of Figures

List of Tables

List of
"Let's Sniff Around"

Chapter 1: Passion

Chapter 2: Long-term Incentives

Chapter 3: Capital Allocation

Chapter 4: Reliable Communication

Chapter 5: Economies of Scale

Chapter 6: Switching Costs

Chapter 7: Network Effects

Chapter 8: Brand Advantages

Chapter 9: Proprietary Resources

Chapter 10: Fair Value Extraction

Chapter 11: Staying Power

Chapter 12: Proven Business Model

Chapter 13: Predictable Demand Drivers

Chapter 14: Reinvestment Options

Chapter 15: Scalability and Low Incremental Costs

Chapter 16: Cyclical Risks

Chapter 17: Other Risks

Introduction

This book attempts to provide practical analytical frameworks for investors to empirically evaluate the quality and durability of any business. The traits of a high-quality, durable company include:

- People who are passionate and make decisions with a long-term perspective for the benefit of all stakeholders, with good skills in capital allocation and proper long-term incentives
- Reliable communication
- A competitive advantage that is both intense and durable
- Modest extraction of the economic benefit generated for customers and suppliers
- The ability to survive and be relevant for many years to come
- Predictable long-term demand drivers
- Lucrative reinvestment options
- A robust and proven business model
- Scalability and low incremental costs
- Manageable risk exposures

I am sure that experienced long-term investors can agree on most of these traits. So, what can I bring with this book? This book provides you with actionable guides on how to empirically evaluate each of these elements, as well as the nuances within them. When combined, these frameworks can also serve as a unified model for the discussion of overall business quality.

Although the book is about the quality of companies, it is by no means limited to the discipline of "quality investing," which focuses only on mature companies with pronounced overall quality. The book is equally intended for investors who focus on less mature companies or those with varying degrees of quality. It is intended for investors in all industries, in both public and private markets, and for investors who buy anywhere from one share to all the shares of the companies in which they invest. It is also intended for non-investors who are just interested in analyzing business quality and risks—for example, business operators.

★ ★ ★

There is a chasm in the analytical mentality among investors. Some appear to operate with mental checklists where each checkpoint is binary and must be ticked off with minimal effort. Obviously, in support of their preexisting investment thesis, that is. Or perhaps sometimes more accurately their boss's investment thesis. They attach "labels" to companies based on broad-level historical pattern recognition supported by anecdotal evidence without further empirical analysis of the current circumstances. For instance, they might conclude that a business has a "competitive moat" because it's evident that the business benefits from some degree of network effect. But what about obtaining specific, empirical data regarding the common causes of network-effect erosion? It seems that this doesn't interest some professionals, who are too busy with other more important things such as making PowerPoint presentations or calculating whether their expected return is 10.1% or 10.11%.

Other investors have a different approach. They know that none of the traits are binary; they are nuanced. They know that they shouldn't be evaluated based on theorizing, wishful thinking, or stock pitch arguments. They know what should be assessed by knowing what specific indicators to look for and evaluating the real-world evidence concerning those indicators. These investors are like *sniffer dogs*. They sense the world. Sniffer dogs are trained to search areas diligently and systematically, following scent trails or detecting specific odors. Sniffer dogs make decisions based on the sensory input they receive from their environment. They gather information from their surroundings and determine the direction and strength of the scent trail. Sniffer dogs undergo rigorous training to harness their natural sniffing ability for specific tasks.

What, then, of those investors not among the sniffer dogs? They are far from sniffer dogs. They are *dowsers*. They wander around with their Y-shaped twig looking for evidence that supports their hypothesis of underground water or precious metals. They do get out and walk around with their twig out, but the observations gathered about the world have little impact on their conclusions. The twig will dip when they pass over a supposed underground asset. This is, however, an unconscious, involuntary physical movement that occurs in response to thoughts or ideas rather than to external stimuli. Dowsers attribute successful finds to their skill and intuition, while failures can be rationalized as interference from other substances. Some dowsers may spend a lot of time and effort dowsing and brag about how diligently they dowsed—not realizing the nonexistent connection to the actual chances of discovering water.

Then there are the experienced *senior dowsers*. They are so senior and high ranking that they are simply above the need to do any real work. They can instantly find underground water and precious metals using

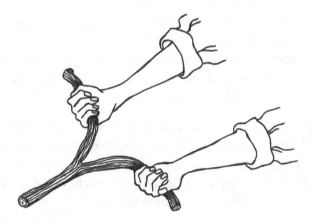

Figure 1   A dowser-investor's dowsing twig.

Source: Original artwork by Henriette Wiberg Danielsen. © 2024 Simon Kold.

only their gut. Or so they think. They don't shy away from overruling diligently collected empirical conclusions based on random anecdotal
experiences.

The investment industry is abundant with massively over-remunerated
dowsers, tarot card readers, Feng Shui consultants, Freudians, and detox
foot bath operators. I don't think the world needs more of these. But I
urge you to be a sniffer dog—like an empirical scientist who forms
hypotheses, gathers empirical observations, and strives for the ideals of
falsification.[1]

Consider this book an attempt to help you be more like a sniffer dog
and less like a dowser. The book attempts to be a sniffer dog training
manual. Specifically, a manual with regards to the question of the quality
and durability of companies.

How to Use This Book Productively. I believe that investment analysis should be based on solid evidence. But it's also important for investors
to use their time wisely. This book provides guides for evaluating different
aspects of business quality. The aim isn't to make you expend enormous
time and effort on every single aspect discussed. Instead, use this book to
focus on what matters most for your investment:

- Concentrate on the aspects from the book that are most crucial for your
  overall investment case in the given scenario.
- Focus on the aspects from the book where your target company shows
  the greatest weaknesses.
- For both points, prioritize seeking empirical evidence that might challenge or undermine your overall investment hypothesis, and critically
  assess your interpretation of this evidence.

I personally seek to find the path of least resistance to "kill" an investment idea. A time opportunity cost is associated with investment analysis.
Analyzing one company means you are missing out on analyzing another.
By focusing on what really matters and by trying to find the shortest path
to rejection, you can hopefully manage this cost.[2]

Let's Sniff Around

In each section, I have created a box labeled "Let's Sniff Around," which contains specific analytical actions that you can take to empirically evaluate that particular subelement of business quality and durability. For readers who are not professional investors and have no ambition to become one, these suggested steps might seem overwhelming or of little use to you. No problem—simply skip them, and you should still be able to enjoy the book!

It is a great pleasure to finally have succeeded in writing a book about the quality of companies, especially considering my earlier, painfully embarrassing failed attempt to write a book about the quality of coconuts. As the first "how to" business book in history, this book doesn't guarantee overnight success (e.g., unlike my book about coconuts). At best, it promises to make you a gazzilionare in a currency where 1 gazzilion is pegged to the exact garage sale value of this book.

Enjoy the book!

Part I

What Makes Some People Create Exceptional Long-term Per-share Business Performance?

Chapter 1

Passion

Control of companies is placed with people spanning a panoply of passion:

- At one end are people for whom the job is a stepping-stone, something they do for a few years until a bigger company calls. They have a history of hopping from one job to another, spanning several sectors. They focus on meeting quarterly targets and maximizing results within a 2- to 4-year time frame and are not accountable for the aftermath.
- At the other end are people for whom the firm is their life's work. They are emotionally enthralled by the enterprise. When the business suffers, they care for it as parents would for a sick child. They feel responsible to all stakeholders and seek a maximum in a further future.

Expecting these two types of people to run a company the same way is like asking the sun to shine at night. But why does such passion matter for investors? Intense emotional investment is indispensable for creating exceptional outcomes in all fields of human endeavor. As Steve Jobs once said, "The only way to do great work is to love what you do." An absence of passion results in complacency, a focus on short-term profits at the expense of long-term value per share, a mindless unwillingness to deviate from peers, or an excessive concentration on a single stakeholder group at the expense of others. To achieve exceptional long-term outcomes, a firm must simultaneously delight its customers, offer superior products, maintain satisfied suppliers, nurture a loyal and contented workforce, and operate within societal norms. A passionate management and workforce is a necessary ingredient to achieve all of these at the same time. It is easy to boost profits in a 2- to 3-year time frame by cutting employee benefits, pressuring suppliers, reducing service quality, or hiking prices. While such measures can enhance short-term profits, they erode long-term value per share.

The longer the investment time horizon, the more management decisions affect the outcome. Over longer periods, the decisions made significantly shape business performance per share. Just as passion drives exceptional results in arts, sports, and science, it also propels success in business. Managers who lack passion also lack the recipe for exceptional results.

Galileo Galilei, famous for his contributions to astronomy and the laws of motion, represents the ultimate level of exceptional results while

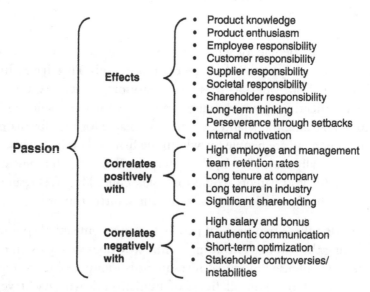

Figure 1.1 Effects of passion and its correlations.
Source: Simon Kold.

embodying characteristics quite opposite to those of most modern corporate managers. These characteristics include perseverance, internal motivation, and independence from prevailing norms. Galilei did not engage in a conflict with the Catholic Church over the heliocentric model because it was beneficial to his short-term incentive program or because it was a "hot trend" at the time. He did it because he was obsessed with the truth and with his scientific work. He was so extremely perseverant in supporting the heliocentric model proposed by Copernicus that he was ultimately sentenced by the Inquisition to spend the rest of his life under house arrest. To the contrary, most managers prioritize short-term gains and align their actions with current trends or the prevailing corporate culture. Unlike Galilei, whose dedication to scientific truth led him to challenge established norms, most in the corporate community shy away from such risks. They focus on strategies that promise immediate returns and favor adherence to established methodologies. This contrast highlights a fundamental difference in approach: whereas Galilei was driven by his devotion to his beliefs and the pursuit of knowledge, most managers are guided by trends, near-term targets, and the immediate expectations of analysts, media, and shareholders.

1.1 Perseverance and Internal Motivations

Perseverance through setbacks is a manifestation of passion. An anecdote featuring Jensen Huang of NVIDIA during the company's existential crisis in 1997 showcases attributes such as resilience, determination, adaptability, and boundless optimism. The company prepared to release the RIVA 128, one of the first consumer graphical processing units to integrate 3D acceleration, essential for rendering 3D graphics on computers. However, the company was running low on cash, with only enough to sustain operations for about 6 months. At this point, most people would have given up. But Jensen and his team decided to take an unconventional and risky decision.

My will to survive exceeds almost everybody else's will to kill me.

—*Jensen Huang (NVIDIA), 2003 presentation at Stanford eCorner.*[1]

Instead of following the conventional course of receiving physical prototypes for testing, NVIDIA chose to conduct the entire testing in simulation, then committed the rest of the company's financial resources to commissioning the production of the RIVA 128 without ever inspecting a physical prototype. NVIDIA bet the house, the silicon ranch, and the transistor tent on a product they had never tested in the real world. Not surprisingly, the product did not work as intended. The RIVA 128 supported only 8 of the 38 so-called DirectX image blending modes for which it had been designed. The team attempted to convince software developers to use only those eight supported modes in computer games and software. Despite the setbacks, the product surprisingly achieved commercial success. NVIDIA was lucky that the product performance, well, worked, despite the lack of prototype testing, and entered the market just as personal computer gaming began to bloom. Although luck contributed to the outcome, without passion, to bankruptcy, the company would have succumb. Still led by Jensen Huang, NVIDIA today is one of the world's most valuable companies.

In a passage from her 1985 autobiography, the then-79-year-old founder of her self-named cosmetics firm, Estée Lauder, answered her own

Figure 1.2   Jensen Huang, the passionate CEO of NVIDIA, has a tattoo of his company's logo on his shoulder.

Source: Reuters/Robert Galbraith

rhetorical question, about what is the most important determinant of business success. According to Lauder, who herself was an exceptionally passionate businesswoman, the single most important trait is persistence.

What makes a successful businesswoman? Is it talent? Well, perhaps, although I've known many enormously successful people who were not gifted in any outstanding way, not blessed with a particular talent. Is it then intelligence? Certainly, intelligence helps, but it's not necessarily education or the kind of intellectual reasoning needed to graduate from the Wharton School of Business that are essential. How many of your grandfathers came here from one or another "old country" and made a mark in America without the language, money or contacts? What, then, is the mystical ingredient? It's persistence. It's that certain little spirit that compels you to stick it out just when you're at your most tired. It's that quality that forces you to persevere, find the route around the stone wall. It's the immovable stubbornness that will not allow you to cave in when everyone says give up.

—*Estée Lauder in* Estée: A Success Story.[2]

Investors often focus on figuring out whether executives exhibit the ideal incentive structure rather than investigating the intensity of their passion. While it's vital to weigh financial incentives, the power of passion as a motivator should not be overlooked. Exemplary executives equate their personal success with the continued prosperity of the company and not solely the lining of their own pockets.

The same year as the launch of the RIVA 128, following Apple's acquisition of NeXT, Steve Jobs returned to the firm he had cofounded and from which he had been fired a decade earlier. Jobs likely rejoined Apple more out of an emotional opportunity to revive his struggling brainchild than out of a financial motive. Ironically, it ended up also paying off financially, as Jobs successfully revived Apple and made it one of the world's most successful companies ever.

Howard Schultz's return as Starbucks' CEO is another well-known anecdote. Schultz joined Starbucks in 1982 when it was a small coffee bean retailer in Seattle. He acquired the business in 1987 and rapidly expanded it until he stepped down as chief executive officer (CEO) in 2000, though he remained as chairman. Schultz returned as CEO in January 2008, during a challenging period for Starbucks, characterized by overexpansion, declining sales, and a diluted brand experience. Similarly, Morris Chang, the iconic founder of TSMC, made a comparable comeback. After retiring as CEO in 2005, Chang resumed his role in 2009 amidst the global economic downturn and production issues.

Let's Sniff Around

Analyze perseverance and internal motivation:

- Study responses to prior crises: history of confronting difficult challenges directly and persistence in the face of setbacks.
- Evaluate product enthusiasm, detailed product knowledge, and personal product use.
- Review interviews, conversations, and media appearances to decide whether management identifies personal success with the success of the business.
- Assess the management's lifestyle and appearance. A modest lifestyle can indicate internal motivation.

1.2   Focus on All Stakeholder Constituencies

A manager's job is to maximize long-term cash profit per share. But these long-term profits aren't achieved by aiming straight at them. Instead, they are the byproducts of delighting customers, offering great products, nurturing a loyal and committed workforce, and operating within the norms of society. Yet, many managers overemphasize certain stakeholder groups and neglect others. A business run solely for shareholders will surely be outrun by its neglect of other interests.

What's good for customers is good for shareholders.

—*Jeff Bezos, 2002 Letter to Amazon shareholders.*

Michael Pearson's tenure as CEO of Valeant Pharmaceuticals is widely regarded as an example of the risks of excessive focus on one particular stakeholder group, in his case shareholders, at the expense of others. He intensely focused on maximizing shareholder value, a practice that led to substantial stock market successes for a few years but eventually culminated in myriad complications. Mike Pearson's playbook at Valeant was to acquire companies with profitable drugs, instead of investing in R&D, and financed these acquisitions with debt. Post-acquisition, Valeant would cut costs, especially in R&D and sales, and often raise the prices of niche drugs with little competition. Prices of heart drugs Isuprel and Nitropress were ruthlessly raised, causing controversy that contributed to a Senate investigation into Valeant Pharmaceuticals in 2015. Shortly after the announcement of the investigations, reports emerged about Valeant's relationship with Philidor Rx Services, a specialty pharmacy that distributed Valeant's drugs. Allegations suggested that Valeant was using Philidor to avoid generic substitutions and inflate sales figures. In early 2016, it also became public that the Securities and Exchange Commission was investigating Valeant's revenue recognition practices and reliance on non-GAAP figures, which, the Securities and Exchange Commission (SEC) believed, could have misled investors. These factors collectively tarnished Valeant's reputation in the pharmaceutical industry and ultimately led to the decimation of shareholder value.[3]

The story illustrates the unsustainability of prioritizing shareholders at the expense of customers, employees, and society. You should recognize and avoid such a narrow focus because it does not lead to permanent shareholder value creation.

Interestingly, Mike Pearson's investor communication would have scored well using the methods for evaluating capital allocation discussed in Chapter 3. Mike Pearson exemplified the rhetoric of an accomplished capital allocator, which enticed some of the world's top investors to invest in his company, despite his imbalance in managing stakeholder constituencies.

People who are passionate about creating value for all parties often demonstrate an undeniable enthusiasm for the products, an emotional duty to employees, and a reverent sense of responsibility toward suppliers and the greater society. By genuine responsibility toward society, I'm not referring to the practice of producing an abundance of soulless zombie corporate ESG content, blindly following the crowd without critical thought. I'm referring to the practice of demonstrating a sincere responsibility that arises from independent initiative and thoughtful consideration, aimed at truly doing good rather than just conforming to norms.

Let's Sniff Around

Analyze the risk of a management neglecting stakeholder groups:

- Evaluate their demonstrated knowledge of product details by reviewing their communication.
- Evaluate the genuineness of enthusiasm for the company's products and product development.
- Research historical controversies: Investigate any past controversies involving stakeholder groups. This information can often be found through search engines, in litigation records, and in the legal proceedings section of the company's 10-K filings.
- Interview customers and ask them about their views on the management's genuine sense of responsibility toward the customers. If available, review customer satisfaction metrics, such as Net Promoter Scores, to understand customer loyalty and satisfaction.
- Look for price surges that are not accompanied by improvements in quality.
- Interview former employees and ask them about their views on the management's genuine sense of responsibility toward the employees and other stakeholder groups. High employee turnover rates can indicate dissatisfaction. This can be supplemented by examining employee reviews on platforms like Glassdoor.
- Analyze changes in suppliers, high supplier turnover, and conduct interviews with suppliers to understand their perspectives if necessary.
- Identify signs of arrogance or disrespect toward employees or suppliers.
- Identify any tendency to evade questions on earnings calls or in direct dialogue.

1.3   Decision-making Time Horizons

Passionate people make decisions with a long-term perspective. These people suffer from competitive paranoia and willingly sacrifice short-term profitability to strengthen their long-term competitive position. They tend to be more conservative during exuberant periods of the business cycle. They go to great lengths to satisfy all stakeholder constituents, even when there isn't an immediate payoff. Unlike their dispassionate, complacent "salary-man" counterparts, they are also unafraid to take risks and deviate from their peers. In contrast, corporate managers concentrating on maximizing near-term performance are averse to compromising short-term profits for a more distant future compensation.

The story of Intel's decision not to produce the chips for Apple's iPhone is a famous example of the unfortunate consequences of too much focus on short-term profitability. Apple had approached Intel, given their existing relationship supplying processors for Apple's Mac computers. The proposed deal with Apple for the iPhone chips had a lower margin than Intel was accustomed to. Therefore, from a short-term profitability perspective, it did not seem attractive. Former CEO Paul Otellini and Intel's leadership therefore decided to pass on the opportunity, leading Apple to turn to Intel's competitor, Samsung, for the design and manufacture of an ARM-based chip. ARM's architecture is more power efficient, making it ideal for mobile devices. This decision paved the way for Samsung, and later TSMC, to become dominant players in the mobile chip market and eventually challenge Intel in its core non-mobile chip segments. In retrospect, in a 2013 interview with the *Atlantic,* Otellini admitted this mistake, saying, "The lesson I took away from that was, while we like to speak with data around here, so many times in my career I've ended up making decisions with my gut, and I should have followed my gut.... My gut told me to say yes."[4]

The Intel example illustrates that even capable managers, versed in their industries' nuances (for context, Otellini was Intel's first CEO who wasn't an engineer, though he had spent his entire career at Intel), can sometimes make decisions that prioritize short-term profits at the expense of significant long-term value, whether due to their incentives or external pressures to meet immediate targets. Note that optimizing short-term performance isn't just about overt actions like slashing benefits or skyrocketing prices; it can also manifest in more subtle decisions, such as whether to pursue a potential partnership with an existing customer, and it can happen even to capable and ethical management teams, such as Otellini and his colleagues at Intel.

Let's Sniff Around

Analyze decision-making time horizons:

- Consider their incentives as decision-making time horizons are often dictated by them. Use methods presented in Chapter 2.
- Interview both former and current employees, seeking examples of short-term decision-making: Those who have had direct interactions with top management often have insights into this matter.
- Identify instances where attractive projects were forgone to meet short-term financial targets.
- Identify instances where monetization was/is intentionally withheld.

However, always approach such accounts with a critical mind, considering the subjective perspective of the individual recounting what they deem an "attractive project." Moreover, **don't mistake prudent cost-consciousness and frugality for a lack of long-term vision**.

1.4   Career Path and Tenure

The career path, the tenure at the company, and in the industry often parallel a person's level of passion. Following, I generalize four types characterized by their career path.

Owner-operators

Owner-operators are often also a firm's founders and have poured in immense effort to build the business, typically considering the company as their life's work. Such specimens have a solemn duty toward their employees. Most founders would explore various cost-cutting measures before resorting to staff reductions. (The point here is the exceptional feeling of care for employees. This should not be confused with poor internal management of resources that allows unproductive activities to continue without eliminating positions.) With their experience managing all facets of the firm, founders usually have an unparalleled understanding of their customer base. They are typically well versed with industry details and have learned from their past mistakes. Founders often draw a modest salary and hold significant ownership in the business.

Owner-operator personas (in-company tenured executives)

Owner-operator personas have extensive tenure at the company, encompassing most or all of their careers. They have either held diverse roles within the firm or served as executives for an extended period and often exhibit characteristics like founders. They can possess an excellent understanding of the customer base if their roles have involved decades of customer interactions. Such specimens have typically learned from past mistakes, are intimately familiar with the industry, and feel emotionally engaged with their employees. Over the years, they've usually amassed a significant shareholding in the company. Their attachment to the business can be as intense as that of founders, and they can view the company as their life's work. Their loyalty indicates genuine passion for the firm and its stakeholders. I call these people "owner-operator personas" because they act and think as if they were long-term owners.

Industry-tenured career executives

A third category comprises executives with extensive industry experience but short tenures at their current companies. Their consistent industry presence suggests they enjoy their work. Such specimens are knowledgeable about the industry and its customers but may not have the same level of commitment to their employees. Often, they're drawn to their roles by lucrative salaries and, due to their short company tenure, possess a smaller shareholding compared to the wealth accumulated from previous positions. Preferably, a manager in this category should at least have spent a long time at the prior company before shifting firms to get a CEO position, rather than having a history of hopping between multiple companies.

Weathervanes

The fourth category includes executives with neither extensive industry nor company experience. These individuals often shift from one position to another, executing 3- to 5-year business plans before transitioning to new roles. They are often averse to straying from the prevailing business trends and conventions. They are like weathervanes: their directions are dictated by external forces. They usually command high salaries but hold negligible shares in the company. Having not been in the industry or company long enough, they haven't learned from relevant past mistakes. Such managers often lack intimacy with customers and industry. They might not have a profound emotional connection to the staff either. While they can be adept at maximizing profits over a 3- to 5-year period—a strategy that has advanced their careers—they don't have accountability for the company's longer-term performance. While these managers can be valuable in turnaround scenarios or as temporary cost-cutters in complacent, cost-bloated, underperforming companies, they generally don't foster exceptional long-term results.

Together, these four generalized types form a spectrum. While many executives of publicly traded companies fall near the third and fourth type, I tend to avoid them, preferring instead to focus on the first two.

 Let's Sniff Around

Analyze career path and tenure as indicators of passion:

- Note founder status: Founder status often beneficial but not always good. The topic of evaluating founders is discussed later in this section.
- Note industry tenure: Longer is preferable.
- Note tenure within the company: A longer tenure is preferable, unless the company has been underperforming for a long time.

- Evaluate experience in sales roles: Having customer experience is favorable, while lacking it is not. This is especially relevant when assessing a CEO, as CEOs should have had extensive customer interaction.
- Note transitions between companies: Fewer transitions are better.
- Note transitions between industries: No shifts is ideal. Recent shifts can be especially alarming.

The career paths and tenures of not only the CEO but also all top decision-makers should be regarded as indicators. A management team where the majority of the people exhibit these positive characteristics is often indicative of passionate leadership and a great culture.

Consider, for instance, the company tenure of Taiwan Semiconductor Manufacturing Company (TSMC)'s management, as illustrated in Table 1.1. TSMC is the world leader in semiconductor manufacturing. Nearly all TSMC's top decision-makers have been with the firm for decades, having come up through the ranks and remained with the firm. They receive modest salaries and own a solid amount of stock.

However, using tenure and career path as indicators has limits. I would rather hug a cactus than invest with a long-tenured executive in a chronically underperforming company.

A note on founders. I think many investors, including myself, have a founder bias. This likely stems from a survivorship bias from studying many of the world's greatest business successes and their founders, like Steve Jobs, Bill Gates, and Estée Lauder, who were incredible businesspeople.

You shouldn't automatically equate founder status with eminent management. For every success story, there are many lesser-known stories of founders who didn't have the correct skill set to scale their business beyond a certain level, or who could not retain key personnel because they were mentally unprepared to share authority. Some founders seemingly confuse being the firm's founder with being its Führer, as they become unfavorably intransigent, autocratic, and fatigue-inducing.

Table 1.1 Overview of TSMC Management's Tenure and Shareholding (as of January 2022)

Name	Role	Tenure in current role, years	Tenure as senior executive in company	Tenure at company	Value of shares (multiple of total cash compensation)
Morris Chang	Founder (retired)	35	22	31	$2800m
Mark Liu	Chairman (former Co–CEO)	4	16	28	$285m (29x)
C.C. Wei	CEO	8	16	28	$160m (20x)
Wendell Huang	VP and CFO	3	3	18	$36m (36x)
Lora HO	SVP Europe & Asia (former CFO)	3	19	22	$100m (~200x)
Wei-Jen Lo	SVP R&D	12	12	18	$31m (~60x)
Rick Cassidy	SVP Strategy	13	13	24	Unknown
YP Chin	SVP Operations	6	6	35	$200m (~400x)
Y.J. Mii	SVP R&D	6	6	27	$22m (~45x)
J.K. Lin	SVP Materials management	4	11	35	$278M (~550x)
J.K. Wang	SVP Corporate planning	4	10	35	$56m (~100x)
Kevin Zhang	SVP Business development	2	5	5	$2m
Cliff Hou	SVP Europe and Asia sales	2	10	24	$10m

Source: Adapted from author's calculations from publicly available TSMC filings...

Let's Sniff Around

Analyze founders:

- Evaluate whether they receive a high salary and benefits by reviewing proxy filings or remuneration reports.[5] This behavior suggests they prioritize their personal financial interests over the broader interest of their stakeholders.
- Evaluate lack of focus on certain stakeholder groups by conducting the analysis discussed in Section 1.2.
- Identify lack of demonstrated willingness to share authority by interviewing former employees.
- Identify inability to build, manage, and retain a strong management team.

For instance, when evaluating the enterprise software firm Salesforce's co-founder and CEO Marc Benioff, you might express concern that all named executives in 2006, except co-founders Benioff and Parker Harris, were no longer executives with the company by 2014.[6] By 2020, all named executives from 2014 had left, except for Benioff and Parker. Benioff tried to transition in a co-CEO twice, and both times, that executive ended up leaving the company within a few years. You might also be skeptical about the necessity for him to receive substantial stock option awards as a founder. However, it should be noted that Benioff appears passionate and skilled at balancing stakeholders, but I would have my concerns regarding the other aspects.

1.5   Retention of People

Passionate people stay. Firms with higher employee retention rates than their peers must be doing something right; the people working there must enjoy their roles, otherwise they would have sought other jobs. The retailer Costco, for example, has a phenomenal retention rate of 90% after

1 year's employment.[7] A retention rate near 90% is generally considered excellent, but benchmarks vary by industry. There is an explanation behind low employee retention rates. The employees were probably not abducted by aliens; they likely left for a reason.

You can evaluate retention rates at various levels, including overall retention rate and management retention rates. For context, the average in-role tenure of CEOs and C-level executives in large US companies is around 7 and 5 years, respectively, according to a study by consulting firm Korn Ferry.[8]

One of the first things I look at when studying a company is how the executive team was composed 5 years ago and how it looks like today. I exemplified this for Apple in Table 1.2. Apple had minimal turnover and planned gradual transitions. I like it when the turnover of a management team resembles that of Apple, not the turnover of the lineup of a reality TV show. I also create another overview that maps the in-company and in-role tenure of each respective current decision-maker. I illustrated this for TSMC's management in Table 1.1.

I prefer companies that promote from within because they bring people to top positions who are more passionate about the company and have a deeper understanding of the industry. It also indicates a culture that emphasizes employee empowerment.

Table 1.2   Apple Leadership Changes from 2018 to 2023

Position	As of 2018	As of 2023
Chairman	Art Levinson	Art Levinson
CEO	Tim Cook	Tim Cook
COO	Jeff Williams	Jeff Williams
CFO	Luca Maestri	Luca Maestri
GC	Kate Adams	Kate Adams
SVP Retail	Angela Ahrendts	Deirdre O'Brien
SVP Services	Eddy Cue	Eddy Cue
SVP Software Engineering	Craig Federighi	Craig Federighi
SVP Hardware Technologies	Johny Srouji	John Ternus
SVP Hardware Engineering	Dan Riccio	Johny Srouji
SVP Marketing	Phil Schiller	Greg Joswiak

Note: Compiled by the author from publicly available information.

Let's Sniff Around

Evaluate retention:

- Examine the paths the executive team members took to reach their positions. If most were recruited externally, it can generally be viewed as a negative sign, unless it happened a long time ago and they have remained in the role since then.
- Evaluate retention levels for executives by reviewing historical filings.
- Obtain general employee retention rates by requesting them from the company or alternatively by interviewing relevant experts.

The generalizability of retention rates as an indicator has limits. Bringing in new blood, new thoughts, and different perspectives and experiences can help avoid tunnel vision, especially in companies that are not already performing exceptionally. So, while I appreciate the tendency to promote from within, I think it is okay for one or two management team positions—although preferably not the CEO—to be filled externally to infuse new thoughts that can challenge status quo.

1.6   Authenticity Indicates Passion

Genuine communication demands the true expression of emotions, honesty, and enthusiasm. Managers who are passionately and emotionally invested in their products, employees, and the challenges they address are more likely to engage in authentic communication. In contrast, the communication of the soulless corporate masses often lacks authenticity to such an extent that it seems devoid of any real sender. A reluctance to deviate from the corporate norm of polished but inauthentic communication suggests a lack of the passionate qualities desirable to long-term investors.

The communication of most corporate managers is less authentic than a pop-star lip-syncing the national anthem. Conversely, passionate managers communicate in a distinctly different manner; they cannot suppress

Figure 1.3 Some managers are so passionate that they cannot confine themselves to the institutional corporate norms of communication. The chart depicts the 2021 annual report of the industrial computer vision company Cognex, which has a unique tradition of creating original annual report covers.

Source: Reproduced with permission of Annual Report 2021, Cognex Corporation.

their emotions and enthusiasm. Consider, for example, the communication styles of Warren Buffett, Jensen Huang, or other notable figures who exemplify passion, all of whom communicate in a very authentic manner:

- Expression of emotions
- Deviation from mainstream approaches
- Product enthusiasm and a "geeky" passion
- Intentional informality

A vivid example of authentic communication is that of Peter Rose, the co-founder and former CEO of the freight forwarder Expeditors. Unlike most public companies, Expeditors does not hold earnings calls for analysts. Instead, it posts written responses to written questions in a Form 8-K filed with the SEC and published on its website. During the tenure of Rose, the Q&As were infamous for their colorful and sharp replies to analysts and shareholders. Today, some investors view these 8-K filings as "cult classics." Here is an example from a Form 8-K filed with the SEC on October 22, 2002:

Question

I just wanted to confirm an anecdote I heard about your CEO, Peter Rose, and Expeditors relative lack of executive perks. Expeditors owns its headquarters building and yet I seem to remember hearing that Peter even pays for his own monthly parking. Is this correct? (Jack).

Answer

We have been asked several times to verify that our Chairman and CEO Peter Rose actually pays to park his car in our headquarters building—which is 100% owned by Expeditors. The answer to the question is yes, Peter Rose pays for his own parking—just as he pays his own utility bills and uses his own funds to buy clothes, groceries, and his tickets to Seattle Thunderbirds hockey games. Frankly, it continues to amaze us that this would be viewed in any way as "novel."

Call us naïve, but long before corporate governance became trendy, we just assumed that personal expenses should be paid for by personal funds and corporate expenses would be paid for with corporate funds. While we realize that many of the "talking head" CEOs, whose names are mentioned in hushed tones on Wall Street and on university campuses, would find our philosophies rather provincial, we have always believed that mixing business and personal expenses causes a form of blindness that results in an inability to put the interests of the shareholders first.

Actually, one of the best illustrations of this part of the Expeditors culture is not about Peter paying for his own monthly parking, rather it is the dinner party catered at Mr. Rose's new house in October 1998. The guests were all the members of senior management who were in town for a semi-annual meeting. Anyone who knows Peter would expect him to host a first-class event, and they would not have been disappointed. From the sterling silver, china crystal on the tables to the large, heated tent erected over his new lawn (this was Seattle after all and October can be a little cold at night and likely "wet"), no shortcuts were taken.

The entire cost of the event, soup to nuts, was paid for by Mr. Rose out of his own pocket. Nothing was charged to the company. While this could have been a company expense, given that it was a company event, it wasn't for a couple of reasons. Our policy is that if you invite co-workers (like guests from other countries) to your home for dinner, you pay and you don't claim reimbursement. In your home, the visitor is your guest—not the Company's. Another reason is that shareholders, and we're all shareholders around here, don't need to foot the bill for the excesses that you might want to provide for a party of close friends.

From a pure social observation, it seems to us that the most effective poster child for raw, vulgar, and unrestrained corporate greed is the multi-million dollar-a-year CEO who is too mean, self-entitled, or greedy to pay for his or her own personal living expenses. Don't get us wrong, we have no problem with management being justly compensated for improving the net worth of the shareholders in whatever format the shareholders agree. However, it seems that recently many companies not only employed their CEO's, they apparently adopted them as well. This behavior fuels the argument that many CEO "did it once for the shareholders and twice for themselves" and specialized in taking their half out of the middle.

We think adoption is best when limited to children in need of support, nurturing and a stable home. It is unconscionable when extended to the corporate CEO caught up in the never-ending quest to satiate egos with the shareholders money. To borrow from Mr. Rogers "Can you say greedy, self-absorbed kleptocrat?"

As a side note, the parking garage in our corporate office, like all our branch offices, is a separate profit center. We use the same incentive bonus system to motivate and reward the people who must valet park cars in our tight and post filled garage as we do in each of our branches. The interesting thing is that our garage is a financial success, and it isn't just because we have a captive audience of tenants in our building. Our people hustle, they share in the profits, and they are very aggressive about reacting to changes in market conditions and maximizing market share. The interesting thing is that the bonus appears to have expanded the number of cars we can park in the garage as to our knowledge we have yet to turn away a single car nor have we as yet ordered a "garage full" sign.

—*US Securities and Exchange Commission, Form 8-K filed by Expeditors International of Washington, October 22, 2002*

Since Mr. Rose retired in 2014, the Q&As have been a lot less entertaining, but Expeditors has continued the practice even to this day.

A perhaps even more vivid case study of authentic, passionate communication is Masayoshi Son, the "larger-than-life" founder and CEO of the telecommunications and technology conglomerate SoftBank. Masa grew up as a third-generation Korean immigrant in Japan. While studying abroad at Berkeley in the United States, he built and sold two businesses for $3.2 million before returning to Japan.[9] In 1981, he started a software distribution business and later began making venture investments. He became the world's richest man for a few days during the dot-com bubble, then lost over 90% of the market value of his assets. Son made a remarkable comeback, first by buying a large stake in Alibaba, which would become one of China's most valuable companies, and later envisioning owning "the highway of the information revolution" (i.e., in reference to the industrial revolution). He first convinced Steve Jobs to grant him the exclusive rights to the iPhone 1 in Japan before he even owned a telephone company, then acquired Vodafone Japan, and years later invested in 5G spectrum in the United States (via T-Mobile and Sprint) and Japan in an aggressive bet on early locking up scarce future high-speed mobile internet assets. He also raised a venture fund seven times larger than the largest private equity fund at the time. To my knowledge, SoftBank is the only publicly traded company with a 300-year plan.

Son often communicates with a level of enthusiasm and emotional investment that reflects his dedication to his ambitions of changing the world. Since his 2016 acquisition of ARM, a British semiconductor IP company, Masa has passionately spoken about AI and "the information revolution," emphasizing his commitment to financing it and thereby "bringing happiness to everyone." With a geeky, emotional, and wildly unconventional approach to communication, he relies on radical intentional informality.

Some consider Masa a controversial figure due to his large-scale, massive bets on companies with power-law distributed outcomes, featuring a few large winners and many losses. This approach is normal in the venture capital landscape but uncommon among publicly traded companies. His

Figure 1.4 Masayoshi Son of SoftBank communicates in an authentic manner. His approach to communication embodies an extreme level of intentional informality.

Source: Reproduced with permission of SoftBank Group Corporation, February 2021 Investor Presentation.

unstoppable optimism has led him to grand windfalls but has also made him vulnerable to trusting people with lower integrity and to making mistakes that, in hindsight, are embarrassing. Due to his unconventional communication style and recent headwinds, the press often ridicules him. However, this hasn't stopped him from maintaining his wildly authentic communication; rather, it seems to have made him communicate in an even more unorthodox and authentic way.

There is always some madness in love. But there is always, also, some reason in madness.

—*Friedrich Nietzsche,* Also sprach Zarathustra *(1883)[10]*

While individuals like Masa and Rose (or Elon Musk of Tesla) represent an extreme degree of authenticity in communication, leading the press to treat them as geniuses when they're in tailwind and as ridiculous fools when they're in headwind, most corporate leaders are at the opposite end of the spectrum. They tend to exhibit communication that lacks emotional depth and enthusiasm, focusing on immediate results and tasks rather than long-term vision and transformative goals. They are simply less passionate. **An element of passion is the willingness to sacrifice, which includes the willingness to risk one's public perception in pursuit of what one believes in.** The point is not that you should only invest with wildly authentic people like Masa, Musk, and Rose, which has its own problems; while it is undeniable that Masa and Musk are extremely passionate, one can debate whether their passion is for transformative societal goals or for their companies. The point is that you should try to stay away from those who demonstrate insufficient authenticity because that likely means insufficient passion. Authentic communication does not need to be wildly vivid; it can also be more subtle, like Figure 1.5 from the Danish regional bank Ringkjøbing Landbobank. It is highly unusual for any firm to include a detailed, year-by-year, 37-year overview of any-thing in their investor deck. But over those 37 years, under the leadership of former CEO Bent Naur Kristensen and current CEO John Bull Fisker (since 2012), the bank has achieved keeping realized loan losses after inter-est at an astonishingly low 6 basis points. Since the bank was and still is managed with a long-term horizon, the management thinks that this table contains important information for contemporary investors, and I think so too. It is often the authentic deviations from conventionality, such as the slide in Figure 1.5, that reveal passion. Under the management of Naur and Fisker, the bank has achieved a 41-fold increase in book equity value per share and 216-fold increase in earnings per share (i.e., respec-tively, 11% and 16% CAGR) during a long period where many regional banks have suffered.[11]

 Let's Sniff Around

Analyze authenticity of management communication:

- Contains expressions of emotion.
- Deviates from fad corporate buzzword vocabulary.
- Exhibits exceptional product enthusiasm.
- Uses intentional informality.

If it doesn't, then you are most likely dealing with management suffering from a severe case of passion-deficit-disorder.

Net losses 1987 - 2023

*) Actual net loss relative to total loans exclusive reverse transactions, guarantees, impairment charges for loans and provisions for guarantees.

1,000 DKK	Actual net losses	Actual net losses after interest	Loans with suspended calculation of interest	Impairment charges for loans and provisions for guarantees	Total loans and guarantees etc.	Percentage loss before interest *)	Percentage loss after interest *)
1987	-6,696	304	10,544	75,000	1,358,464	-0.49%	0.02%
1988	-14,205	-5,105	4,522	93,900	1,408,830	-1.01%	-0.37%
1989	-16,302	-5,302	13,107	117,270	1,468,206	-1.25%	-0.36%
1990	-15,867	-1,867	47,182	147,800	1,555,647	-1.02%	-0.12%
1991	-11,429	3,571	47,626	170,000	1,805,506	-0.63%	0.20%
1992	-32,928	-14,928	43,325	177,900	1,933,081	-1.70%	-0.77%
1993	-27,875	-6,875	30,964	208,700	1,893,098	-1.47%	-0.36%
1994	-14,554	4,446	33,889	223,500	1,938,572	-0.75%	0.23%
1995	-10,806	10,194	27,292	238,800	2,058,561	-0.52%	0.50%
1996	-19,802	-1,802	18,404	233,400	2,588,028	-0.77%	-0.07%
1997	-31,412	-12,412	39,846	236,600	3,261,429	-0.96%	-0.38%
1998	-2,914	18,086	4,905	263,600	3,752,602	-0.08%	0.48%
1999	-442	21,558	18,595	290,450	5,148,190	-0.01%	0.42%
2000	-405	27,595	12,843	316,750	5,377,749	-0.01%	0.51%
2001	-8,038	20,962	14,222	331,950	6,113,523	-0.13%	0.34%
2002	-8,470	20,530	26,290	382,850	7,655,112	-0.11%	0.27%
2003	-22,741	2,259	23,412	394,850	8,497,124	-0.27%	0.03%
2004	-14,554	9,446	18,875	404,855	11,523,143	-0.13%	0.08%
2005	-22,908	192	35,796	357,000	15,522,264	-0.15%	0.00%
2006	-13,531	7,028	20,578	295,000	17,858,787	-0.08%	0.04%
2007	-15,264	4,888	13,190	289,097	19,227,572	-0.08%	0.03%
2008	-34,789	-10,237	22,110	356,083	16,475,975	-0.21%	-0.06%
2009	-73,767	-47,658	62,649	467,025	14,890,027	-0.50%	-0.32%
2010	-69,428	-40,207	66,237	565,035	14,758,234	-0.47%	-0.27%
2011	-78,813	-43,073	61,419	649,856	14,448,638	-0.55%	-0.30%
2012	-90,022	-48,337	113,312	758,363	14,849,602	-0.61%	-0.33%
2013	-69,030	-25,117	85,258	853,421	16,604,640	-0.42%	-0.15%
2014	-53,427	-9,206	58,244	931,398	18,073,200	-0.30%	-0.05%
2015	-87,250	-48,815	74,220	942,950	20,194,063	-0.43%	-0.24%
2016	-86,666	-54,300	59,904	937,128	20,878,475	-0.42%	-0.26%
2017	-45,769	-16,414	24,995	931,035	23,465,775	-0.20%	-0.07%
2018	-251,451	-200,376	209,642	2,040,407	43,220,158	-0.58%	-0.46%
2019	-187,787	-118,934	212,195	2,031,645	47,161,735	-0.40%	-0.25%
2020	-120,051	-60,373	264,721	2,204,620	48,257,615	-0.25%	-0.13%
2021	-49,541	71	97,757	2,283,320	53,680,913	-0.09%	0.00%
2022	-42,658	6,401	81,176	2,302,171	58,213,791	-0.07%	0.01%
2023	**-36,968**	**26,626**	**119,789**	**2,334,589**	**59,534,652**	**-0.06%**	**0.04%**
37-year average (1987-2023)						-0.46%	-0.06%
10-year average (2014-2023)						-0.28%	-0.14%

Figure 1.5 Example of a subtler form of authentic communication: The Danish regional bank, Ringkjøbing Landbobank, includes an unconventional slide in its corporate presentation, providing a comprehensive overview of its actual losses since 1987.

Source: Courtesy of Ringkjøbing Landbobank.

Passion is necessary for exceptional business outcomes, and exceptional outcomes mean a lot in investment. As demonstrated by economist Hendrik Bessembinder,[12] the aggregate long-term wealth creation of stocks is highly concentrated, with the top 50 firms accounting for more than 40% of aggregate wealth creation. Nearly 6 out of every 10 stocks contribute negatively to lifetime shareholder wealth creation (specifically underperforming T-bills). The truly long-term investor must increase the likelihood of hitting the big winners and reduce the likelihood of loss. I postulate that seeking passionate people is the best way of doing so.

Chapter 2

Long-term Incentives

In the pact that Dr. Faustus made with the Devil, the Devil at least granted Faustus 24 good years until he took his soul. In contrast, in the incentive pact that shareholders make with executives, the executives often don't even grant shareholders more than a year or two of earnings growth before they take their money.

It is in the interest of long-term investors that the people responsible for running their businesses think like long-term owners. One way such people can think like a long-term owner is by literally being a long-term owner. *There is a difference between being a long-term owner and a profusely paid employee.* There is a different degree of exposure to one's own deficient decisions. Managers with most of their money invested in the enterprise are exposed to the long-term consequences of their own decisions. Those with staggering salaries and minimal investment at risk are not.

There is an old saying, "Don't trust a chef who doesn't want to eat his own cooking." You should be wary of entrusting your hard-earned money to people who don't want to share in the financial downside of the company they are controlling. A chef who eats his own cooking is more likely to do a better job—and especially have better hygiene than one who doesn't. It doesn't matter how many other incentive plans the chef has—for example, a short-term "Chef of the Month" prize for "most dishes prepared in a month"—if that is unrelated to the likelihood that he washes his hands. The same goes for executives who don't want to eat their own cooking, who have all kinds of incentive plans, but ultimately do not have to bear the grave consequences of their eventual bacteria-infected shrimp calzone.

The topic of incentives isn't limited to CEOs. It involves board members, other executives, and even general employees. Ideally, each of these individuals should bear personal financial consequences for poor decisions.

Long-term owners are motivated to act in the best interest of the business over an extended horizon. Their exposure to poor decisions ensures that they consider actions carefully, especially those that could erode long-term per-share value, such as major acquisitions. To mirror the financial incentives of a long-term owner, a manager should have minimal cash compensation and substantial stock ownership. But what about the internal motivation praised in the previous chapter? From my observations, managers with a strong internal drive often also become significant shareholders relative to their personal wealth over time.

 Let's Sniff Around

Analyze long-term incentives:

- Calculate the value of personal stock holdings in relation to cash compensation for the CEO and all key decision-makers. As a rule of thumb, I typically require CEOs to hold stock worth at least four times their annual cash compensation. To me, this seems modest: if they make a decision that decreases the intrinsic value per share by 25%, it will cost them a year's salary.
- Estimate the manager's shares against their estimated personal wealth; begin by examining the company's filings to determine the number of shares owned by the manager. Then, estimate their personal wealth by summing up their historical salaries, as detailed in the filings, subtracting a rough guesstimate of living expenses, and consider any other known investments.

Executive Directors' and their connected persons' interests in shares and share ownership (Audited)

	Share ownership guideline as % of fixed pay (as at 31 December 2022)	Have guidelines been met (as at 31 December 2022)	Actual share ownership as a % of fixed pay as at 31 December 2022[(a)]	Shares held as at 1 January 2022		Shares held as at 31 December 2022[(b)]	
				PLC	PLC ADS	PLC	PLC ADS
CEO: Alan Jope	500%	Yes	894%	43,251	223,140	55,271	237,881
CFO: Graeme Pitkethly	400%	Yes	831%	182,058		206,108	

(a) Calculated based on the minimum shareholding requirements and methodology set out above and the headline fixed pay for the CEO and CFO as at 31 December 2022 (€1,560,780 for the CEO and €1,175,719 for the CFO).

(b) PLC shares are ordinary 3⅑p shares. Includes annual bonus deferral shares dividend accrual, which is reinvested.

Figure 2.1 Unilever is an example of a European company that has stock ownership guidelines for executives (screenshot from Unilever's 2022 Annual Report).

Source: Reproduced with permission from Unilever.

That said, there are limits to the benefits of high management ownership. It doesn't automatically solve everything. For example, even if management has high ownership, having wrong incentive plans (see the following section on disincentives) can still sway them to make suboptimal decisions. Some managers who own stock begin to fixate on short-term stock price movements. This tendency is often observed in their public frustration about the stock price or their excessive attendance at investor events. Conversely, management with modest holdings but with thoughtful long-term incentives tied to relevant per-share KPIs can be adequately aligned.

The approach to management shareholding and incentives differs across the Atlantic Ocean. In the United States, it is much more common to find managers with high ownership and aggressive incentive packages, while in Europe, it is more common to see the "salary-man" CEO with a high base salary, a modest incentive package, and low ownership. While I, on average—with some distinct exceptions—prefer the US model, it is worth noting that many passionate CEOs in Europe don't necessarily own an exorbitant number of shares in the companies they run, but they are dedicated to their work and committed to creating value for all stakeholders, including shareholders.

A notable example of a firm with a unique long-term incentive structure is Florida-based Watsco, which is the largest distributor of air conditioning, heating, and refrigeration equipment and related parts and supplies in North America. Watsco grants restricted share awards to employees, which cliff-vest toward the end of an employee's career. Here is a short excerpt from their 2023 proxy statement filing:

Our executive compensation program is grounded in the principle that compensation should be highly dependent on long-term shareholder returns. This key tenet of our compensation philosophy has driven the unique design of our program for many years and has enabled our leadership team to remain solidly focused on long-term performance. Watsco's entry into the HVAC/R distribution industry began in 1989. Since that time, we have generated cumulative total shareholder return of 21,739% (18% compounded annual growth rate).

Our approach to long-term incentives is unique. Unlike most companies, which grant their officers and employees restricted shares that vest over a period of a few years, our restricted share awards cliff-vest toward the end of an employee's career (age 62 or older). For employees extending their careers beyond age 62, vesting may occur even later. If, for any reason other than death or disability, a holder of restricted shares leaves the Company, 100% of his or her restricted shares are forfeited. This means our key leaders do not know and cannot realize the value of their restricted share awards until they have spent their entire careers with the Company. Restricted share awards are subject to significant market, performance, and forfeiture risks. During the vesting period, shares of restricted stock include the right to vote and the right to receive dividends.

The Company began granting restricted shares in 1997. As of the record date, 137 of the Company's key leaders, including the NEOs, hold restricted share awards that cliff-vest between 2023 and 2054.

2.1   Board of Directors

The idea behind a board of directors is to have a representative democracy, where the directors represent the shareholders. However, these representatives are usually incentivized to represent themselves rather than the shareholders.

In most public companies, the members of the board of directors often have little or no personal exposure to the consequences of poor decisions. Many professional board members earn board fees that become their primary source of income. The dependability of this income can disincentivize them from challenging the CEO and the consensus of the board. Instead, they are incentivized not to deviate from the institutional imperative, to remain on the board, and to continue collecting their comfortable board fees. This stands in stark contrast to the board of directors at Berkshire Hathaway, where all directors have significant ownership stakes, and none depend on income from board fees. Berkshire does not even provide insurance for its directors because the directors should face the consequences of their own decisions.[1]

Let's Sniff Around

Analyze incentives of directors:

- Compare the personal shareholding of each director to your estimate of that individual's personal wealth. This estimate can be based on their previous roles and other known investments. You can assess the board fees they receive and estimate what fraction of their personal income these fees constitute.
- Evaluate whether the board is "weak," i.e. whether they are not truly independent, experienced businesspeople with the authority to challenge the CEO and board consensus.

Stock Ownership Guidelines

Apple has stock ownership guidelines for our CEO, executive officers, and Non-Employee Directors. Under the guidelines, each Non-Employee Director is expected, within five years after joining the Board, to own shares of Apple's common stock that have a value equal to five times their annual cash retainer for serving as a director. Shares may be owned directly by the individual, owned jointly with, or separately by, the individual's spouse, or held in trust for the benefit of the individual, the individual's spouse, or the individual's children. Other than Ms. Lozano and Mr. Gorsky, who joined the Board in calendar year 2021, each Non-Employee Director currently owns shares of Apple's common stock that have a value at least equal to five times their annual cash retainer.

Director Compensation—2022

The following table shows information regarding the compensation earned or paid during 2022 to Non-Employee Directors who served on the Board during the year. Mr. Cook's compensation is shown in the table entitled "Summary Compensation Table—2022, 2021, and 2020" and the related tables under the section entitled "Executive Compensation."

Name	Fees Earned or Paid in Cash ($)	Stock Awards ($)[1]	All Other Compensation ($)[2]	Total ($)
James Bell	100,000	274,941	8,773	383,714
Al Gore	100,000	274,941	7,405	382,346
Alex Gorsky	100,000	348,235	4,950	453,185
Andrea Jung	130,000	274,941	4,568	409,509
Art Levinson	275,000	274,941	12,517	562,458
Monica Lozano	100,000[3]	274,941	1,533	376,474
Ron Sugar	135,000	274,941	14,006	423,947
Sue Wagner	125,000	274,941	5,477	405,418

Figure 2.2   Details on board compensation can be found in DEF 14A Proxy Statements filed with the SEC: Apple's directors receive substantial stock compensation, and the company imposes rules on minimum board member stock ownership.

Source: Apple Proxy Statement January 2023 / Public Domain.

2.2 Disincentives

To provide financial upside for executives, some boards design incentive packages that inadvertently introduce new incentive problems. Following, I discuss the three common disincentive problems.

Incentive to boost the stock price. Simply giving people stock options creates an incentive to try to boost the stock price. Long-term investors should not favor a company that merely boosts its communication and earnings to temporarily elevate the share price. They should seek permanent long-term intrinsic value per share appreciation. Thus, such incentives directly counteract the interests of long-term shareholders.

While stock option programs can be designed in many ways and some might be more acceptable, one positive side-effect is that they can increase actual management shareholding over time if the manager retains the shares post-exercise. You should evaluate the specifics of each option program to determine if it causes problematic disincentives. In high-tax countries, stock schemes can be burdensome in the sense that managers are asked to invest post-tax money in the company's shares. This limits how much one can realistically invest, especially for managers below the executive level, which may make option schemes more acceptable (if properly constructed!). Details on specific programs can often be found in proxy filings.

Incentive to maximize short-term profits. Giving individuals an incentive to increase short-term profits is like promising a marathon runner a bonus for leading after the first mile. It may be productive for his chances of leading after the first mile but not for his chances of winning the race.

It's common for corporate managers to have a variable compensation component linked to short-term (1–3 years) profit and revenue gains. They might also receive options or restricted stock units that vest if profits or revenues meet certain targets within this period. Both incentives can be problematic as they motivate managers to prioritize short-term gains.

Some incentive programs are better than others. If such programs are linked to KPIs measured on a per-share basis and are measured over a more extended period (e.g., 5 years), and if they vest in the form of shares instead of cash, then they are more aligned with the interests of long-term shareholders.

Incentive for value destructive growth. Disincentives for making a business larger but not better can lead to the destruction of shareholder value. Financial bonuses tied to revenue growth, volume growth, market share, or growth milestones, without considering the capital consumed or the number of shares outstanding, can easily create an incentive to pursue low-quality growth. Such growth yields a low or negative return on the capital it consumes. It's like a professional bodybuilder who gets paid per pound gained, regardless of muscle or fat. The easiest way to get paid is to eat counterproductive candy bars all day long. The worst kind of disincentive in this category is when management is financially incentivized to grow by acquiring other companies, as this is a common source of value destruction.

Let's Sniff Around

Analyze management incentives:

- Calculate the value of personal stock holdings in relation to both cash compensation and estimated personal wealth for the CEO and all key decision-makers in the company.
- Check minimum shareholding guidelines for management and board members.
- Analyze disincentives to increase stock price, including options and PSU (Performance Share Units) vesting criteria, by reviewing compensation details in proxy statements.
- Analyze disincentives to maximize short-term profits.
- Analyze disincentives for value-destructive growth.

2.3 Transactions in Own Shares

When executives or directors buy or sell stock, it can be a signal of where they truly think the firm is headed. It's preferable to focus on managers who almost never sell their shares, and when they do, it's mainly for tax purposes. Managers who continuously increase their holdings in their own companies are particularly interesting, as illustrated in Figure 2.3 showing the cumulative shareholding in the freight forwarder Expeditors of its CEO Jeff Musser, who has been with the firm since starting as a part-time messenger in 1983.

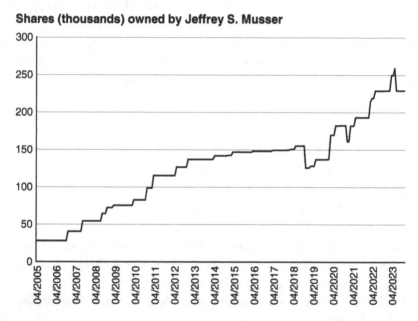

Shares (thousands) owned by Jeffrey S. Musser

Figure 2.3   It is always reassuring to see a CEO's ownership steadily increasing over time. The figure shows the shareholding of Jeffrey S. Musser, CEO of the freight forwarder Expeditors, evolving over time. Musser joined the company in 1983, initially working part-time as a messenger.

Note: Adapted fom publicly available SEC filings.

You should try to understand the motivations and reasons behind the buy and sell transactions of executives and directors. While the reasons for buying stocks are often clear, there can be countless reasons to sell. It's not entirely black and white. Executives often sell stock to cover tax liabilities resulting from option exercises. They may have previously taken loans to cover taxes on earlier option exercises; these loans must be repaid, often by selling stock. There may also be personal reasons, such as a divorce, which are typically not disclosed to the investment community. While there can be reasonable grounds, you should understand the reason for selling.

 Let's Sniff Around

Analyze management's transaction in own shares:

- Review the company's own filings (e.g., Form 4) regarding management transactions. These are filed with the local stock exchange and/or financial supervisory authority and are typically aggregated by financial data service providers.
- Investigate the background of the sale by reviewing disclosures and directly questioning the company. It is usually a red or yellow flag if a manager sells stock without any specific reason.
- Consider the company's share price at the time of sale. Executives who sell when the share price is low should warrant extra diligent review.

Toward the end of Dr. Faustus's 24-year pact with the devil, he was filled with regret and despair as he contemplated the impending eternal torment. Hoping to escape his doomed fate, he prayed to God for forgiveness, but it did little to help, given the binding nature of his pact with Lucifer. Similarly, at the end of the short-term *incentive pacts* that shareholders often make with executives (via the institutional imperative zombies representing them on the board), shareholders must bear the tormenting long-term consequences of decisions made under the short-term incentives inherent in the pact.

One particular benefit of proper long-term incentives is that it predisposes people to think more carefully about how they allocate profits. This leads us to the next chapter, Capital Allocation.

Chapter 3

Capital Allocation

S implified, the job of a business manager can be broken down into two things: (1) optimizing long-term profits and (2) investing or allocating those profits. This chapter is about the latter.

A business can raise capital four ways and allocate its profits five ways.

The four ways to raise capital
- Use internal cashflows
- Raise debt
- Raise equity
- Sell assets

The five ways to allocate profits
- Reinvest in existing operations
- Acquire other companies
- Reduce debt
- Distribute dividends
- Repurchase its own stock

In the short term, the decision to allocate profits one way or another may seem insignificant, but over long periods, these decisions have a huge

impact on per-share outcomes. A CEO should be both a proficient operator and capital allocator. Typically, a CEO becomes an adept operator but
may not necessarily be a capable capital allocator. This isn't something
CEOs usually learn on their way up the corporate ladder.

> Over a long period of time, the decisions CEOs make across those alterna-
> tives have an enormous impact on per-share values. If you took two com-
> panies at the same level with identical operating results, but with two
> different approaches to capital allocation, then over long periods of time,
> they would drive two very different per-share outcomes for their
> shareholders.
>
> —*William Thorndike, investor and author, Talks at Google*[1]

William Thorndike wrote a brilliant book about capital allocation:
The Outsiders. If you haven't read it already, I would highly recommend it.
Before reading it, consider watching the YouTube video interview,
"William Thorndike—Talks at Google," in which William Thorndike
summarizes his findings. This serves as a great introduction to the book.
(I would recommend watching the interview even if you have already
read the book.) This chapter uses examples from his book.

Strategy and capital allocation are intertwined. Every strategic decision
is a capital allocation decision. The decision to do something that consumes resources is a decision to not do other things with those resources.
Those resources could have been used in other ways—particularly the five
ways listed previously—and therefore the strategic decision is a capital allocation decision.

The best example of incredible value creation through capital allocation is Henry Singleton, founder and CEO of a conglomerate named
Teledyne in the 1960s, 1970s, and 1980s. Even to this day, he remains a
legend, receiving praise from icons like Charlie Munger and from the
book by Thorndike. Over Singleton's 27-year tenure, an investment in
Teledyne generated a cumulative return that was 12 times larger than that
of the S&P 500—a money on invested capital (MOIC) of 180 times.[2]

During the 1960s, the stock market favored Teledyne and other conglomerates. Teledyne traded at high multiples and acquired 130 companies using its inexpensive capital that traded at high values. However, in
1969, the entire conglomerate sector came out of favor. This marked the

new chapter of Singleton's journey. From this point onward, Singleton never made another significant purchase and never issued another share of stock. He dismissed his business development team, choosing instead to focus on optimizing his existing operations and initiating a unique stock repurchase program. This marked a complete 180-degree pivot from his previous business strategies. Over the subsequent two decades, Singleton succeeded in buying back 90% of the company's outstanding shares using internal cash flows. Toward the end of this period, he turned to spin-offs, further enhancing value for shareholders.

Singleton conducted the buybacks opportunistically, making large tender offers on his own shares when he believed them to be significantly undervalued. For extended periods, he would patiently do nothing other than accumulate cash, waiting for the share price to drop again so he could repurchase more. According to Thorndike's book:

> In early 1972, with his cash balance growing and acquisition multiples still high, Singleton placed a call from a midtown Manhattan phone booth to one of his board members, the legendary venture capitalist Arthur Rock (who would later back both Apple and Intel). Singleton began: "Arthur, I've been thinking about it and our stock is simply too cheap. I think we can earn a better return buying our shares at these levels than by doing almost anything else. I'd like to announce a tender—what do you think?" Rock reflected a moment and said, "I like it."[3]

3.1   Value-accretive Buybacks versus Buybacks

Buybacks have become increasingly common over the past decades. However, because of the way they are implemented, it is unlikely that they will create value. The most common way buybacks are implemented is through the board of directors approving an amount designated for buybacks. This is typically executed quarterly, often to offset options grants, resulting in minimal net reduction of the share base. Moreover, public companies, on average, tend to repurchase the most shares at inopportune times and the fewest shares when it would be most beneficial. In times of crisis, they focus on preserving cash and liquidity, often suspending buyback programs. Yet, it is during these periods, when many halt their repurchases and share prices are at their lowest, that they should be buying. Conversely, when the economy is thriving and companies report impressive earnings, public companies tend to be more aggressive in buying stock, often at peak prices. Such practices do little to increase intrinsic value per share. For instance, in Q1 2009, during the depth of the Great Financial Crisis, American public companies (S&P500) recorded a quarter with historically low buybacks as percentage of market value.[4]

Some individuals and executives believe that share repurchases aim to drive up the share price by increasing demand for the shares. They completely miss the point. Such supply–demand effects are temporary and don't create any permanent value; in fact, they can be outright value-destructive. In Singleton's case, it was about increasing the intrinsic value per share for shareholders by reducing the number of outstanding shares under opportune conditions. This concept is straightforward, but for some reason, it seems elusive to many corporate individuals who blindly follow the institutional imperative.

Consider the words "value per share." Most business managers focus solely on the numerator and overlook the denominator. Singleton, however, had a different approach. Even today, few execute buybacks the way he did. Unlike corporations with a mindless capital allocation priority, Singleton did nothing for extended periods. Then, when he had accumulated enough

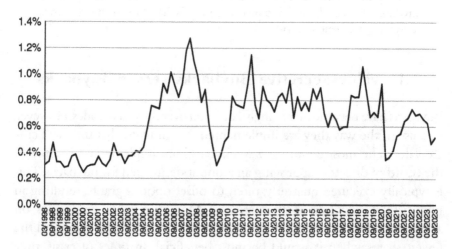

Figure 3.1   Buyback as a percentage of market capitalization of the firms in the S&P500 Index over time.

Data source: With permission of S&P Dow Jones Indices.

Note: Data contained within this illustration is proprietary to S&P Dow Jones Indices and cannot be used or reproduced without their explicit consent.

cash and believed the share price was sufficiently undervalued, he would launch public tender offers for large portions of stock. While some business managers conduct opportunistic buybacks when they perceive the share price to be low relative to their view of intrinsic value, they don't do it as decisively as Singleton. They engage in open market purchases and only when they believe the share price is undervalued. Such an approach can, of course, also add value.

While a company mechanically returning capital to shareholders without thoughtful consideration of its own valuation is often not value accretive, it's not the worst capital allocation scenario either. After all, some companies reinvest capital in projects or acquisitions with low or negative returns, which is a less favorable outcome. Moreover, accumulating cash on the balance sheet to seize opportunities in downturns, akin to strategies employed by Berkshire Hathaway or Henry Singleton, also necessitates prudent contrarian action at times of low sentiment. Simply letting cash sit idly on the balance sheet indefinitely, as has been the case with many Japanese companies for years, is obviously an awful approach to capital allocation.

Let's Sniff Around

Evaluate management's approach to buybacks:
Buybacks aren't inherently value-accretive, but those that are targeted and bolder in their buyback approach can create value through it.

- Evaluate whether management justifies buybacks by enhancing intrinsic value per share or by mechanically returning capital to shareholder.
- Assess if the company has routinely allocated a portion of profits to buybacks, or whether it has been more active during periods with low share prices and less so at other times.
- Evaluate if the current management has historically paused or slowed buybacks to conserve cash in times of market distress.
- Examine the evolution of net shares outstanding over time by reviewing historical company financial statements.

3.2 Hurdle Rates Should Be Determined by Alternatives

I once had a private meeting with the chairman of a sizable listed company whose share price was trading at historic lows. I asked him, "When you decide to invest in new activities that tie up capital, or merely choose to continue activities that don't release capital, how do you determine the hurdle rate that this tied-up capital must meet to justify its use?" He told me that the company used its cost of capital, which their financial advisors had determined to be an 8% WACC. He added that any project that tied up capital had to meet that hurdle rate, with an additional premium for extra risk.

I responded, "I have in front of me your recently published financial and strategic 3-year plan. If you achieve those targets—your own targets—and by the end of the 3-year period your company is valued at a 12x PE, then the implied annual return from now to then is roughly four times higher than your WACC. If you believe in your own public targets, wouldn't it be a better idea to use more of your capital to buy back your own shares now rather than tie it up in projects you believe yield 8%?"

He paused for a moment and pondered. I could tell the idea had never occurred to him. The board was merely following the industry's norms and not thinking independently about how capital allocation could be used to increase per-share outcomes. Neither he, any of the board members, nor the CEO held any significant shareholding, which might explain their perspective.

Hurdle rates should be determined in reference to the set of opportunities available. The cost of capital for organic investments or acquisitions should be viewed as a function of the incremental shareholder return from any other uses of capital. A company's management should have a clear understanding of what they believe the business is worth. They have access to all the relevant information; therefore, they should have a good idea of the expected incremental IRR over the next 5–10 years (or whatever the longest internal forecast the business conducts) if they were to repurchase shares today. What often doesn't make sense—and I see this frequently—is when the management publicly and privately communicates a promising outlook for the company over the next 5–10 years, which starkly contrasts with its depressed stock price, yet isn't willing to

Balancing the numerator and denominator   prosus

We allocate our capital so that we can **drive the highest risk-adjusted return.**

Investment		Buyback
Opportunity-specific	**VS.** Elevated	Discount to NAV
Potential returns (IRR)		
Risks are up	High	NAV accretion

At the moment, invest in things we know well and shift capital to buyback given market conditions and level of discount

Figure 3.2   Page from the 2022 Capital Markets Day of Dutch conglomerate Prosus: According to the slide, the company's investment hurdle rates are determined by the attractiveness of buybacks.

Source: With permission of Prosus Services BV.

allocate capital for aggressive buybacks. Either the management doesn't believe in its own optimistic forecasts, is mathematically illiterate, or simply doesn't prioritize long-term per-share performance. Unfortunately, one of these three reasons must be true; otherwise, the situation cannot be logically explained.

Let's Sniff Around

Analyze a manager's capital allocation mentality:

- Evaluate how they have justified investments and other uses of capital. Have they justified them relative to other uses, as Singleton did in his phone call to Arthur Rock?
- Ask management how they determine the hurdle rate for investments. You'll find that many companies, unfortunately, adopt a mindless institutional imperative approach, like the chairman

I mentioned earlier. Other companies are somewhere in between. They might not be as aggressive as Singleton, but they might answer, "Projects must yield a 15% IRR plus project-specific risk premiums, and then we adjust the hurdle rate up or down based on our own valuation." Such approaches are much more acceptable than institutional imperative WACC considerations.

- Review past capital allocation decisions made by those individuals as a manager's historical capital allocation actions are a good indicator of how that manager will handle capital allocation in the future. Note that this analysis is tied to individuals, not companies.

3.3   Value Destructive Acquisitions

Executives who excel at capital allocation focus intensely on maximizing long-term value per share. To achieve this, they consider both the numerator and the denominator. Sadly, most corporate managers only concentrate on the numerator, like a race car driver with a ruler instead of a speedometer. This mindset becomes particularly risky when these individuals venture into large acquisitions. Large acquisitions represent the most common source of shareholder value destruction. Frequent issues include the following:

- Buying at the peak of the cycle
- Paying too much
- Overestimating synergies
- Failing to integrate successfully and in a timely manner

However, executives with an emphasis on the denominator tend to approach acquisitions in a different way. They only purchase other companies when they are confident that the incremental risk-adjusted return from doing so is justifiable compared to other uses of that capital, including buybacks, debt reduction, and internal projects.

Let's Sniff Around

Analyze a manager's historical capital allocation track record in relation to acquisitions:

- Check for examples of walking away from deals. This is a positive indicator because it demonstrates price discipline.
- Evaluate the share price of the manager's own company at the time of purchase. A high share price at the time of acquisition indicates that management believed buybacks were not attractive, while a low share price at the time of purchase is problematic.[5]
- Assess integration track record and synergies achieved relative to the targets set when justifying the acquisition.
- Note timing of acquisitions: Making acquisitions at the peak of a cycle is problematic, while economic or industry-specific troughs are usually good times to buy.
- Evaluate whether the acquisitions were financed organically or in a manner that resulted in significant shareholder dilution or increased leverage.

Financial databases such as CapitalIQ contain data on all disclosed acquisitions, including storage of the original press releases. If you don't have access to such databases, you can map it out yourself using advanced Google search functionality to find the original press releases and log the relevant details in a spreadsheet.

3.4   Unsung Capital Allocators

One might assume that the stock market would place a premium on skilled capital allocators, especially those with a track record of opportunistically acting to enhance value per share. Logically, one would expect that capital allocation ability would trade at a premium multiple. However, this is often not the case and for several reasons.

Firstly, the stock market hates complexity. It penalizes businesses that are complex, challenging to analyze, and possess corporate structures that deviate from the norm. Many of those who excel at capital allocation tend to create complex business structures over time. Their intent is not to create complexity for its own sake. The complexity arises as a byproduct of their efforts to minimize taxes. Over extended periods, reducing taxes can enhance value per share. This tax optimization often goes hand in hand with increased complexity, making these businesses harder to analyze. Managers recognize the market's aversion to complexity, yet they continue to pursue it because (1) they prioritize long-term per-share business performance over short-term valuation multiple optimization and (2) they possess personal characteristics that render them indifferent to deviating from standard corporate practices.

Second, some of these contrarian capital allocators tend to say and do things that deviate from the corporate norm. The institutional imperative exists not only in the realm of corporate managers but also among investment managers. These investment managers might be hesitant to take on the career or commercial risk of investing in a company led by a controversial madman capital allocator,[6] even if they appreciate the investment and believe the manager will excel. Their decision to pass on the investment may therefore be influenced by factors other than their assessment of the investment's inherent attractiveness.

3.5   Metrics and Vocabulary

Investors can also examine management's metrics and vocabulary as indicators of their approach to capital allocation. A prerequisite for such an analysis is having sufficient data. Ideally, CEOs should be in their position for at least a few years to have produced enough statements and actions to analyze.

To our shareholders:

Our ultimate financial measure, and the one we most want to drive over the long-term, is free cash flow per share.

Figure 3.3   The first 21 words of Jeffrey Bezos's 2004 letter to Amazon's shareholders.

Source: Amazon 2004 Letter to Shareholders. Public domain.[7]

Let's Sniff Around

Analyze management's vocabulary as indicator of capital allocation skill:

- Review sources such as shareholder letters, earnings call transcripts, annual reports, and materials from investor days and webcasts. You can look for the following positive indicators:[8]
  - Consistent use of "per share": Managers who frequently use the term "per share" in their writings and during calls highlight their consideration of both the numerator and denominator. Whether discussing financial targets or company goals and achievements, it's reassuring when they mention "growth in profits per share." When reflecting on past accomplishments, observe whether they emphasize total revenue and profit growth or emphasize "per share" milestones.
  - Usage of IRR or other return metrics for investment justifications: When managers take the time to detail and ideally quantify the expected returns from both organic and inorganic investments, it's a sign that they are conscious of the opportunity cost associated with capital consumption.
  - Emphasis on unit economics: Managers discussing unit economics indicate their comprehension of growth and customer acquisition. They view it as an investment made not merely for growth's sake, but because each additional customer or unit offers an attractive IRR or another return metric, making it a worthy use of capital compared to other options.
  - Frequent reference to "cash": Managers who consistently mention terms like cash investment costs, cash profits, or cash flows signal their focus on the real use and returns of cash resources, as opposed to mere accounting figures.

While a CEO's vocabulary can be a positive sign, the case of Mike Pearson at Valeant Pharmaceuticals demonstrates that vocabulary is not enough. CEOs like Pearson, who communicate effectively with shareholders and mimic great capital allocators, may still neglect other stakeholder groups. Such skewed focus can ultimately be detrimental to long-term investors. Furthermore, some companies say the right things but then fail to follow through when actually allocating capital. Therefore, it's important to be wary of "imitators." The analysis of metrics and vocabulary alone cannot suffice in assessing capital allocation qualities.

Historical management communication is not only a great source of observations for evaluating their capital allocation mindset, it can also be used to evaluate the reliability of the statements they make about the future, a topic explored in the next chapter.

Chapter 4

Reliable Communication

There once was a shepherd-boyish CEO who was bored as he sat on the hillside watching the corporate sheep. To amuse himself he took a great breath and sang out, "W.O.L.F. (a local acronym for Windfall of Lucrative Fortunes)! W.O.L.F.! The W.O.L.F. is here!"

The village investors came running up the hill to capture the W.O.L.F. But when they arrived at the top of the hill, they found no W.O.L.F. "Don't cry W.O.L.F., shepherd-boyish CEO," said the village investors, "when there's no W.O.L.F.!" They went grumbling back down the hill.

When forming and evaluating an investment case, you substantiate it based on the information available to you. Much of this information originates from the management of the company you invest in, whether provided directly to you, shared publicly with all investors, or given to resources you trust for secondary information. In fact, nearly all the characteristics discussed in the subsequent chapters of this book cannot be assessed without considering information originating from the company's management.

How can you mitigate the risk of relying on future-oriented information provided by management today, only to be disappointed later? You can start by examining their past predictions and the outcomes of those predictions. By reviewing management's past communications and determining whether they historically have acted in line with their statements, you can attempt to minimize the risk of unpleasant surprises when relying on their current information about the future. You may also want to evaluate the genuineness of their communication as it can be an additional indicator of their honesty and reliability.

There are two dimensions to the problem of the reliability of management communication. The first is the extent to which past predictions have accurately reflected ex post outcomes. The second is whether there are enough observations of past predictions to form an informed view about the reliability of current predictions. In Figure 4.1, I have illustrated three different scenarios:

- Scenario A: The manager has a long history of making predictions, and most of these have proven accurate. One can attribute a reasonable degree of reliability to what the manager says today about the current state and the future.
- Scenario B: The manager has a long history of making predictions, but many of these have turned out to be incorrect. One should discount the predictions made by this manager about current affairs and the future, or even choose not to invest at all.
- Scenario C: The manager has made only a few past predictions because the manager is new to the role. In this situation, there's not enough data to determine the reliability of the manager's predictions about current and future outcomes. One should therefore discount the predictions made by this manager, or opt not to invest at all.

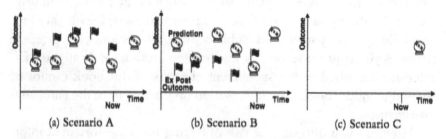

|(a) Scenario A | (b) Scenario B | (c) Scenario C |

Figure 4.1 Predictions versus ex post outcomes: Three scenarios each indicating varying degrees of reliability. (Flag = Outcome; Crystal ball = Prediction).
Source: Simon Kold.

Usually, it's better to give credit to predictions made by someone with a history of reliability like that of an atomic clock than one with a history of reliability like a doomsday cult on April Fool's Day.

4.1 Past Predictions and Ex Post Outcomes

One way I review the reliability is to collect every letter to shareholders issued by the company from the year before the current CEO took office up to the present day and then read them in chronological order in one session. Even without systematically identifying patterns, such simple analysis delivers a decent preliminary understanding of a manager's reliability. The evaluation can be enhanced by copying predictions to a list. Once you have completed the list, go back and find historical evidence on how each prediction compares to the ex post historical outcomes. This is not a statistical investigation. The conclusion is often obvious.

Please note that the analysis of past predictions should not be misunderstood as merely an examination of whether a company has a history of meeting its quarterly guidance targets. This is not the purpose. It's about the broader, more long-term, and even qualitative predictions about the future and how these predictions compared to real-world outcomes.

Transcripts of earnings calls, especially the question-and-answer sessions, can serve as sources of historical management predictions. Analysts often query managers about their perspectives on future developments, and management responses often contain predictions.

Let's Sniff Around

Analyze past reliability of managements predictions:

- Methodically review historical earnings call transcripts, catalogue predictions, and compare them with actual outcomes (as illustrated for Apple in Table 4.1).

Table 4.1 Example of Predictions and Outcomes from Apple's Earnings Calls

Earnings call	Prediction	Ex post outcome
Q1 2014	Emphasized strong confidence in the new product pipeline	They were right.
Q2 2014	The tablet market would surpass the desktop computer market in size within a few years	That did not happen (Based on Gartner's worldwide unit shipments data).
Q2 2014	Increase capital return program to over $130 billion: highlighted as a signal of the board and management team's strong confidence in the future of Apple	They were right.
Q3 2014	Partnership with IBM mentioned as catalyst for iPad growth in enterprise segment	Effect unknown
Q4 2014	Optimism about the future, mentioning the introduction of Apple Pay and Apple Watch, and hinting at other projects in development without giving specifics	They were right.
Q2 2015	Pointed out that only a small fraction of the iPhone's installed base had upgraded, suggesting future upgrade revenues	They were right.
Q3 2015	Many, many years of innovation left for the iPhone	They were right (as of 2023).
Q4 2015	Expressed confidence in the iPhone long-term supported by the rate of Android users switching to iPhone, iPhone's momentum in emerging markets	They were right.
Q1 2016	Expressed optimism about virtual reality, stating that it is not just a niche market but something with cool and interesting applications	To be decided. Launched VR headset in 2024.
Q3 2016	Implied that the current state of Apple TV and tvOS is just the beginning and that Apple plans to build upon this foundation to expand its business in this area	Launched Apple TV+ in November 2019.
Q1 2017	Smartphones become integral to people's lives with rising usage, ongoing innovation from app developers, and exciting things in Apple's pipeline	They were right.
Q1 2017	Goal to double the size of services business in the next 4 years	Services increased 2.2 times, and number of paid subscribers quadrupled.

Note: Adapted from publicly available historical earnings calls

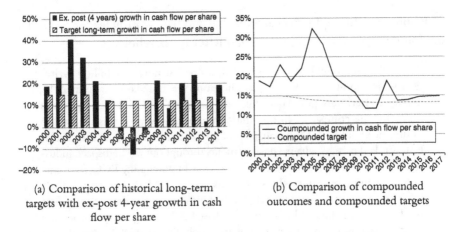

(a) Comparison of historical long-term targets with ex-post 4-year growth in cash flow per share

(b) Comparison of compounded outcomes and compounded targets

Figure 4.2 Alternative asset manager Brookfield's CEO, Bruce Flatt, has a long track record of delivering on ambitious targets.

Source: Adapted from author's calculations of data from public filings.

Executives' explanations for outcomes that diverge from their prior expectations should be scrutinized. The willingness to acknowledge misjudgments and discuss challenges, rather than attributing them to external factors, is an indicator of reliability. However, avoid dismissing a management team because of a solitary, albeit significant, predictive error made in the distant past. Perhaps that mistake provided a pivotal learning experience, enhancing the accuracy of their subsequent predictions.

4.2   Genuineness as Indicator of Reliability

If prior communication has consistently demonstrated genuineness, honesty, and transparency, and if it has expressed thoughts and feelings sincerely, without pretense or hidden agendas, then this forms a crucial input for evaluating the reliability of what that person says today about the future.

There is hardly a better example of this than Warren Buffett. Throughout his career, Buffett has been known for his straightforward and honest communication. He writes personal detailed letters to shareholders where he discusses not only his successes but also his mistakes and the lessons learned from them. This level of transparency is rare in the corporate world and has contributed to his reputation as a reliable and trustworthy leader. Consider the following example from the 2020 letter to shareholders:

> The final component in our GAAP figure—that ugly $11 billion write-down—is almost entirely the quantification of a mistake I made in 2016. That year, Berkshire purchased Precision Castparts ("PCC"), and I paid too much for the company. No one misled me in any way—I was simply too optimistic about PCC's normalized profit potential. Last year, my miscalculation was laid bare by adverse developments throughout the aerospace industry, PCC's most important source of customers. In purchasing PCC, Berkshire bought a fine company—the best in its business. Mark Donegan, PCC's CEO, is a passionate manager who consistently pours the same energy into the business that he did before we purchased it. We are lucky to have him running things. I believe I was right in concluding that PCC would, over time, earn good returns on the net tangible assets deployed in its operations. I was wrong, however, in judging the average amount of future earnings and, consequently, wrong in my calculation of the proper price to pay for the business. PCC is far from my first error of that sort. But it's a big one.

Let's Sniff Around

Analyze genuineness of investor communication:

- Assess whether shareholder letters are written by the CEO or by the corporate communications department.[1] Is the style of the letters personal or impersonal?
- Evaluate whether investor communication reports on both challenges and mistakes or only highlights successes.
- Evaluate whether communication is filled with corporate buzzwords (e.g., "strategic," "deep dive," "post-pandemic," "key," "transformational") or with unique phrases that aren't typically found in soulless corporate language.

Some companies actively deviate from the norm of investor communication. Consider Apple, for instance. Even though it is one of the world's largest companies, Apple doesn't have an investor presentation. Apple doesn't provide a letter to shareholders. Apple's annual report is black text on white paper with no corporate fluff. Apple doesn't provide an annual guidance. Apple doesn't provide many nitty-gritty details, but it has a solid high-level reporting structure that represents how the company thinks investors should view the business. Such actions, which actively deviate from typical communication norms, are often positive indicators of reliability.

Sometimes managers are promotional—they are so-called "selling the stock" to investors. They spend too much time talking to investors, attending investor conferences, etc. This is a red flag. Managers should run the business and increase per-share business performance, not stock market perception. There are a few exceptions where it is perhaps more acceptable for management to be slightly promotional, such as when they are trying to raise or refinance debt, but you should always carefully note examples of promotional communication as significant proof points against the reliability of their communication. I generally try to avoid CEOs who transform into snake oil salesmen during the full moon. Even during the waning moon, I keep a safety perimeter and carry a silver shield of skepticism.

Apple Inc.

CONDENSED CONSOLIDATED STATEMENTS OF OPERATIONS (Unaudited)
(In millions, except number of shares which are reflected in thousands and per share amounts)

| | Three Months Ended | | Nine Months Ended | |
	July 1, 2023	June 25, 2022	July 1, 2023	June 25, 2022
Net sales:				
Products	$ 60,584	$ 63,355	$ 230,901	$ 245,241
Services	21,213	19,604	62,886	58,941
Total net sales [(1)]	81,797	82,959	293,787	304,182
Cost of sales:				
Products	39,136	41,485	146,696	155,084
Services	6,248	5,589	18,370	16,411
Total cost of sales	45,384	47,074	165,066	171,495
Gross margin	36,413	35,885	128,721	132,687
Operating expenses:				
Research and development	7,442	6,797	22,608	19,490
Selling, general and administrative	5,973	6,012	18,781	18,654
Total operating expenses	13,415	12,809	41,389	38,144

Figure 4.3 Neither the word "Adjusted" nor "EBITDA," so frequently combined in investor presentations, exists in Apple's financial vocabulary. There are no fancy charts. There are no adjustments. There is not even an investor presentation. There is just an earnings report with black print on white paper.

Source: Apple's Quarterly Report for the July Quarter 2023 filed with the SEC. Public domain.

Finally, there are rare examples of the phenomenon where market-leading firms actively downplay their market positions in investor communication due to fear of antitrust intervention. In these instances, they define their markets as a union of several large markets to disguise their monopolistic market positions.[2] Most companies, on the contrary, exaggerate their distinction by defining their market as the intersection of various smaller markets, making them appear more dominant than they are. When it is obvious that a company is actively downplaying its own market position or earnings, this strengthens its reliability and indicates that it probably has a mighty market position. What leads to such mighty market positions? This is the topic explored in the following chapters.

Part II

What Makes Competitive Advantages Intense and Durable?

Introduction

A great company is characterized by having at least one considerable competitive advantage against every competitor. This attribute is so essential that I have dedicated an entire part to discussing it. A tenet of microeconomic theory is the idea that excess profits are competed away. In the absence of a durable competitive advantage, high profits attract more competitors. More players mean lower prices and thinner profits. Companies might cut costs or innovate, but without barriers, others quickly copy. This creates a cycle where no one can keep high returns for long. Over time, competition ensures that firms can only earn returns equal to their cost of capital because competition balances out any excess profits.

Warren Buffett introduced the famous metaphor for competitive advantages—the "economic moat."[1] The metaphor illustrates the business and its excessive profits as an economic castle, encircled by a moat. The moat makes it challenging for competitors to penetrate the castle. The presence of a moat is not an all-or-nothing situation. The moat can be qualified:

it can be "wide," "proved illusory and soon crossed," or even "unbreacha-ble," and corporate managers can invest in "moat-widening opportunities" as per Buffett's metaphorical terminology. Buffett also stresses the impor-tance of the moat being "enduring." In his 2007 letter to shareholders, he explains that companies in industries that are prone to rapid and continuous change do not meet his criterion of an enduring moat. The moat must be able to withstand changes and not require continuous rebuilding:

> Our criterion of "enduring" causes us to rule out companies in industries prone to rapid and continuous change. Though capitalism's "creative destruction"[2] is highly beneficial for society, it precludes investment cer-tainty. A moat that must be continuously rebuilt will eventually be no moat at all.

Hamilton Helmer's 7 *Powers* framework has become increasingly popular among investors since the publication of the book in 2016. The framework centers around the concept of "power," which Helmer defines as "the set of conditions creating the potential for persistent differential returns on capital." For each of the 7 Powers (economies of scale, network effects, switching costs, branding, cornered resource, counter-positioning, process power), Helmer describes their "unique Benefit/Barrier combi-nation." Each Power creates benefits in the form of increased prices, reduced costs, and/or lessened investment needs relative to competitors. The Power must also create a Barrier: some aspect of the Power conditions that pre-vents existing and potential competitors from engaging in value-destroying arbitrage.

Throughout this book, when referring to a competitive advantage, I follow Helmer's definition of Power, in the sense that the term *competi-tive advantage* should be understood as a set of conditions that create the potential for persistent differential returns on invested capital by gen-erating both

- a benefit in the form of increased prices, reduced costs, and/or lessened investment needs relative to competitors,
  AND
- a barrier that prevents existing and potential competitors from compet-ing away the company's excess future risk-adjusted profits.

Unless stated otherwise, when referring to a competitive advantage, I refer to a situation in which the business has a competitive advantage over all competitors. These competitors may vary, and the target company can have different types of competitive advantages against each of the major competitors. This is acceptable, if there is a competitive advantage against every single competitor (at least in regard to the company's existing customer base). There need only be two mutually powerless competitors to arbitrage away the excess profits.

In numerous markets, two or three companies often hold competitive advantages over the remaining participants, but not against one another. These oligopolistic market scenarios, characterized by minimal differentiation among the leading companies, can result in "rational competition" with respectable capital returns for these select industry frontrunners.[3] Nonetheless, the term should, by default, only be applied to situations where there is an advantage over all competitors, including the nearest followers.

For investment purposes, I believe **it is crucial that a durable competitive advantage can be empirically verifiable.** In the following chapters, I discuss how each type of competitive advantage should

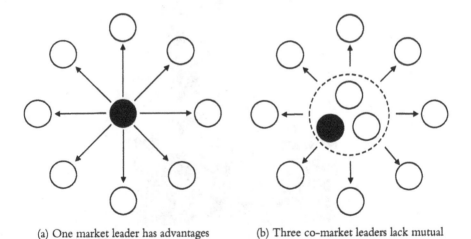

(a) One market leader has advantages   (b) Three co-market leaders lack mutual
over all competitors   market power

Figure P.1   My definition requires at least one type of competitive advantage over each competitive interface. (Label: Black circle = Target company)
Source: Simon Kold.

manifest in specific, observable differences between a company and its competitors. By seeking empirical evidence for these predicted differences, investors can form an informed and empirically based evaluation of their hypothesis regarding the company's possession of a durable competitive advantage. Using the moat metaphor, investors should attempt to measure the moat's width and depth rather than merely theorizing about its existence.

I like to think of competitive advantages in **two dimensions**. The first is the **intensity** of a competitive advantage, meaning whether it results in a weak or strong competitive advantage. The second is the **durability** of the competitive advantage, meaning whether it will provide an advantage for a short time or a long time.

It is also helpful to think of the first-order derivatives of these, i.e., the **direction of the competitive advantage** intensity, whether I expect the intensity to increase or decrease from the current level—and similarly

Figure P.2   The Colossus of Rhodes is believed to have stood for only about 54 years. While it existed, it was a magnificent wonder, but it was taken down by the forces of nature. Similarly, competitive advantages can be intense but not durable.

Source: Augé de Lassus / Wikimedia Commons / Public domain.

with the durability: whether the perceived durability seems to increase or decrease.

Although some companies may possess multiple competitive advantages, which is undoubtedly advantageous, having a single intense and durable competitive advantage is sufficient. For example, having a distinctive old brand that no competitor can ever replicate is more valuable than a combination of a negligible procurement scale advantage, a modest brand awareness, and a soon-to-expire patent.

Competitive disadvantages

Many investors emphasize competitive advantages. That's commendable. However, perhaps they don't concentrate enough on competitive disadvantages. Searching for a competitive advantage is like trying to validate a preconceived belief. Searching for competitive disadvantages is the opposite. I hear the term "competitive advantage" 500 times for every time I hear "competitive disadvantage." With so many companies and investors touting competitive advantages, statistically a lot of companies must have competitive disadvantages. It's weird that I never hear about them!

In recent years, some investors have begun to debate whether "moats" have become overrated. Investors have experienced losses betting on companies they thought had impenetrable positions, only to see these businesses lose market share to later entrants. I think some of these disappointments are due to the disproportionate focus on competitive advantages relative to the focus on competitive disadvantages.

For instance, the company you're examining might possess a distinct scale advantage, and you may have found empirical evidence supporting this belief. However, the closest competitor might have a proprietary product technology advantage. Another competitor could have a radically different business model, placing your company at risk of counter-positioning. While your company might have a competitive advantage, it could also simultaneously have competitive disadvantages. Empirically evaluating these disadvantages may be even more crucial than trying to validate your initial presumed advantage.

The heavyweight boxing champion Sonny Liston had an extraordinary reach of 84 inches. This impressive reach gave him a significant advantage in the ring, allowing him to land punches while keeping his opponents at a distance. In 1964, the champion Liston faced the upcoming Cassius

Clay (later known as Muhammad Ali). Most people considered Liston a heavy favorite, among other things, due to his reach advantage. However, his opponent Clay managed to win the match due to his exceptional speed and "ring IQ." The way some investors analyze competitive advantages is akin to focusing only on the reach advantage. They may go out and do due diligence and, in fact, find that Liston's reach was 84 inches versus Clay's 78, validating their thesis of a competitive advantage. Later, when Liston lost the fight, they were puzzled: *How could this happen? We analyzed his competitive reach advantage. What's wrong with our damn measuring tape?*"[4]

Instead of solely attempting to empirically test your hypothesis that the company possesses an advantage, try to invert your hypothesis and focus on disadvantages. Methods introduced in the subsequent chapters can be used to empirically assess both advantages and disadvantages. You just have to invert the roles.

Opaqueness of competitive advantages

Some advantages are easier to see than others. Companies that have dominated industries for decades and consistently generated high, industry-leading returns on invested capital likely possess some of the strongest advantages out there. However, these tend to be obvious to most observers. There is low likelihood of seeing an advantage that others don't. However, the chances of gaining such differential views are much higher in situations where the company's advantage isn't readily apparent. This is especially true for those who get into detailed analysis of the causes of competitive advantages and understand the characteristics to look for, rather than merely observing symptoms of fully developed competitive advantages, such as high returns on invested capital. I hope that the methods provided in Part II will enable you to identify opportunities in the latter category—that is, companies that are building or expanding their competitive advantages through investments or withheld monetization, making their advantages less obvious for those who only study the symptoms, not the causes, of competitive advantages.

However, I must also acknowledge that even the first category, where the symptoms are evident to all, can sometimes offer very attractive opportunities. An example of this was when Apple's cash-adjusted market capitalization was valued as low as 10 times its cash earnings in the mid-2010s, potentially even lower if one considered the expansion costs of developing new product lines included in the reported operating expenses. Such opportunities become available when the investor community is overly focused on a negative narrative. But even in such situations, an investment hypothesis can be pursued with even greater conviction if one has empirically analyzed each of the causes of competitive advantage rather than merely its symptoms—even if the symptoms are evident to everyone.

For these reasons, I firmly reject the notion that the analysis of competitive advantages can be solely reduced to metrics such as ROIC (return on invested capital).[5] However, I do accept the premise that if a company does not possess an attractive ROIC—both absolute and relative to the industry—yet is presumed to possess a strong competitive advantage, then the investor must confidently understand the reason for the temporarily suppressed ROIC.

Chapter 5

Economies of Scale

I t's not the size of the boat, but the motion of the ocean. Yet, under specific conditions chronicled in this chapter, the big boat certainly gets a bigger bang for its buck. Economies of scale is the reduction in per-unit costs of a product (or operation or function that contributes to the production of a product) as the total output per period increases.[1] This means achieving enhanced efficiency as size expands.

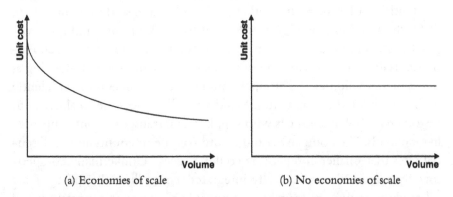

(a) Economies of scale   (b) No economies of scale

Figure 5.1   Simplified illustration of a situation with and without economies of scale.

Source: Simon Kold.

This phenomenon occurs when a firm's average costs per unit decline with rising production volumes. Consequently, smaller competitors, despite having similar access to technology and resources, may find it challenging to match the lower costs of a larger firm. This situation enables the larger firm to achieve profitability at a price point that leaves smaller competitors unprofitable due to their higher average costs. The cost structure underlying these economies of scale often includes a considerable proportion of fixed costs.

For the scale advantage to be noteworthy, a pronounced portion of the total unit costs must be scale-dependent. Although commonly seen in manufacturing, economies of scale can appear in some degree in nearly every business function, including manufacturing, distribution, purchasing, marketing, service networks, sales force utilization, and R&D.[2] Later in the chapter, I go into detail on the following four types of scale advantages:

• Distribution network density
• Purchasing scale economies
• Marketing scale economies
• Production scale economies

John D. Rockefeller's Standard Oil is one of history's most prominent holders of scale advantage. Standard Oil consolidated refineries, pipelines, and distribution networks. The company achieved an astounding cost advantage over its competitors, allowing it to undercut them and gain substantial market share. Its market position became so dominant that, in 1911, the US Supreme Court ordered it to break up into multiple, geographically split businesses. Many unit costs related to extraction, refining, transportation, and distribution of oil decreased with output. Operating at much higher volumes, the business could use its resources more efficiently within each of these activities. Standard Oil's large scale enabled it to negotiate favorable contracts with suppliers and transportation companies, like railroads. The company could secure volume discounts and preferential rates that smaller competitors couldn't access. Unlike many competitors, Standard Oil was vertically integrated, controlling all aspects of the oil production process, from extraction and refining to transportation and distribution.

Smaller competitors faced higher per-unit production and operational costs, making it hard for them to compete on price. Due to its better unit cost, Standard Oil could set prices that either eradicated profits for competitors or led them to experience outright negative unit economics, with losses increasing as volume grew. This created a barrier for competitors, as they couldn't afford to operate at the lower price points set by Standard Oil.

5.1   Relative Scale and Relevant Market

The advantage of scale does not depend on the absolute size of the dominant firm, but rather on the size difference between it and its competitors. I use "relative scale" to refer to the size differential between the leader and its rivals. The size difference can be in terms of volume, market share, or other measures of scale. A low relative scale often indicates minimal or no cost advantage.

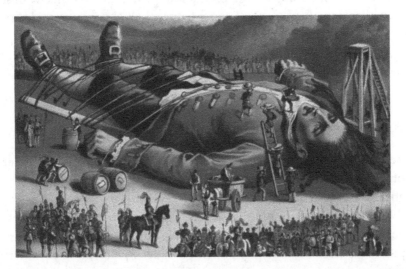

Figure 5.2   Under the right conditions, as in *Gulliver's Travels,* having a relative scale can lead to benefits.

Source: Haaretz newspaper publishing Ltd. / Wikimedia Commons / Public domain.

The relative scale should be assessed within each "relevant market," i.e., the market where the economies of scale effect is applicable. A mere comparison of two corporations' total sizes is often not the appropriate comparison. In brewing, the relevant market is often national since costs such as distribution and production depend on proximity to customers. Carlsberg has a scale advantage over Heineken in Denmark, where it has a larger market share, even though Heineken is a larger global enterprise. For waste management businesses, relative scale should be assessed at an even more localized level, while cloud computing services should be assessed on a more international level. The determination of whether a market is local or global for relative scale assessment often depends on factors like transportation cost, local regulations, and the extent of specific localized needs.

Bruce Greenwald elegantly defines "relevant market" in his book, *Competition Demystified*, as "the area—geographic or otherwise—in which the fixed costs stay fixed."[3] Plant-level relative scale can also be relevant. For instance, two brewers with equal domestic market shares in a small country, one with a single large production plant and the other with several smaller ones, may see the former having a production cost advantage due to economies of scale.

Assessing the relevant market is crucial because an incorrect assumption about it invalidates any empirical analysis of economies of scale.

5.2   Prohibitive Costs

A scale advantage necessitates a barrier to competition. This barrier is prohibitive costs, which prevent competitors from arbitraging away its higher risk-adjusted returns on capital.

Prohibitive costs imply that a follower would either incur losses, or at least fail to achieve a return on capital sufficient to satisfy its cost of capital, if it tried to match the market leader's prices, due to differing incremental costs between the two. The presence of prohibitive costs makes it unappealing for the follower to try to capture market share from the market leader, thereby creating a protective barrier around its existing business.[4]

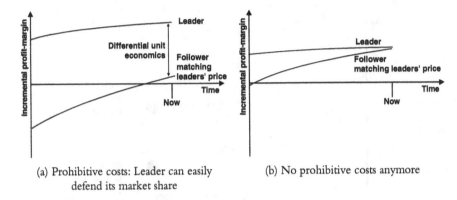

(a) Prohibitive costs: Leader can easily   (b) No prohibitive costs anymore
defend its market share

Figure 5.3 Comparing two scenarios of differential unit economics between leader and follower.

Source: Simon Kold.

5.3 Evaluating the Intensity and Durability of Economies of Scale Advantages

5.3.1 *General analyses*

A scale advantage can be intense and durable, and it can be insignificant and diminishing. In this section, I will discuss some general empirical analyses that you can conduct to evaluate the intensity and durability of scale advantages. After going through these general analyses, I will discuss how the evaluation can be tailored to specific types of scale advantages. The general analyses are as follows:

- Relative scale
- Historical unit cost and volume relationship
- Correlation between market share and cost efficiency
- Prohibitive costs
- Plateau in unit costs and catch-up risk

Relative scale. If the relevant market is local, then relative scale must be assessed within each local market. If the relevant market is broad, then relative scale must be observed within this broad market. This has implications for the sources of information required to conduct the analysis because local information is usually much more difficult to obtain.

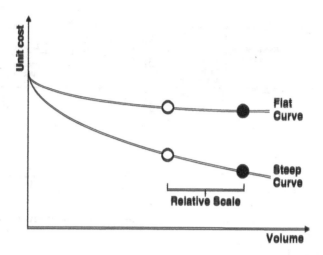

Figure 5.4   Necessary conditions for advantage: a steep cost curve and relative scale.
Source: Simon Kold.

Let's Sniff Around

Analyze the degree of relative scale:

• Obtain data on measure of scale (market share, volume, or revenue) of the target company and its competitors by reviewing financial statements. This can provide information on firm-wide or continent-wide scale (if reporting segments are geographic).[5]

   However, if scale must be assessed more locally, you can:

• Obtain data on more local measures of scale via desk research, expert interviews, or by asking the company. Sources of information on (or indicators of) local revenue, volume, or market share include industry reports and market research, trade associations, third-party data providers, industry studies, antitrust court cases, and online sentiment analysis.

The goal of the analysis is not to obtain the exact measure of relative scale but to test if the relative scale is roughly sufficient and whether the relative scale is decreasing.

Historical unit cost and volume relationship. Relative scale only matters if a significant portion of the total unit costs decreases with increased volume. If it does, one should expect to empirically observe that unit costs have decreased as volumes have grown (refer to Figure 5.1 for a graphical illustration).

Let's Sniff Around

Analyze cost curve steepness from historical data:

- Calculate the historical development of total unit costs as volumes have increased or decreased over time. The analysis may need adjustments for inflation and historical fluctuations in raw input costs.
- Calculate the development at both the company and industry level.

To support your thesis of economies of scale, your empirical findings should indicate that unit costs have historically decreased as volumes increased (or vice versa), suggesting a sufficiently steep cost curve.

To illustrate this, let us consider Anheuser-Busch InBev's (ABI) North American segment. ABI reports regional sales volume in hectoliters and provides revenue and earnings before interest and taxes (EBIT) data for the region, enabling the calculation of a cost measure that combines the cost of goods sold and the cost of doing business. Using inflation data, we can adjust the total cost for inflation and compare it against the reported hectoliter beer volumes. A unique aspect of this example is that the volumes have decreased during the period under evaluation from 2010

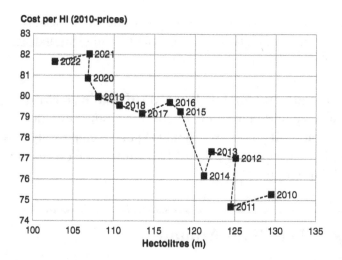

Figure 5.5 Anheuser-Busch InBev's North American segment: Inflation-adjusted cost per hectoliter as a function of volume.

Source: Adapted fom public filings and inflation data from St. Louis Fed.

to 2022. (For context, the decline in beer volumes is attributed to a shift toward specialty beers, Mexican beers, and low-calorie alcoholic beverages like hard seltzer, often at the expense of mass-market American beers.) The data indicate that the inflation-adjusted (2010 price level) cost per hectoliter has increased as the volumes have decreased. This is consistent with the hypothesis of a correlation between historical volumes and unit costs.

We can also infer from the data that if ABI's North American volumes were to increase, then the data would support the thesis that the inflation-adjusted cost per hectoliter should decrease.

Correlation between market share and cost efficiency. A pattern of correlation between market share and cost efficiency across the industry, as illustrated in Figure 5.6, can serve as a relevant indicator. It is expected that smaller players incur higher costs per unit than larger ones.

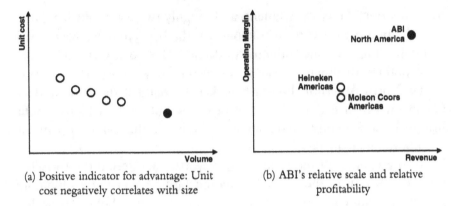

(a) Positive indicator for advantage: Unit
cost negatively correlates with size

(b) ABI's relative scale and relative
profitability

Figure 5.6 Positive indicator for advantage: Unit cost negatively correlates
with size.

Source: Adapted from public filings.

Let's Sniff Around

Analyze correlation between market share and cost
efficiency:

- Obtain data from the financial statements of the company and its
  competitors to see how both overall costs and specific costs vary
  among competitors on a per-unit basis. If a comparison of unit
  costs is not feasible, then compare profit margins.
- Evaluate how these metrics correlate with measures of scale across
  the industry.

   If the data needed for this analysis are not available in the financial statements, then it may require inquiries with the companies or
industry experts.

Let's again consider the North American brewery industry. In this
case, we don't have perfect data based solely on public filings, but I will try
to illustrate it based only on information from the 2021 annual reports of
ABI, Molson Coors, and Heineken. As illustrated in Figure 5.6(b), ABI's
North America segment is nearly twice as large as both Heineken's and

Molson Coors' Americas segments and roughly twice as profitable. Note that it's not a perfect comparison, but it is the best proxy we have based on public filings. See the endnotes for details.[6] These data seem to support the hypothesis that there is a causal connection between size and unit cost in the North American brewery market. I excluded the Boston Beer Company, which had 1/8th of the revenues and an even higher profit margin, because I considered it an outlier, as it is in the craft beer segment and not the mass-market.[7]

In the context of the example, it is worth considering the so-called three-tier system in the United States, established after the prohibition; this system requires breweries to first sell their beer to wholesalers or distributors. These intermediaries then distribute the product to the retailers, bars, and liquor stores. This arrangement curtails the scale advantage in sales and distribution that large breweries would otherwise possess.

Prohibitive costs. If the follower matches the leader's price and attempts to steal market share, will it still profit or generate an incremental return on invested capital (incremental ROIC) exceeding its capital cost? If so, this supports the falsification of the thesis of prohibitive costs. The prohibitive cost can be estimated based on unit cost structures for both the leader and the follower. Remember to not only focus on product prices but also take into consideration the sales and marketing investments needed to steal market share.

Let's Sniff Around

Analyze the thesis concerning the existence of prohibitive costs:

- Simulate the competitor's hypothetical financials if they match the leader's price and attempt to capture market share (e.g., by investing sufficiently in marketing, promotions, etc.).
- Evaluate the incremental ROIC of such a scenario.
- Debate your assumptions with representatives of direct competitors, who may offer opposing views and highlight flaws or pitfalls in your assumptions.

Can a company possess a scale advantage without its competitors incurring massive prohibitive costs, like the competitors of Standard Oil? Certainly, it can, but this represents a less intense and less durable form of scale advantage compared to scenarios where modest or high prohibitive costs are present. With nearly no prohibitive costs you can be sure that the advantage will be more subtle than Mona Lisa's smile.

The discussion of prohibitive costs in the case of ABI vs. Molson Coors became somewhat technical.[8]

Plateau in unit costs and catch-up risk. You likely prefer situations where your companies maintain a durable advantage over all competitors. If no further scale benefits are achieved, competitors can catch up and eliminate the cost advantage. Investors should focus on advantages in the future, not in the past.

Let's Sniff Around

Analyze the likelihood of a plateau in scale benefits:

- Obtain data on the company's unit costs and adjust them for inflation, raw input fluctuations, and cyclical fluctuations.
- Calculate incremental profit margins of these adjusted numbers and evaluate whether they have been stable for a while.
- Ask the company about continued cost efficiency gains, and cross-check this information with relevant experts.

If the plateau has been reached, then the thesis of prohibitive costs becomes even more important.

The example of Anheuser-Busch InBev's North American business is unique in this respect because volumes have decreased. As illustrated in Figure 5.5, the inflation-adjusted cost per hectoliter has increased, while volumes have decreased. This suggests a cost structure that has not plateaued. We would expect the cost per hectoliter to decrease if volumes were to increase again.

But wait, there's more! In the following subsections, I discuss some common types of scale advantages and how to tailor additional analysis to each specific type.

5.3.2   Distribution network density

Distribution network density is a type of scale advantage where a more efficient distribution within a given area allows a company to serve a greater number of customers at a reduced cost per unit. This type of scale advantage is geographically limited, often necessitating assessment on an area-by-area basis. It is also sometimes referred to as route density.

A distribution network consists of various operations that facilitate product distribution within a designated area. They typically include delivery fleets, warehouses, sortation centers, delivery stations, retail stores, third-party logistics partnerships, reverse logistics facilities, and more. By having a denser network than competitors in each area, market leaders often achieve lower distribution costs per unit.

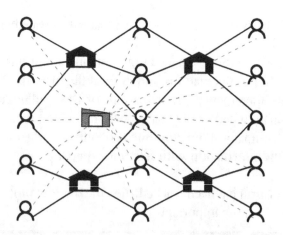

Figure 5.7   Distribution network. Black is denser than Gray.
Source: Simon Kold.

USD per package including fuel

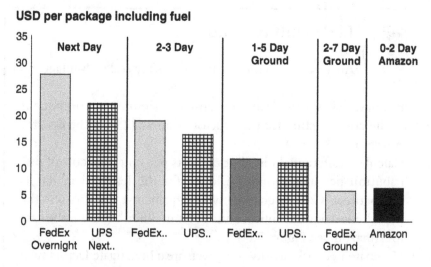

Figure 5.8   Price per package, by delivery service product and carrier CY2023, estimate by Barclay's Research.

Source: Adapted from Barclay's Research.

For instance, Amazon has developed a superior fulfillment and logistics network that allows faster and more cost-effective delivery of products in many areas. This lower distribution cost, combined with a consumer-focused pricing strategy, creates prohibitive costs of taking market share from Amazon, helping to defend its market share in areas where this distribution network density advantage exists. Given the significance of distribution costs within the cost structure for Amazon, this cost advantage is meaningful.

Another example of a company benefiting from route density advantage is the uniform rentals and facilities services company, Cintas. The drivers of Cintas are responsible for picking up soiled garments and delivering fresh ones each week. The cost effectiveness of a given route is a function of the density of drop-off and pick-up points, owing to reduced fuel expenses and enhanced revenues per route. Cintas is more than twice the size of each of its nearest competitors in uniform rentals. Given the significant scale of Cintas, this cost advantage is considerable.[9]

Let's Sniff Around

Analyze distribution network density scale advantages:

- Evaluate whether distribution cost is a significant component of the cost structure for this type of business. (This is the case for Amazon.)
- Calculate differential distribution costs per unit: The cost of distribution per unit should be lower for the leader than for its competitors. Collect quantitative or qualitative data to test the hypothesis that distribution costs per unit differ.[10] (This is the case for Amazon; see Figure 5.8.)
- Compare network density in a given area: Investigate factors such as the number of warehouses, warehouse locations, the number of distribution centers, and the transportation modes employed.
- Compare time to deliver: If the target company can deliver products more quickly than competitors, it may indicate a more efficient distribution network. Compare delivery times between the target company and its competitors.

Sometimes data can be obtained through secondary sources instead of primary sources. For instance I found the data presented in Figure 5.8 in a sell-side research report.

5.3.3   Purchasing scale advantages

Purchasing scale economies occur when a company achieves cost savings by buying goods or services in larger quantities, resulting in a lower cost per unit. These cost advantages arise from the increased bargaining power with suppliers due to high-volume purchases.

Companies that possess purchasing scale advantages often enjoy lower prices, more favorable payment terms, and better access to scarce resources. This advantage is probable when the volumes purchased by the company are significant relative to the size of the supplier. If the supplier does not rely heavily on the revenues from the purchaser, then the supplier will prioritize maximizing their own profits. However, if a particular purchaser accounts for a large portion of a supplier's volume or profit, suppliers will want to protect this through reasonable pricing. On the other hand, if purchases are large compared to the supplier, most bargaining leverage may have already been exhausted. The scale effect also depends on the concentration of the supplier groups, as a concentrated supplier group will have higher bargaining power than a fragmented one.[11]

Costco is an example of a business with purchasing scale advantages. As one of the largest wholesale club operators, it buys products in vast quantities. This purchasing volume gives it bargaining power with suppliers. As a sidenote, Costco's practice of passing on cost savings to customers is the example that led famous investors Nick Sleep and Qais Zakaria to coin the term "scale economies shared." As the firm grows in size, it passes scale savings back to the customers in the form of lower prices. Consequently, customers purchase more goods, which provides the firm with greater scale, allowing it to pass on additional savings as well. Furthermore, I acknowledge that Costco's cost leadership is attributed not only to its purchasing scale but also to a myriad of small decisions aimed at saving money.

 Let's Sniff Around

Analyze purchasing scale advantages:

- Determine the extent of volume discounts, for example, by conducting supplier interviews.
- Evaluate supplier concentration: Purchasing economies of scale may be more pronounced in industries where the supplier group is fragmented.
- Compare prices and profit margins: Being a price leader is a positive sign, provided it's not at the expense of having a functional business model. Likewise, achieving better profit margins at comparable prices is indicative of an advantage.
- Note access to unique resources: The scale of purchasing can offer access to exclusive product lines, e.g., Costco's exclusive Kirkland Signature brand.
- Evaluate the risk of over-pressuring suppliers: Be cautious of companies excessively squeezing suppliers because this can lead to long-term repercussions. (Refer to Chapter 10 on value extraction for more details.)

5.3.4 *Marketing scale advantages*

Marketing scale economies is the cost advantages a company can achieve through large-scale marketing efforts that result in reduced per-unit marketing costs. As a company's marketing budget and campaigns grow, the cost per customer reached or acquired typically decreases. This advantage arises from factors such as the ability to spread marketing costs over a larger customer base, more efficient use of marketing channels, better negotiating power for advertising rates, and increased brand recognition.

Certain brand names have a carryover effect among geographic markets, though usually, the company must invest to establish its brand name in each market. Nonetheless, some brand names achieve international recognition due to trade press, technical literature, cultural prominence, or other factors that do not necessitate investments by the company.

Nike, with a large consumer base and extensive distribution network, can spread its marketing costs, such as athlete endorsements, sponsorship, and advertising production, across a higher volume of product sale. The company's global presence also enables it to effectively target marketing efforts across different regions, maximizing the impact of its marketing investments.

Coca-Cola, as one of the world's most recognized brands, also enjoys marketing economies of scale due to its size and extensive reach, which allow Coca-Cola to spread its marketing costs, such as advertising and global promotional campaigns, across a higher volume of product sales.

While many aspects of marketing must inherently be conducted within each national market, some industries may have potential for international marketing scale economies. This isn't just consumer brands like Nike and Coca-Cola. For example, in turbine generator production, which involves a complex sales process, the fixed cost of a specialized salesperson can be utilized across multiple national markets.[12]

Let's Sniff Around

Analyze marketing scale advantages:

- Consider whether the marketing cost is a significant component of the company's and its competitors' cost structures. (In Nike's case, advertising and promotion costs are $4bn relative to $16bn of total SG&A expenses and a $22.2bn gross profit.)

- Compare the marketing spend as a percentage of revenue or gross profit to competitors. (In Nike's case, the advertising cost corresponds to 18% of gross profit. In Adidas' case, that number is 26%. Nike is roughly 2x relative scale of Adidas in terms of revenue.)
- Compare the average customer acquisition cost to competitors.
- Compare measurements of brand recognition and loyalty to competitors.

5.3.5 Production scale advantages

Production scale economies is the cost advantages a company can achieve as its production output increases, resulting in lower per-unit production costs. As a company increases its production volumes, it can distribute fixed production costs, such as equipment, facilities, and management, over a larger output. This advantage arises from factors such as more efficient use of resources, better utilization of technology, reduced labor costs per unit, and optimized production processes. Anheuser-Busch, which we have already discussed in this chapter, is an example of this type of scale advantage.

Taiwan Semiconductor Manufacturing Company (TSMC) is another example of how economies of scale in production can lead to advantages. As the world's largest dedicated independent semiconductor foundry, TSMC's vast production output allows it to distribute fixed costs like advanced fabrication facilities and R&D across a significant volume of chips, leading to lower per-unit costs. This scale empowers TSMC to invest heavily in cutting-edge technologies, maintaining its lead in the rapid-evolving semiconductor manufacturing industry.

Let's Sniff Around

Analyze production scale advantages:

- Compare production costs per unit and incremental production cost per unit to those of competitors.
- Compare industry-specific measures of plant-level production efficiency to competitors.
- Compare utilization rates to competitors.

5.3.6 Related concepts

Economies of scale is often related to vertical and horizontal integration, and often coexists with learning curve benefits. Cost leadership often result from economies of scale, but this is not the only contributing factor. Consider each of these related concepts when evaluating potential scale advantages and disadvantages of your target company versus its competitors.

Vertical and horizontal integration. A scale advantage can arise when a firm is more vertically integrated (i.e., involved in successive stages of production or distribution[13]) than its competitors. Standard Oil is as an example of this. However, there are numerous instances of companies specializing in a specific stage of production that obtain a scale advantage (TSMC being a well-known example). As such, the relationship between vertical integration and scale advantage should be recognized but not excessively generalized.

Similarly, firms operating across multiple horizontally related businesses can sometimes achieve economies of scale advantages over competitors that do not, provided they can share operations, sales force, distribution, and purchasing across business units. An example would be Procter & Gamble or large pharmaceutical companies.

Learning curve and cost advantage. The learning curve effect occurs when unit production costs decrease as a firm gains more experience in producing a product. This effect often coexists with economies of scale. The decrease in unit costs due to accumulated production experience can result from factors like enhanced worker productivity, specialized equipment and processes, more efficient machinery, product design simplifications, improved quality controls, and better monitoring and management of operations.

Ford's introduction of the moving assembly line in 1913 is a well-known example of Ford's historical learning curve advantage, enabling more efficient production than its competitors and making the Model T the most affordable car available. Tesla is a contemporary example of the learning curve effect, where the company has a cost advantage due to its cumulative learning in electric vehicle manufacturing. Some pharmaceutical companies can produce certain off-patent drugs more cheaply than competitors can, due to their accumulated specialization in manufacturing those particular drugs.

The evaluation of how learning curve advantages contribute to cost advantages must focus on the barriers that prevent competitors from replicating such manufacturing processes. Factors such as the complexity of the processes, the extent of proprietary processes, and proprietary employee training all increase the difficulty of replicating these processes.

Frugality and cost advantage. Costco has scale advantages, but these alone cannot fully explain the magnitude of their cost leadership. This is because Costco also benefits from a differentiated business model and a frugal culture. Despite paying its employees above the industry average and not squeezing suppliers, Costco's operations are more cost effective. By fostering a culture where every level of the enterprise is obsessed with keeping unnecessary costs low, many small gains add up to become a meaningful cost advantage.

Cost leadership very often involves scale advantages, but cost leadership should not be explained solely by economies of scale. Frugal cultures, cost-effective organizational structures, and business models also contribute lollapaloozably[14] to achieving cost leadership. As Benjamin Franklin said: "Watch the pennies, and the dollars will take care of themselves."

Chapter 6

Switching Costs

Dearly beloved, we are gathered here today to celebrate the words that shall unite this couple in an everlasting contract of commerce. We have come together in the presence of God to witness and bless the joining together of this customer and this producer in holy subscription agreement. Today, as customer and producer join hands and hearts in premium membership, they embark on a journey together, a journey of auto-renewals, add-on sales, and never-ending termination fees. As they say their vows, they promise to love and cherish each other, in uptimes and downtimes, through usage-limits and lack of data-portability, amid service interruptions and automated replies, till bankruptcy do them part. And so, without further ado, let us proceed with the exchange of vows and rings, the symbols of their unbreakable bond and eternal entanglement.

Switching costs are the expenses that customers face when they shift from one product to another. These expenses include the customer's direct financial costs of switching, the need for procedural adaptations, and the established relationships with the current supplier. High switching costs can deter consumers from switching providers, even when better alternatives are available, because the transition can be costly, time-consuming,

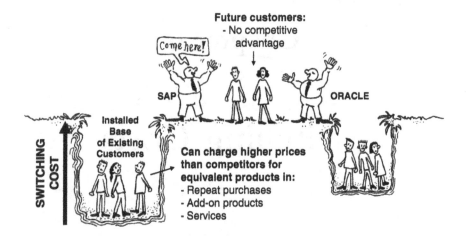

Figure 6.1   Metaphorical illustration of switching costs.

Source: Original artwork by Henriette Wiberg Danielsen based on idea by Simon Kold.
© 2024 Simon Kold.

or risky. This phenomenon, also known as "customer captivity," often leads to customers being "locked in" with their current providers.

Switching costs give firms more power over their existing customers because they are less likely to switch to competitors. In the presence of switching costs, competitors need to provide substantial cost or performance improvements to convince buyers to leave the incumbent.

Enterprise software, especially enterprise resource planning (ERP) systems, often comes with high switching costs. An ERP system integrates the company's order processing, sales, purchasing, inventory management, and financial system into one common database for the entire company. Replacing an ERP system involves retraining the organization's application users, replacing processes and systems built on the ERP system, and dreading the "haunted house"-level of horror associated with potential operational disruptions adversely affecting customers. Companies often hesitate to leave a working system behind, particularly for crucial operations like order entry, inventory management, invoicing, shipping, patient records management, or bank transactions. Even though a new system might promise productivity improvements, the risk of systemic operational failure often discourages firms from making the transition.

6.1   Sticky Customers, Add-on Products, and "Cost of Switching"

The benefit of customer switching costs is the ability to charge existing customers higher prices and to be better positioned to sell follow-on products. However, switching costs offers no advantage with potential customers. It is important to understand that switching costs represent an advantage only in relation to existing customers. Companies that possess advantages solely with their existing customers can be good, but seldom great. The truly excellent "switching cost companies" are those like Apple, that combine switching costs with other forms of competitive advantages (such as brand, network effect, proprietary technology), enabling them to have an advantage in acquiring new customers, retaining existing ones, and monetizing their customer base. Switching cost as a standalone advantage, without the combination of other forms of advantages, is not optimal. A business relying only on switching costs has no way to lure customers in. It's like a man selling Geiger counters and protective Tyvek suits in the Chernobyl Exclusion Zone. It's a lucrative niche, but finding new customers can be challenging.

Figure 6.2   Switching cost as a standalone advantage, without the combination of other forms of advantages, is kind of like darts without beer. It is functional alone but works much better in combination.

Source: Author's private photo collection.

The barrier of switching costs is the unattractive proposition for challengers to entice existing customers away. Competitors offering equivalent products must offset customers' switching costs to encourage them to switch, making it less appealing for competitors to challenge.

Switching costs were a central contributor to IBM's dominance in the mainframe computer market during the 1960s and 1970s. When introduced in 1964, IBM's System/360 mainframe line secured a major market share. Buying an IBM mainframe was a major investment. The costs of hardware replacement made customers hesitant to consider competitors. IBM's mainframes came with unique operating systems, programming languages, and components. Opting for a competitor meant not just changing the mainframe hardware, but also overhauling software applications. Employees were already trained in IBM's mainframes. Plus, IBM mainframes were optimized for other IBM products, complicating any transition due to potential compatibility challenges. It was easier to escape from a black hole than to switch from IBM.

High switching costs meant IBM could charge premium prices and was well-situated to offer additional products and services. Existing IBM customers leaned toward continuing with IBM for additional purchases, ensuring compatibility and leveraging their existing infrastructure.

To entice customers to switch, competitors would need to compensate for these costs either by lowering prices or by offering technological advancements. This put competitors at a disadvantage, requiring them to sacrifice profits.

A property of switching costs is that customers who have previously bought from a particular supplier continue to purchase from that same supplier. Often, switching costs arise from investments that the customer cannot transfer to another supplier. Therefore, repeat purchases can lead to economies of scale for the customer (i.e., a benefit that customers get in terms of reduced per-unit costs when they buy in larger quantities from the same supplier). Once a trading relationship is established, both parties may benefit from continuing their collaboration instead of engaging with different partners. For instance, a supplier might have to make special equipment just for a buyer's specific order. This is an investment in their partnership. Likewise, a buyer might spend money on advertising a final product before getting a part from the supplier needed to make the product.[1]

6.2 Switching Cost Multipliers

Switching costs can arise when a customer values compatibility across multiple products from a specific firm. These costs may result from repeat purchases of an identical product or from the purchases of complementary products. Such costs are referred to as switching cost multipliers. Apple is a good example of switching cost multipliers. Apple has a strong ecosystem of integrated products and services, such as iPhones, iPads, Macs, Apple Watch, Apple TV, AirPods, and iCloud. This integration makes it easier for users to synchronize and share data across devices, creating a seamless user experience. As a result, switching to another platform, such as Android or Windows, would require considerable effort in transferring data, learning new interfaces, and losing cross-device functionality. Apple uses proprietary software and operating systems like iOS and macOS, which are exclusive to their devices. Users who have invested time and effort in learning these systems may find it difficult to switch to another platform that uses different software. Many users have purchased apps, games, and media content through the App Store, as well as subscribed to Apple's services like Apple Music, Apple TV+, and iCloud storage.

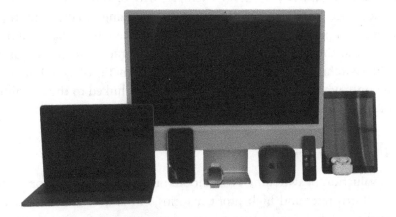

Figure 6.3 Apple's integrated hardware, software, and service ecosystem is an example of "switching cost multipliers."

Source: Author's private photo collection (of his own Apple captivity).

Switching to a different platform would mean losing access to these paid apps and services or having to repurchase them on the new platform.

6.3   Evaluating Intensity of Switching Cost Advantages

Switching costs can vary in their intensity and durability. Some may initially be intense but not be durable over time. This section discusses how to empirically evaluate the intensity and durability and will include an examination of the cost of switching and metrics like churn, retention, and cohort analysis, which can indicate the intensity of switching costs. We will also consider risks to switching cost advantages, such as standardization, increased customer acquisition costs, and risks associated with excessive value extraction.

Even if a customer incurs costs when switching from a product, no future revenues will be linked to that product unless there are recurring payments for its use, such as service arrangements, spare part sales, upselling, or cross-selling opportunities. **Without a clear path to new product or service sales from existing customers, switching costs become irrelevant.** This is, for example, why on-premise ERP enterprise software companies were acquisitive, buying smaller enterprise software companies with more narrowly focused uses that could be cross-sold to the larger company's existing customer base. It's important that the switching cost analysis considers that benefits of switching costs accrue only when substantial future revenues are linked to the continued use of the product.

6.3.1   Costs of switching

Your evaluation of switching costs should not only assess symptoms, such as low churn rates and high profit margins, but also consider the actual financial, procedural, and relational costs that customers face when switching. This is crucial because competitors must compensate customers for these costs if they wish to entice them to switch. If the cost of switching is not high or appears to be diminishing, then it will not serve as a durable advantage.

Financial switching costs are the expenses customers face when transitioning between products or service providers and may include the following:[2]

- **Fees and penalties:** early termination fees, account closing fees, or penalties for breaking contracts or agreements
- **Setup and installation costs:** initial setup, installation, or equipment costs
- **Transfer or migration costs:** moving data, balances, or customer records from one provider to another that can incur expenses related to data transfer, conversion, or migration services
- **Loss of discounts or incentives:** discounts, loyalty rewards, or other incentives

Procedural switching costs are the time, effort, and resources required to change from one product, service, or provider to another. The following are common determinants of procedural switching costs:

- **Risk of errors and disruptions:** Transitioning to a new system or product increases the potential for errors and operational disruptions, adversely affecting productivity and customer satisfaction. It can cause downtime, leading to substantial financial losses for the company due to lost customers and reduced business volume, as well as unexpected costs. Even the slightest fear of such issues can make chief financial officers and chief technology officers averse to risking their jobs by switching a business-critical system (i.e., career risk).
- **System or data migration:** Transferring data, customer records, or other information between systems can cause delays or data loss, which result in downtime and significant financial losses.
- **Retraining and process adaptation:** Retraining employees in a new system or product requires time and resource investments.
- **Compatibility issues:** Integrating a new product or service into existing infrastructure may present compatibility challenges with current hardware, software, or systems.
- **Time and effort for evaluation:** Before switching, customers often need to invest time and effort in evaluating and comparing alternatives.

Relational switching costs are the emotional, social, and psychological expenses associated with changing a relationship or service provider. Following are common determinants of relational switching costs:

- **Community:** Value the community of other users of a product or service.
- **Loss of established relationships:** Personal connections with a provider's sales and service teams.
- **Trust and reputation:** Trust in current provider's reliability and reputation. Switching to a new provider introduces uncertainty regarding the quality and dependability of the new offering.

 Let's Sniff Around

Analyze the customers' costs of switching:

- Interview a representative sample of the company's customers. The interview guide should cover the determinants mentioned earlier that are deemed most relevant for the company in question.
- Quantify the costs of switching based on the information gathered in the interviews.
- Identify customers who have switched and inquire about the monetary and nonmonetary costs associated with changing providers.
- Ask customers about their methods for reducing switching costs and whether they anticipate a reduction in these costs.

6.3.2 The arbitrage of switching costs

Companies with switching costs understand the lifetime value of attracting new customers. They therefore compete fiercely to win over these customers, aiming to profit from their eventual lock-in. New customers are valuable, since they are not yet attached to any provider (see Figure 6.1 for a graphical metaphorical illustration). As a result, firms should increase their bids for new customers by spending more on customer acquisition.

In economic theory, this should go on until the expected lifetime value of these customers is fully priced in. At this point, there is no excess risk-adjusted return for businesses to make on these new customers, as the price of acquiring them has fully reflected their value. For this reason, you should be skeptical about the idea that companies with customer switching costs can continue to generate the same returns on customer acquisition investments as they have in the past.

Customers also play a role in fighting switching costs. They can maintain relationships with multiple suppliers to avoid the risk of being locked into a single source. They can reduce switching costs by using the service in a way that lowers the difficulty and cost of transitioning to another supplier. Negotiating short-term contracts is another strategy. They can also utilize third-party platforms or intermediaries to assist in comparing and transitioning between different suppliers.

Let's Sniff Around

Analyze the arbitrage of switching costs:

- Obtain empirical observations—either as hard data or anecdotal evidence—of how customer acquisition costs have evolved over time for the company in question and its direct competitors.
- Conduct customer interviews to understand both existing and emerging methods for customers to counteract switching costs.

6.3.3   Churn, retention, and cohorts

High revenue retention is usually a symptom of switching costs. Measures such as gross customer churn, gross revenue churn, net revenue retention, and customer cohort data can be used in the evaluation of switching costs.

Churn, retention, attrition. Customer churn, also known as attrition, is the rate at which customers cease doing business with a firm over a specific period, typically 1 year or 1 month. A low churn rate can indicate high switching costs. In contrast, a high churn rate could suggest low switching costs or that the company's offerings fail to sufficiently engage customers to retain them. Typically, consumer and small business segments experience higher churn rates compared to those in enterprise and government segments. For benchmarking purposes, it is often useful to compare churn rates with those of leading companies in similar or related industries.

Gross churn numbers reflect the specific impact of customers (weighted by number, revenue, or volume) who have ceased doing business during a period, exclusive of the effects of additional sales and increased volumes and prices among existing customers. This measure purely represents the extent of loss. Some companies may hesitate to reveal gross churn figures. A reluctance to disclose gross churn, particularly when it is commonly shared among peers, should often prompt additional scrutiny.

Net revenue retention measures the percentage of revenue that a company retains from its existing customers over time.

$$\text{Net revenue retention} = \frac{\text{Starting revenue} - \text{Gross churn} + \text{Net change in revenues from existing customers}}{\text{Starting revenue}}$$

Net revenue retention is a function of factors that are relevant to switching costs, including gross churn and increased volume with existing customers, which is a function of add-on sales (i.e., one of the benefits of switching costs). Sometimes, the metric is reported alongside gross churn, enabling assessment of the amount of both switching and growth or contraction from existing customers. If the net retention rate exceeds 100%, it means that the increase in business with existing customers more than offsets the loss from churn.

A high revenue retention rate is a positive indicator of switching costs because a company can only achieve a high net retention rate if it has reasonably low churn and is able to increase business with existing customers. However, net revenue retention is also a function of other factors, such as product quality, customer care, and price levels.

Let's Sniff Around

Analyze churn and retention rates as symptoms of switching costs:

- Request the information directly from the company.
- Search historical earnings calls for relevant keywords, which can sometimes yield this information even when it is not formally mentioned in reports.
- Consult industry experts or analysts who may have a sufficiently accurate understanding of churn levels.
- Be alert to varying ways of defining retention rates among companies that report them.

Customer cohort analysis. Customer cohort analysis data can indicate the strength of a company's position, which depends on switching costs, customer satisfaction, and the quality of product offerings. It is commonly disclosed in only a limited number of industries, but I personally believe it is a relevant indicator of strength for almost any business.

By analyzing the revenues generated by various customer cohorts defined by the year they first started doing business with the company, you can identify patterns suggesting the presence or absence of switching costs. For example, if older cohorts consistently show higher revenue retention or lower churn rates than newer cohorts, this might indicate higher switching costs for long-term customers. This could mean that switching costs increase over time. If newer cohorts demonstrate higher revenue retention than older cohorts did when they were at similar maturity level, then it may indicate that switching costs are becoming stronger over time. Conversely, if the opposite is true, it could indicate that switching costs (or customer satisfaction) are eroding.

It may also be relevant to consider the size of the latest cohort and compare it with the sizes of other cohorts in their respective entry years. If the business consistently adds new cohorts that are larger than those of the previous year, this suggests that the company's offerings are compelling and that the potential switching costs for new customers are not

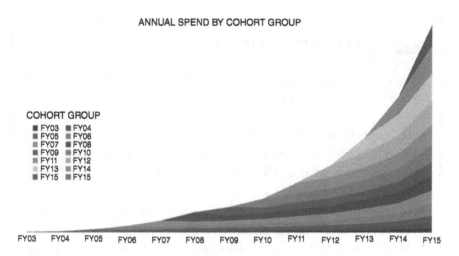

ANNUAL SPEND BY COHORT GROUP

COHORT GROUP
- FY03 - FY04
- FY05 - FY06
- FY07 - FY08
- FY09 - FY10
- FY11 - FY12
- FY13 - FY14
- FY15 - FY15

FY03 FY04 FY05 FY06 FY07 FY08 FY09 FY10 FY11 FY12 FY13 FY14 FY15

Figure 6.4 Enterprise software firm Atlassian demonstrated impressive revenue cohort data in its S-1 filing in 2015.

Source: U.S. Securities and Exchange Commission / Public Domain.[3]

prohibitive for acquiring new customers. Conversely, if the size of new cohorts suddenly seems to decrease compared to the sizes of older cohorts, this could indicate that the company's switching costs and product offerings are hindering its continued growth. However, this could also be a sign of having reached a certain maturity level in market penetration, especially if such a pattern is also observed among peers.

Even if a company does not disclose customer cohort data, you can still try to gather relevant information. For example, you can ask management or investor relations about the sizes of recent customer cohorts. If they are reluctant to provide sufficient information, you could then inquire with former employees or other relevant experts.

6.3.4 Risk of standardization

Standardization of products is a kryptonite-like antidote to switching costs (unless the standards are proprietary). When products follow standardized guidelines, they have common features, interfaces, or protocols that make them compatible with other products. This allows customers to replace or upgrade components without the need to replace the entire system. As a result, standardization promotes a more competitive market, incentivizing companies to innovate and improve their offerings to attract and retain customers.

In the 1960s and 1970s, corporations relied heavily on mainframe computers from IBM. However, the emergence of standardized UNIX-based systems in the 1980s and 1990s offered flexibility and vendor-neutral solutions. As businesses transitioned to these open platforms, the costs of migrating away were reduced. This shift toward standardization fostered a more competitive market. Good for customers. Bad for IBM.

 Let's Sniff Around

Analyze the risk that standardization poses to switching costs:

- Evaluate increasing standards adoption in the industry as well as industry collaborations.
- Check if products increasingly integrate with competing products (interoperability).
- Follow open source initiatives.
- Study and monitor regulations that enforce or promote standardization.

Third-party service. Original equipment manufacturers (OEMs) that generate profits from aftermarket services and spare parts often benefit from some degree of switching cost. One example could be the elevator OEM Otis Worldwide, discussed in Chapter 14. Such OEMs face a threat from third-party service providers increasingly gaining the ability to perform these services. This is particularly relevant to consider in industries with lucrative aftermarket service.

To assess the likelihood that a third-party service provider will capture service business from the OEM, you can consider what prevents the third-party service provider from delivering a sufficient service as well as customer preferences for switching from OEMs to third-party providers based on factors such as service quality, reliability, and pricing. Some companies transition from OEM services during industry peaks and back to third-party services in industry troughs.

6.3.5   Risk of excessive value extraction

While the topic of value extraction is covered in more depth in Chapter 10, the risk factors should be briefly mentioned here in relation to the evaluation of switching costs. The risk of excessive value capture should be addressed assiduously in the context of switching costs, as it poses a grave danger to the durability of the advantage derived from switching costs.

The optimal pricing strategy for a company with switching costs is one that maximizes the net present value of all future profits, rather than prioritizing short-term profits at the expense of the company's future competitiveness. Specifically, among firms with switching costs, some prioritize value over an inappropriate time horizon, leading to excessive value capture and temporarily inflated earnings. Investors should remain extra vigilant regarding the combination of switching costs and excessive value extraction, as it presents two risks: first, overpaying for an inflated income stream, and second, a decline in future market power due to dissatisfied customers and diminished competitive strength.

Companies that overexploit switching costs are like King Louis XVI of France. He imposed unsustainable taxes on the commoners to finance extravagant court expenses, and in the end, he was decapitated.

Chapter 7

Network Effects

Network effects, also known as demand-side economies of scale, occur when the value a user derives from a product increases with the number of other users of the same product.

Not all things exhibit network effects. For example, the value you derive from eating an apple is independent of the number of people consuming apples. The apple's taste and nutritional value remain the same, irrespective of how many other people are eating apples. However, when it comes to learning a new language, you are more inclined to learn Spanish than Somali because Spanish enables you to communicate with more people. Although it would likely also be wonderful to speak with some nice Somalians, the utility of being able to communicate in Spanish is just higher because there are way more Spanish speakers (unless you are based in Mogadishu). Languages are types of human systems in which the value to each person speaking the language depends on how many other people understand that language. Languages have proven to possess very durable network effects. Consider the challenge of disrupting the English language, which has achieved global network effects. It would be quite challenging. Nice try, Esperanto!

Network effect can be both positive and negative with the value of the good increasing or decreasing as more users adopt the same products.

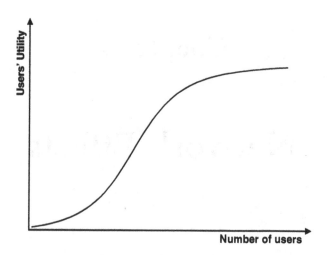

Figure 7.1 Network effects: Utility increases with number of users.
Source: Simon Kold.

Network effects can also be indirect, such as when a growing user base leads to increased complementary product offerings and reduced prices (e.g., more software options for a popular computer).

One of the earliest recorded observations of network effects as a business advantage can be traced back to the 1907 and 1908 annual reports of the American Telephone & Telegraph Company (AT&T). Theodore Vail, the company's president at the time, highlighted the difficulties faced by rival telephone companies attempting to compete with AT&T once it had secured a majority of customers in a local area. Vail stated in his annual report that:

> Two exchange systems in the same community, cannot be a permanency. No one has use for two telephone connections if he can reach all with whom he desires connection through one.
>
> . . .
>
> A telephone without a connection at the other end of the line is not even a toy or a scientific instrument. It is one of the most useless things in the world. Its value depends on the connection with the other telephone and increases with the number of connections.[1]

A telephone network in the early twentieth century that allowed users to call every household in a city was much more valuable than a telephone network with no one to call. A local newcomer attempting to establish a network in an area already served by an existing telephone network faced the challenge that its potential customers would obtain a lower utility from the new product, making it nearly impossible to capture market share. This unattractive cost/benefit for competitors trying to gain market is the barrier side of network effects.[2] Consider a city in 1908, where AT&T had connected every household with telephone cables and managed all calls through a central office. A competitor emerges and begins building its own network. Few people are interested in subscribing to the new network since they can already call everyone in the city using AT&T's service. Why would they switch to a new network that only connected them to a fraction of the population of the city? Consequently, the new entrant must offer a discounted price to attract any customers. From the entrant's perspective, the proposition of overbuilding the AT&T network is unattractive: the cost of building the network is high, its product offers lower value to customers, it can only charge a discounted price, and uncertainty regarding customer adoption is significant.

The benefit of network effect advantages lies in the ability to charge higher prices due to the increased value perceived by users. It doesn't necessarily have to be in the literal sense of prices; it can also take the form of other monetization methods, such as higher level advertising.

Network effects can take various forms, including the following:

- Direct network effects (e.g., early twentieth-century landline telephone networks, LEGO bricks, iMessage)
- Standards/protocol network effects (e.g., Microsoft Office file-formats, VHS versus Betamax)
- Two-sided networks (e.g., auction houses, operating systems, stock exchanges)
- Expertise ecosystem network effects (e.g., Adobe Photoshop, professional tools)
- Data network effects (e.g., Waze, Google Search)

Later in the chapter, following my guide to a general empirical evaluation of network effect advantages, I will discuss each of the types just mentioned in more detail, aiming to help you further tailor the general evaluation to each specific type.

7.1   Boundedness

Network effects are often limited by factors such as geography, language, interoperability (e.g., messaging between iOS and Android devices), user segments, and character of the network (e.g., private networks like Facebook and professional networks like LinkedIn). It is crucial to understand these bounds when evaluating network effect. Comparing the scale of Facebook to China's WeChat is not meaningful, as they operate in distinct markets with minimal overlap. A classifieds business that enables users to buy and sell used goods locally possesses local network effects. Being "the largest classifieds business on the continent" holds no value unless the business is also the largest locally. Analysis of network effects often requires assessment at a local level, which can complicate the analysis due to difficulty of obtaining data.

7.2   Critical Mass and Relative Scale

In the context of network effects, the term "critical mass" refers to the point at which a network can grow independently, without substantial marketing or user acquisition investments. Network effects are fascinating when they result in a considerable market share gap between the leader and the nearest follower. Once a firm with a powerful network effect reaches a sufficient relative scale compared to its follower, the network effect can occasionally become so strong that the market transforms into a near "winner-takes-all" scenario. Most network effects are subtle and not powerful enough to create such drastic market concentrations, but there are rare examples of the latter, such as Windows OS in the 1990s or the LinkedIn professional social network. Be mindful that these rare extreme cases of network effects do not disproportionately influence your perception of network effects. Such rare network effects are almost as hard to find as the Loch Ness Monster itself. Although they are fascinating, they are not representative of the typical network effect scenario.

Firms with products that exhibit network effects, or believe they do, might temporarily delay monetizing their products in an attempt to achieve a critical mass installed base before rivals. By reaching critical mass first and gaining a significant relative scale, they create a network effect advantage, enabling them to monetize more later without risking market share loss.

This strategy has been widely adopted by growth-stage consumer internet companies over the past two decades.

An interesting investment inflection point can occur when the market leader has established a significant relative scale to the nearest competitor—such as twice the market share—but has not yet begun to monetize its product and market position. The absence of an earnings stream due to a lack of monetization can make it difficult for investors to recognize the full value of what has been created.

Network effects are known for occasionally creating very intense competitive advantages that result in exceptional market shares and profits. However, it is important to note that this can also work against you. If scale goes down, then utility also goes down. Therefore, history includes spectacular examples of **reversals of network effects, where a dominant leader collapses with the same speed as it obtained its dominant position,** as seen in the case of MySpace. If users leave a network or decrease their engagement, then the value for the users that remain is reduced. This can create a cycle of network effects in the opposite direction of how investors typically think about it. A good example of this is dying shopping malls, whose two-sided network effects (shoppers and shops) once made them great but now work in the opposite direction.

7.3   Evaluating the Intensity and Durability of Network Effect Advantages

7.3.1   General analyses

Network effects can vary in intensity and durability. How can you evaluate the likelihood of intensity and durability of a particular case? I suggest you empirically evaluate your specific case with regards to following five indicators discussed in this section:

- Relative scale to the nearest follower.
- Utility curve steepness: incremental utility to each user of new users joining
- Network effect saturation point
- The extent and cost of multi-homing
- The extent and risk of interoperability

Later in the chapter, I discuss how such general assessment can be further tailored to the specific types of network effects mentioned earlier.

Relative scale. A ride-hailing customer in London does not gain higher utility because the service adds an extra driver in Sydney. For many firms, the relative scale must be measured at a local level. I try my best to measure relative scale in the market where increased utility is derived from an increasing user base, although it is not always possible to obtain the desired data.

The degree of relative scale that sufficiently allows a leader to monetize its position without risking a follower taking share is a function of the steepness of the utility curve, i.e., how much more valuable the product becomes to users by adding extra users. If there is a flat utility curve, as illustrated in Figure 7.3.b, then having a significant relative scale does not matter. A rule of thumb can be to require the leader to be twice as large as its nearest competitor. Such size difference is often sufficient for the network effect to be meaningful.

Let's Sniff Around

Analyze relative scale:

- Obtain data on installed user base for the company and its competitors by examining company filings, investor materials, or broader communications. Since most companies are not shy about boasting how many users they serve (and many report numbers such as monthly-active-users or daily-active-users), these numbers are often easy to find.
- Calculate relative installed base on both sides of the network, if the business is a two-sided network.
- For businesses operating across numerous local markets, each with local network effects, it can be more challenging to obtain the data, as it is seldom reported with such geographic detail. In these cases, you can seek alternative sources of information about local installed base, such as industry reports, interviews with industry experts, local media reports, and data aggregation websites.

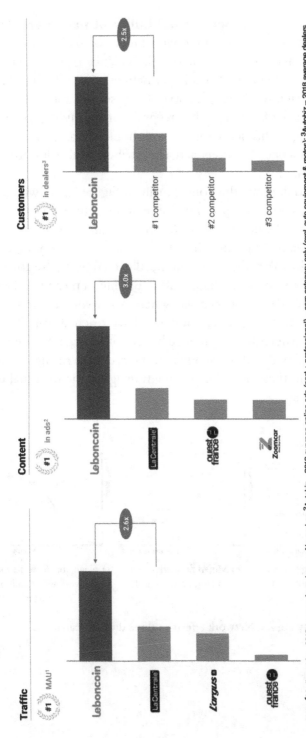

Note: [1]Mediametrie – 2018 average from January-November; [2]Autobiz – 2018 average online ads (part + professional) – cars category only (excl. auto equipment & motos); [3]Autobiz – 2018 average dealers

Figure 7.2 Page from the 2019 Investor Day presentation of Adevinta, an online classifieds group. The company argues that its French operation, Leboncoin, possesses considerable relative scale in the used car vertical.

Source: With permission of Adevinta.

Utility curve steepness: Incremental utility of new users. Having more users doesn't matter if each individual user doesn't benefit from the larger network. Therefore, you should seek evidence that can determine whether users value being part of a larger network, i.e., whether the utility curve is sufficiently steep. I'm sorry if this sounds more dry than a mummified econ textbook, but the steepness of the utility curve helps explain the concept. This doesn't mean you should try to quantify a slope but just seek evidence that users actually attribute real value to adding incremental users.

I have tried to illustrate this conceptually in Figure 7.3(a), which illustrates a situation with a steep utility curve and significant relative scale, indicated by a thumbs up. Figure 7.3(b) presents an often-seen scenario where there is relative scale, but the added value of having more users is so small that it doesn't really move the needle. Despite the relative scale, the network effect is so subtle that it fails to produce a meaningful advantage. Figure 7.3(c) depicts a scenario where a network effect has now diminished, as both the leader and follower have reached scale. They are both in a plateau where the incremental benefit of adding new users levels off. This is marked with a thumbs down because, despite strong utility and some relative scale, there is no longer an advantage as the marginal utility increase is minimal.

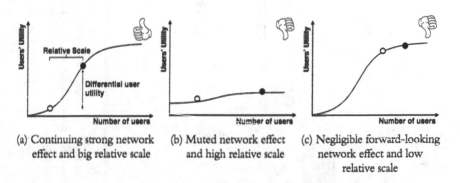

(a) Continuing strong network effect and big relative scale

(b) Muted network effect and high relative scale

(c) Negligible forward-looking network effect and low relative scale

Figure 7.3   Utility curves: Network effects in three distinct scenarios.
Source: Simon Kold.

Let's Sniff Around

Analyze utility curve steepness:

- Interview a sample of users about the following:
  - their willingness to switch to the smaller network
  - their willingness to pay the same amount on the smaller network
  - their willingness to pay more for the existing network
  - how being on a larger network creates more value for them

- Observe the industry dynamics of similar network effect businesses in other geographies.[3]
- Compare user engagement levels: Compare the ratio of daily to monthly active users (or monthly to yearly active users) between the leader and its competitors. This reveals which network has a more engaged user base, which is indicative of network utility.
- Compare user retention levels: Compare user retention rates and cohort statistics between the leader and its competitors. Higher retention is indicative of higher utility.
- Compare the development of user acquisition cost for the company and its competitors. If the utility curve is steep, it should become cheaper to acquire customers as the installed base grows because the value to each customer increases. The per-user cost of customer acquisition should be a decreasing function of the installed base. Specifically, you can evaluate the balance between organically acquired users and those acquired through paid or subsidized means, comparing these metrics for both the company and its competitors.

Network effect saturation point. If all investor presentations claiming a "flywheel effect" were stacked, then they would reach the moon. However, many businesses have enjoyed network effects, only to reach a point where adding new users no longer benefits existing ones. For most firms, this plateau occurs quite early, leading to a muted network effect that doesn't result in a meaningful advantage and therefore no differential returns on capital.

To illustrate what I mean by saturation point, consider the online multiplayer game *World of Warcraft*. In its early years, the game's growing user base enhanced its appeal due to a vibrant in-game economy, a variety of players to team up with for quests, and a large community for social interaction. However, the game reached the limits of network effects. Beyond a certain user threshold, additional players did not improve the experience for existing players. In fact, excessive crowding in popular areas, longer queues for in-game events, and the dilution of community engagement could detract from the experience. There is simply a point at which the scale leads to what economists call diseconomies of scale, even for products with very strong network effects like *World of Warcraft*.

Why should investors care about such economist mumbo jumbo? Well, investors should concentrate on competitive advantages in the future, not in the past. It is easy to be blinded by historical network effect advantages, but if a company has already reached the saturation point at which adding extra users does not benefit existing ones (as illustrated in Figure 7(c)), then it becomes easier for the competitors to catch up and erode the advantage.

One determinant of whether this saturation point occurs early or late appears to be the degree of variation in how each user utilizes the network, hereafter referred to as the variation in "user preferences."[4] To exemplify this, consider a job classifieds business versus a ride-hailing business. Both exhibit network effects and involve two sides: drivers and passengers in the ride-hailing business, and job seekers and employers in the job classifieds business. Both types of businesses have demonstrated their ability to result in high market concentration locally, likely due to the potent network effect. However, there is a difference between job classifieds and a ride-hailing service in terms of user preference

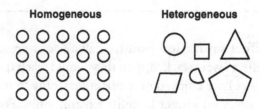

Figure 7.4   Variation in user preferences is a determinant of a network's utility flattening point.

Source: Simon Kold.

variation. Passengers using the ride-hailing service want to get from point A to point B as quickly and efficiently as possible. They benefit from having more drivers on the platform because it reduces waiting times and the cost of the trip. However, their preferences regarding the trip itself are homogeneous; they just want to go from A to B. Similarly, drivers just want to get some trips.

Job seekers certainly benefit from a larger supply of job offerings, but their preferences vary more. They are not just looking for "a job"; they are seeking a specific job that interests them. Employers who advertise on the job classifieds are looking for the most qualified candidate, not just any random person to fill the job. This difference in user preferences variation has implications when the added value of more users diminishes.[5]

The marginal utility of adding extra users eventually diminishes, even for networks with heterogeneous user preferences, such as social networks or *World of Warcraft*.

 Let's Sniff Around

Analyze the diminishing of user utility gains:

- Interview users about the value they would attribute to an increased supply on the network.
- Calculate the penetration of the addressable user base in existing markets.
- Consider the uniqueness of individual users' network usage. This should be based on an overall understanding of the network and its typical user, rather than reviewing each user individually. If necessary, conduct multiple user interviews and evaluate the variation among the answers.

The extent and cost of multi-homing. Something must be preventing competitors from achieving an equivalent value proposition as the leader. If users can effortlessly switch between networks, then relative scale becomes irrelevant.

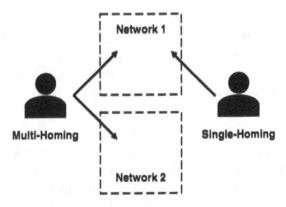

Figure 7.5   Multi-homing: A network effect "party-killer."
Source: Simon Kold.

The phenomenon of users utilizing multiple platforms or networks is known as "multi-homing" or "multi-tenanting." For example, a person using both Uber and Lyft ride-hailing services exemplifies multi-homing. Similarly, posting the same video on both YouTube and Vimeo is another instance. Multi-homing undermines network effects. If users frequently multi-home, the value created by the networks gets arbitraged away, benefiting customers but not the network owners.

I try to gather information on the extent of multi-homing as well as get a decent understanding of users' reasons to multi-home or not.

Network effect durability is a function of the cost users incur from using multiple networks as well as their switching costs from leaving the incumbent network. For instance, game consoles demonstrate high costs of multi-homing for consumers. Most people are unlikely to purchase and set up both a PlayStation and an Xbox due to the costs, space requirements, and the inability to transfer purchased games from one platform to another. Social networks have low multi-homing costs, as it requires minimal time and effort for users to create accounts on multiple platforms like Facebook, Instagram, TikTok, Snapchat, and Twitter simultaneously.

If the network is multi-sided, then data on the extent of multi-homing must be obtained separately for each side of the network. For example, in the case of game consoles, multi-homing is low on the consumer side but higher on the developer side, as some developers create games compatible with both PlayStation and Xbox. If the company's operations span multiple local networks, then the extent of multi-homing must some-times be assessed at each local level.

I suggest you also try to get a decent idea about the trend in degree of multi-homing: The current extent of multi-homing might be accept-able, but is it increasing?

Let's Sniff Around

Analyze the extent of multi-homing:

- Search investor materials and earnings call transcripts for men-tioned data points.
- Directly ask the management or investor relations of both the tar-get company and its competitors about the extent of multi-homing.
- Search for information in market research reports and analyst reports.
- If necessary, for a localized assessment and when information can-not be obtained from the company, consider gathering data from a sample of local markets through local sources, then extrapolate from that sample.

A company with network effects but no multi-homing frictions is like a polygamist's wife. The polygamist's wife is consumed by jealousy and must constantly compete for the polygamist husband's attention. The wife is vigilantly aware that he could always bring home a new wife—nothing prevents him—there is no friction cost of multi-wifing. The polygamist's interests and attention are unpredictable, and she must be adaptable to remain his favorite wife. The wife can't even scold him too much for forgetting their anniversary, because that just shifts his attention to his other wives. Compare this with my wife. For context, I'm a monog-amist, and I'm pretty sure there are extreme friction costs to me multi-wifing. I can't even forget to put my socks in the laundry basket without it turning into a topic for our next "household summit." My wife is in a more advantageous position (although she might argue against that, given that she is married to me!).

When analyzing companies with network effects, you want to identify companies that are much more like my wife than the polygamist's wife.

Let's Sniff Around

Analyze the users' costs of multi-homing:

- Quantify monetary losses of multi-homing, such as hardware costs (e.g., buying smartphones with different operating systems), subscription costs (e.g., paying for both Spotify and Apple Music), account management (e.g., managing advertising campaigns on Google Ads and Facebook Ads), regulatory compliance costs (e.g., being listed on two stock exchanges), compatibility issues (e.g., integrating software between Windows and Mac systems), and lower ROI (e.g., diminished sales on a secondary e-commerce platform).
- Evaluate the switching costs if the user were to replace the incumbent network for the competitor. The entire framework for evaluating switching costs in Chapter 6 can be relevant for assessing the frictions that prevent users from multi-homing.

Extent and risk of interoperability. Two systems function separately. A link between the two systems is introduced. Increasingly, the two systems operate together, serving the users of both systems. Users begin to view the two systems as one.

Interoperability is beneficial for consumers, but for a company with network effects, its introduction often represents an existential risk. If two commercial networks become compatible, they can merge in an economic sense, meaning the network effect applies at the industry level rather than the firm level.

In 1908, it was challenging to interconnect with other telephone networks. Each company had its own systems of cables and equipment. A customer on AT&T's network could make local calls to someone who was also on the AT&T network, but not on a competing network. This enabled AT&T to become a monopoly.

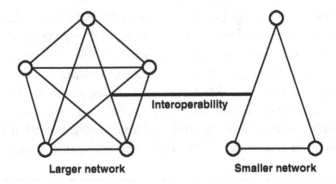

Figure 7.6 Interoperability between two networks: A network effect "party killer."
Source: Simon Kold.

The competitive strength of modern telecommunication firms is nothing compared to the old AT&T because there is interconnectivity between the physical mobile telecom networks. T-Mobile customers can call AT&T customers, and so on, which eliminates the firm-level network effect.

LEGO bricks exhibit network effects. The more compatible bricks you have, the greater the building possibilities. Since LEGO's building block patents expired in 1978, the company has aggressively protected its trademarks and other intellectual property rights by filing lawsuits against competitors like Mega Bloks. LEGO has attempted to prevent competitors from selling blocks compatible with basic LEGO bricks. I suspect the company does this because it understands the significance of compatibility in relation to the erosion of network effects.

Technology can introduce interoperability. The advent of advanced, cross-platform game engines like Unreal Engine and Unity reduced the network effect of console manufacturers. These engines facilitate easier and more economical game development for multiple systems. Developers can now reach broader audiences across various consoles and computers.

Regulatory risks, which are covered in more depth in Chapter 17, must always be considered in conjunction with network effects, especially if the network effect holder provides some kind of societal infrastructure, similar to what the railways and AT&T did, or what social media and search engines do currently. In fact, one could argue that regulatory risks are increasingly relevant for modern-day network effect "information utilities." For instance, the European Union's Digital Markets Act (DMA) regulation, set to be implemented in 2024, includes provisions that would require large messaging services to be interoperable with other services. This would potentially affect major messaging platforms like iMessage, WhatsApp, and Facebook Messenger, mandating them to enable communication capabilities such as message exchanges, video calls, and file sharing with smaller messaging services. Noncompliance with this legislation could result in fines, up to 10% of the company's global annual turnover.

Let's Sniff Around

Analyze the extent and risk of interoperability:

- Evaluate the degree of proprietariness of the technical standards used by the target company. Proprietary standards can increase the risk of interoperability issues.
- Analyze the movement toward open standards, which are often driven by regulators or industry collaborations.
- Assess the likelihood of government intervention.
- Gain an understanding of how emerging enabling technologies might enhance interoperability.

But wait, there's more! In the subsequent sections, I discuss specific types of network effects and how additional analysis can be tailored to each specific one.

7.3.2 *Protocol network effects*

Languages are hard to disrupt due to durable network effects. You can think of products exhibiting protocol network effects as abstract forms of languages. Protocol networks form around communication and computational standards.

On May 24, 1844, Samuel Morse, the inventor of the telegraph, famously sent the message "What hath God wrought" to his assistant, Alfred Vail, using a system of dots and dashes that represented letters and numbers, known as Morse code. More than 150 years later, on January 31, 1997, the French Navy broadcast a message over the airwaves in Morse code that translates to "CALLING all. This is our last cry before our eternal silence," marking the end of their use of Morse code in maritime communication.[6]

Another 25 years later, the author of an investment book of lava-lamp-level-of-kitschiness, sent the following morse code: -.-- --- ..- / -.. --- .-- . . . . .-. .* Morse code was indeed a very durable communication standard.

There is a good chance you are already familiar with the case of VHS versus Betamax, which was a case of two competing standards, where the technically less sophisticated standard (VHS) prevailed due to higher adoption. This is the essence of protocol network effect advantages. The standard is the best standard not because it is technically the best, but because its wider adoption makes it the best.

Once a protocol has been widely adopted, it becomes very difficult to replace, for example, the continued use of the SWIFT protocol for payments or the TCP/IP protocol despite the existence of technically better alternatives. This is also the explanation why fax machines continued to be in use so long after the emergence of better communication methods.

Protocol network effects can be proprietary to a single company, for example AT&T's proprietary telephone protocol in the early twentieth century, hereafter "firm level" protocol network effects. However, it is more common to see protocol network effects benefit the entire industry instead of creating advantages for individual participants within it (hereafter "industry level"). For instance, the QWERTY typewriter keyboard became standard for typewriters without creating a particular advantage for its inventors. It is still the standard today, despite technically better layouts, such as the Dvorak layout.

Protocol network effects at the firm level, rather than at the industry level, are the relevant sources of competitive advantage. When protocol network effects occur, it is often a firm that is dominant in the early phase of an industry that manages to set a standard (regardless of whether the protocol remains associated with that firm in the long run). For example, IBM played a crucial role in imposing standards in the computer industry, and Home Box Office led in defining a signal-scrambling standard.[7] ARM's instruction architecture exhibited a protocol network effect in mobile CPUs. Examples of other well-known contemporary products that exhibit firm-level protocol network effects include Apple's AirPlay, Microsoft Office file formats, and Dolby codecs and audio formats.

*This Morse code can decoded as follows: YOU DOWSER.

Figure 7.7 "Video Wars": Sony's Betamax vs. JVC's Video Home System (VHS). VHS became the standard "protocol" due to wider adoption, despite Betamax being technically superior.

Source: inBaliTimur / Flickr / https://www.flickr.com/photos/thisisinbalitimur/31640036170/ / Last accessed on April 27, 2024.

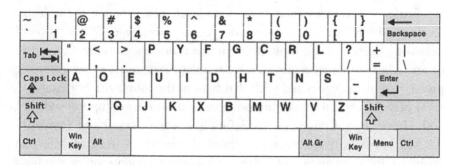

Figure 7.8 The Dvorak keyboard layout was designed to increase typing speed and reduce finger movement. However, its adoption has been limited due to the strong network effects of the established QWERTY standard.

Source: Unknown / wikimedia Commons / Public domain.

Let's Sniff Around

Analyze protocol network effects:

- Evaluate the ability to capture value (many businesses with proto-col network effect lack the ability to sufficiently capture value). For instance, you can interview users about their willingness to pay for use of the protocol/standard.
- Assess the degree of standardization (adoption-level by users, developers, or other industry players) and interoperability between the protocol and other systems, platforms, or devices.
- Evaluate the degree of technological lock-in associated with the protocol.
- Assess the ecosystem of complementary goods and services sur-rounding the protocol.
- Evaluate the relative adoption to competing protocols.

7.3.3 *Expertise ecosystem network effects*

Expertise ecosystem network effects occur when a product or service becomes more valuable as more professionals become proficient in using it. Certain products, typically tools used by professionals to conduct their jobs, can exhibit expertise ecosystem network effects. If a professional tool is sufficiently difficult to operate, the tool requires expertise of its own. Employers require proficiency in such tools when hiring. Professionals have a strong incentive to develop expertise for the tool with the widest adoption so that they can use the expertise as a selling point on the labor market. Companies are also likely to use the tool with the widest adop-tion. Every new person on the labor market who specializes in the tool adds value to the other users of that tool.

Popular programming languages, for example, exhibit developer eco-systems where knowledge and methods of using the tool (the program-ming language) are shared in the ecosystem. Microsoft's Excel, Word, and PowerPoint also serve as examples of expertise network effects. Expertise network effects are often found in industry-specific professional software, such as programming languages and frameworks, computer-aided design

(CAD) software, 3D animation and visual effects software, data analysis and visualization tools, advanced photo and video editing software, electronic design automation (EDA) tools, geographic information systems software, computational biology tools, digital audio workstations (DAWs), and high-performance computing (HPC) tools.

It can also be found in hardware products that require a high level of expertise to operate, for example: specialized surgical tools, microsurgical instruments, diagnostic devices, spectrometers, chromatography, electron microscopes, computer numerical control (CNC) machines, professional-grade cameras and photography equipment, musical instruments, precision measurement tools, etc. Essentially, any type of professional tool that requires a high level of tool-specific expertise to operate and has wider adoption than competing tools could potentially have an expertise ecosystem network effect.

The da Vinci Surgical System, developed by Intuitive Surgical, exemplifies how a physical product can benefit from ecosystem expertise network effects. Introduced in 2000, the system is designed for minimally invasive procedures, primarily in abdominal surgery. Intuitive has introduced four generations of the da Vinci and announced a fifth in 2024. This ongoing innovation necessitates that medical professionals continually update and advance their skills.

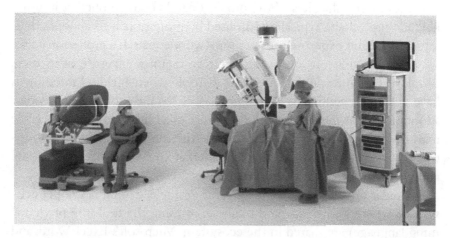

Figure 7.9   Specialized tools for professionals, such as the da Vinci Surgical System above, can possess expertise network effects.
Source: Courtesy of Intuitive Surgical Press Resources, 2024.

The company initially competed with a firm called Computer Motion, which it later merged with. Today, the system holds a highly dominant market share in robotic surgery. Given its profitability and under-penetration, the growing robotic surgery market will inevitably attract competitors.

Competing with Intuitive is daunting for several reasons. There are significant costs involved in developing such tools, obtaining FDA approvals, and bringing them to market. However, even more challenging is the task of contending with the network effects of Intuitive's established ecosystem of specialized users.

Operating the da Vinci system requires expertise highly specific to the particular tool. The da Vinci Surgical System integrates into medical education. The next generation of surgeons develops proficiency in robotic surgery through the da Vinci system. Over the past two decades, Intuitive has nurtured the ecosystem that includes a vast installed base of surgeons, hospitals, and academics. There is extensive ecosystem dissemination and collaboration. For example, there are 38,000 peer-reviewed academic articles published relevant to robotic surgery, and the vast majority of this research is done independently of Intuitive.[8] Young surgeons are motivated to learn the da Vinci system due to its widespread use. Hospitals prefer to invest in systems with proven clinical benefits and familiarity among existing specialized surgeons.

Let's Sniff Around

Analyze expertise ecosystem network effects:

- Evaluate the degree of tool-specific expertise required.
- Quantify the switching costs of users of the tool switching to a competing tool: There must be a significant switching cost - cost of expertise loss - when switching from the tool to another tool. Certifications of expertise in using that specific tool are an indication of increased switching costs.
- Evaluate and compare user loyalty and retention metrics: Experts who have invested time and effort in mastering a specific tool are more likely to remain loyal to that tool and resist switching to

alternatives. Analyze the retention rates and loyalty of expert users to evaluate the strength of the expertise network effects.
- Gauge extent of ecosystem dissemination and collaboration: Assess the extent to which knowledge is being shared and collaboration occurs within the expert community.
- Assess the degree of compatibility between the tool and the competing tool (low compatibility is a good sign).
- Specifically for medical devices, try to figure out if it is being used in universities and teaching hospitals; i.e., will the next cohorts of doctors be trained on it and is this first training experience powerful enough that they will keep advocating for its use?

7.3.4 Two-sided networks

Two-sided networks consist of two user groups: supply-side and demand-side. Each group joins the network for distinct reasons and provides complementary value to the other. For instance, a new store in a shopping mall creates value for shoppers by diversifying the supply of goods, while an additional shopper represents potential revenue for existing stores.

While two-sided networks are frequently associated with indirect network effects, it's worth noting that they can also exhibit direct network effects on one side, however often negative (e.g., a congested parking lot at a shopping mall).

Most cities have or used to have a weekly marketplace at a square in the city. Supply-side users (farmers, artisans, grocers, etc.) came to the marketplace to sell to demand-side users (citizens of the city). These marketplaces take many forms, including specialized craft marketplaces, local professional auctions (e.g. fish actions, car auctions, etc.), shopping streets, and shopping malls. By aggregating competing sellers in one physical location, sellers can obtain more business than those that are spread out. This makes it practical for competitors to co-locate. Although the proximity of competing sellers can increase price transparency and reduce prices, it is worthwhile for suppliers as a group because of the higher density of customers. Businesses that own a marketplace and can monetize it, for example, by charging a "take-rate" on the revenues of the supply-side users might have a competitive advantage over other marketplace owners if they possess sufficient relative scale over competing marketplaces.

Many businesses can be thought of as two-sided marketplaces, such as stock exchanges and other types of exchanges. In the case of stock exchanges, companies issuing shares (supply side) are sellers, and investors are buyers. The more companies issuing shares on a particular exchange, the more attractive it is for investors to participate in the buying of shares. The high cost of multi-homing on the supply side (i.e., companies being less willing to pay to be listed on several exchanges) means that in most countries, it only makes economic sense to have one domestic stock exchange.

With the emergence of the internet, entrepreneurs have been able to create new forms of marketplaces. Many of these online marketplaces remain local, like their physical counterparts (e.g., general used goods classifieds), while some are national and a few even international (e.g., Airbnb). Today, the internet hosts numerous niche marketplaces that exhibit network effects.

More business models than one might intuitively think can be considered two-sided marketplaces. Many media companies, for example, function as two-sided marketplaces. Advertisers on the demand side purchase the attention of readers, viewers, or listeners on the supply side of the media marketplace. Younger readers might not view national and regional newspapers as businesses with a significant competitive advantage, but they undoubtedly held very potent local advantages in the pre-TV and pre-internet era, as they were inevitable advertisement outlets with substantial indirect network effects. For decades, these businesses maintained a robust advantage until technology eventually developed newer forms of advertisement infrastructure.

Once a successful two-sided marketplace reaches critical mass, it can be challenging to disrupt. A new solution must provide a better value proposition for both supply- and demand-side users; otherwise, one side won't leave without the other.

Other examples of companies that can be viewed as two-sided marketplaces include print classifieds, online classifieds, media, matchmaking services, e-commerce, various types of auctions and exchanges, shopping malls, software and games, freelance services, dating apps, online travel agencies, vacation rental platforms, job boards, real estate listing websites, flea markets, trade shows, talent agencies, business conferences, and farmers markets.

Another general type of two-sided network is what is often referred to as "platforms." Platforms are like two-sided marketplaces in the sense that they have two sides with different groups that benefit from each other. The difference between a platform and a marketplace is that the supply side of the platform creates products that are only available on the platform. There is an integration between the supply-side product and the platform itself.[9]

A computer operating system, such as Windows, is an example of a platform. The developers of software applications that can run on Windows are the supply side. They create products that the demand side (i.e., the users of that software) can consume through the intermediating platform (i.e., Windows). A higher supply of software applications for the operating system benefits the users of the operating system. More users of the operating system benefit the software developers as it expands their addressable market. The intermediating platform itself can play a more significant role in the value generated for users. For example, consumers who buy a Sony PlayStation game console might purchase it for the games ecosystem available on the PlayStation (i.e., the network effect), but they also buy the PlayStation due to the graphics and performance of the system itself.

Few platforms, specifically operating systems, exhibit direct positive network effects in addition to indirect network effects. Windows users, for example, benefit directly from being able to share files with other users (i.e., a rare positive direct demand-side network effect).

Two-sided platforms include examples such as PC operating systems, mobile operating systems, other operating systems (e.g., Kindle eBook), game consoles, video-sharing platforms, and OS-integrated app stores.

Some marketplaces and platforms have more than two sides. For example, in the case of food delivery apps, the network connects independent riders who transport the food, restaurants that sell food, and consumers who purchase and consume the food and transportation. In this case, with two complementary supply sides (riders and restaurants), all three sides benefit from the increased usage of each of the other two sides. Visa and MasterCard can also be viewed as multi-sided networks, facing many "sides": consumers, banks, acquirers, merchants, as well as governments (in cross-border transactions).

Credit rating agencies like S&P and Moody's can be considered as specialized platforms. On the supply side, they provide credit ratings and research on various entities like governments, companies, and financial instruments. On the demand side, investors, financial institutions, and other market participants use these credit ratings to make informed decisions about their investments. In this case, credit rating agencies create products (ratings and research) that are tightly integrated with their platform (rating methodologies and research databases).

Let's Sniff Around

Analyze two-sided network effects:

- Test whether users (on the side of the network that is monetized) are willing to pay a higher price for the leading network over the subsequent network (or accept a higher degree of other forms of monetization, such as ads). Test this statement with users on the paying side of the network.
- Evaluate whether there is a sufficiently high cost of multi-homing. This is a typical weakness of two-sided networks. See the box on evaluating the extent and cost of multi-homing described earlier in this chapter.
- Evaluate negative direct one-side network effects (if relevant)

Specifically for marketplaces that match supply with demand, it is relevant to evaluate the following:[10]

- Evaluate and benchmark match rates. Match rates or success rates are measures of how successfully the two sides can find each other.
- Analyze market depth. A marketplace without sufficient supply will be dysfunctional. Evaluate the limitations for increased supply.
- Evaluate and compare metrics concerning the time to find a match between supply and demand (also referred to as "days to turn").
- Analyze the fragmentation of supply and demand: Marketplaces with greater fragmentation on both the supply and demand sides are more valuable and defensible. Marketplaces can measure concentration by calculating the percentage of Gross Merchandise Value (GMV) that the top sellers or buyers represent.

7.3.5 Data network effects

A data network effect occurs when the value of a product or service increases as the amount of data collected and processed grows. This type of network effect is commonly seen in data-driven applications, recommendation engines, and machine learning systems. As more users generate and contribute data, the system becomes more effective, accurate, and valuable for all users. Data network effects often result in improved personalization, recommendations, or predictions, benefiting both users and the company providing the service.

A good example of data network effects would be the GPS smartphone application, Waze, which enables users to obtain real-time travel times, route details, traffic updates, and location-dependent information. Users are encouraged through points and badges to report accidents, traffic jams, speed and police traps, as well as to update roads, landmarks, etc.[11] The more users contribute information, the more useful the service Waze offers becomes. Waze collects anonymous information about its users' speed and location and processes this data to improve the service. The application requires a critical mass of users in a region to have real utility.

Some examples of products and services exhibiting data network effects include:

Navigation apps (e.g., Waze)
Search engines (e.g., Google)
Machine learning algorithms (ChatGPT)
Language translation services (e.g., Google Translate)
Recommendation engines (e.g., TikTok)
Autonomous vehicles (e.g., Tesla)

With the emergence of machine learning algorithms being embedded in products in the years to come, data network effects seem to play an increasingly important role as a competitive advantage in the future than they have in the past.

Be aware that the strength of data network effects can be overstated. Data network effects are only significant when data is central to how the product benefits users. If data is merely peripheral to the product, then the data network becomes irrelevant. I've heard many companies tout their "data," but to me, it seems that the evidence of its actual advantage is less accessible than Area 51.

Let's Sniff Around

Evaluate data network effects:

- Evaluate whether the relative data amount is really a significant contributor to the product's value proposition. If data is merely peripheral to the product, then the data network becomes irrelevant. Many data network effects can be overstated.
- Benchmark user engagement metrics to competitors.
- Consider the data exclusivity and quality.

You've successfully made it through the longest and densest chapter of the book. I surely managed to overcomplicate network effects, huh? Good thing the next chapter is about something as simple as brands. Brands must surely be obvious advantages, right?

Chapter 8

Brand Advantages

A firm with a brand, a firm with brand awareness, and a firm with a brand advantage walked into a bar. They each ordered a beer, but when they had to pay, the firm with the brand said, "Sorry, I don't have any cash. Do you accept logos?" to which the bartender winced. Then the firm with brand awareness, realizing it also didn't have any cash, said, "Don't you know who I am?" Embarrassed by his two companions, the firm with the brand advantage took out his big, fat wallet, paid for the round, and gave the bartender a tip. True story!

The term "brand" means different things in different contexts. In this book, I adopt a narrow definition of brand. If not constrained by the length considerations for chapter titles, this one would likely have been titled "Advantages of Products Exhibiting Affective Value from Identity Creation or Uncertainty Reduction, Established over a Long Time in the Minds of the Consumer Base." But that title is perhaps one or two words too long.

Brand as a competitive advantage refers to a unique, hard-to-replicate proprietary asset that evokes positive emotions in customers, prompting them to pay a higher price for a product than they would for an otherwise equivalent offering. This concept is different from brand awareness, which is about how familiar consumers are with a specific brand. The mere

135

presence of a brand, meaning just having a brand name or logo linked to a company or product, differs greatly from the advantage I discuss in this chapter. Although many companies have a brand, few possess the type of advantage I refer to here.

The benefit of brand advantage is the ability to charge higher prices for a company's offerings compared to functionally equivalent products. Customers' willingness to pay these higher prices stems from two sources: first, the positive associations built up with the brand, which elicit good feelings about the offering, independent of the product's objective value; and second, uncertainty reduction, because customers are more familiar with the branded product, they know that it will meet their expectations—as opposed to taking the chance with an unknown product.[1]

Note that the ability to charge higher prices does not need to be exercised by the company. For instance, it could be argued that Tesla has a brand advantage, yet it doesn't price its cars higher than those of similar technical quality. Costco's Kirkland Brand is another example. In these cases, the surplus is passed on to the consumer, and the firm instead benefits from higher market share.

A durable brand can only be developed over an extended period through consistent, reinforcing actions. This is the barrier that prevents competitors from arbitraging away the superior economics that the brand enables. Not only would competitors have to invest significant amounts of money in creating such a replication of the brand, but they would also have to do it over a lengthy period, and the outcome would be more uncertain than the quantum state of Schrödinger's cat. Achieving the desired customer emotional impact after investing substantial time and resources is not guaranteed, making such investment risky and outright unattractive. Efforts to mimic another brand may result in trademark infringement lawsuits, which can be costly and have uncertain outcomes.

Let's take, for example, the benefit of Harley-Davidson motorcycles' brand:

- The company cultivated an emotional connection with its customers, who associate the brand with freedom, adventure, and the American spirit. The brand's distinct, rumbling exhaust and the classic cruiser design evoke a sense of nostalgia.

- The company's reputation for quality and reliability provides customers with peace of mind, knowing that they are investing in a product that will meet their expectations.

Now for the barrier side: Harley-Davidson has built its brand identity and emotional connection with customers over more than a century, through consistent marketing efforts, rallies, and events that celebrate the brand's heritage and foster a sense of community among riders. Competitors who would try to arbitrage away this brand advantage would have to invest a significant amount of money over a long time, hoping to replicate its brand appeal. Doing so would involve substantial investment, with no guarantee of success. Additionally, competitors risk trademark infringement if they attempt to imitate the distinctive design elements of Harley-Davidson motorcycles.

Branding is a nonexclusive type of advantage. A direct competitor might have an equally impactful brand that targets the same customers. All competitors with brand advantage, however, will still earn returns on capital superior to those without it.

Figure 8.1 Customers buy Harley-Davidson motorcycles because of the sense of identity they obtain from the product.

Source: Visitor7 / Wikimedia Commons / CC BY SA 3.0.

Don't confuse brand advantage with economies of scale in marketing. While Coca-Cola is a strong brand with brand advantages, its advantages also lie in its economies of scale in marketing. For example, Coca-Cola can sponsor Olympic Games, while smaller competitors cannot because the advertising cost is only justifiable for an entity of Coca-Cola's size that can spread the investment over more customers. A smaller competitor, even with amazing brand benefits, would still be at a disadvantage due to negative relative scale.

8.1   "Identity Creating" or "Uncertainty Reducing"

Not all types of goods can have brand advantages—even though they might still have brand awareness. If the brand itself does not justify a pronounced price premium, then it is not a brand advantage but merely brand awareness. Many business-to-business goods typically fail to exhibit meaningful emotional price premiums since most purchasers are only concerned with objective features. Those consumer goods associated with a sense of identity tend to have purchasing decisions more driven by emotions.

Products that evoke emotions and foster a sense of identity often share several common characteristics:

• Allow users to showcase their personality or uniqueness
• Signal belonging to a community or fan base
• Indicate wealth, success, or aspirational status
• Align with personal beliefs, e.g., eco-friendly or cruelty-free
• Tie to one's hobbies or interests
• Offer genuine, artisanal, or original appeal
• Are associated with admired personalities, e.g., athletes or celebrities

Examples of product categories that elicit such emotions include sports and hobby equipment, designer handbags, musical instruments, vintage cars, exclusive alcohol, eco-conscious sustainable products, and limited-edition sneakers.

For example, a friend of mine bought an expensive vintage bamboo fly fishing rod. Even though the brand name and model of the rod are barely visible, and certainly not to others than himself, I would still categorize this purchase as "brand." He paid a significant price premium over its functional value due to an emotional "affective value" that ties to his "identity" in his fly-fishing hobby. In fact, even though the rod is eight times more expensive than my modern graphite rod, the functional performance of the expensive vintage rod is, of course, much lower. Brand is really all about affective nonfunctional value that is nearly impossible for other things to replicate.

Affective value is depicted brilliantly in a scene from one of my all-time favorite movies, *Pulp Fiction*, where the character "Butch" (played by Bruce Willis), upon realizing that his girlfriend has accidentally left his watch behind at their apartment, decides to risk his life to return to the apartment despite being chased by mobsters. The watch is not just a time-piece; it is a symbol of his father's time as a POW during the Vietnam War. In the real world, most people would perhaps not risk their life for things that have affective value, but I'm sure they would do some pretty extraordinary things. This dynamic is evident, though in a less dramatic way, when consumers have affective value for things they desire to purchase and are willing to pay a substantial price premium for affective value related to their sense of identity.

Consumers are also willing to pay more for a product that reduces uncertainty because they believe the downsides of uncertainty with unknown products outweigh the additional cost of the known product. Goods like safety, medicine, and transport can benefit from this psychological dynamic. This is the case for most goods associated with avoiding worst-case outcomes. The willingness to pay a premium for the known product is justified by the perceived reduction in the likelihood that the otherwise similar unknown product will fail in a worst-case scenario or cause the problem itself.

Common determinants drive the willingness to pay a premium for products, due to reduced uncertainty:

- Offer critical health or safety benefits
- Have potential severe consequences if they fail
- Are associated with vulnerable populations, e.g., babies or elderly
- Have a strong track record or reputation for reliability
- Are endorsed by trusted professionals or institutions
- Comply with strict regulatory or quality standards
- Benefit from strong word-of-mouth or community recommendations
- Offer guarantees, warranties, or strong post-purchase support

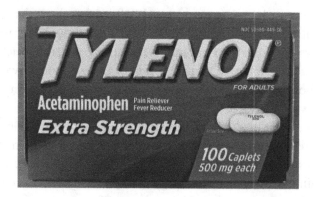

Figure 8.2 "Uncertainty reduction": Due to its long-standing presence in the market and extensive marketing over the years, many consumers trust Tylenol more than generic acetaminophen products, even though the active ingredient is the same.
Source: Author's private photo collection.

Examples of such product categories include life-saving medical devices, baby and infant products, home security systems, car safety equipment, tires, home and property insurance, fire safety equipment, child safety seats and restraints, medical and dental services, high-quality automotive parts and repair services, and branded medicine.

Let's Sniff Around

Analyze the customer utility from "identity creation" or "uncertainty/risk reduction":

- Assess whether the determinants mentioned previously are the primary drivers of the average customer's utility from the products.
- Conduct interviews with customers to evaluate the proposition that these factors contribute to a higher perceived value.

8.2 Brand Time Constraints

Fostering a sense of identity and reducing uncertainty are not enough for a brand to be durable. It must have a barrier rooted in time and uncertainty. If the benefits were achieved quickly, it would likely be easy for others to replicate them. The establishment of the brand should have been the result of consistent actions that are hard to replicate over a very long time. More specifically, the brand should have consistently provided the following:

- Delivered product quality and differentiation
- Created emotional connections and/or a sense of familiarity and confidence
- Maintained trust with its customers and benefited from natural brand ambassadors
- Invested considerable sums in effective marketing and advertising (often but not always)

8.3   Luxury Brands

Luxury brands serve as a case study for brand advantage because the price premium for "identity creation" is taken to an extreme level.[2]

Luxury brands often aim to have full control over their distribution channels and the brand experience. By controlling every aspect of the customer experience, from product presentation to the sales process, luxury brands can manage the emotional connection with the customer. Controlling distribution also allows for better price regulation, preserving the brand's status and appeal to consumers who associate a higher price with superior quality and exclusivity. Controlling distribution channels further protects against counterfeiting, mitigating the risk of damage to the brand's reputation. Luxury brands are often so concerned with owning the distribution process and maintaining exclusivity that many of them practice the disposal or destruction of unsold inventory.

Consider Hermès. Founded in 1837 as a harness workshop in Paris, Hermès initially catered to European noblemen, producing some of the finest wrought harnesses and bridles. Over the years, it evolved to offer leather bags, accessories, and fashion items. Throughout its long history, Hermès has maintained a consistent dedication to craftsmanship. For instance, the iconic Hermès Birkin bag is handcrafted by a single artisan and can take anywhere from 18 to 25 hours to complete. Hermès products are exclusive, and some are even hard to buy. Both the Birken and

Kelly bags have waiting lists that can span years. Hermès tightly controls their own distribution through its own boutiques. While other brands might expand rapidly into numerous product categories, Hermès has been careful about its expansion.

Emerging brands that attempt to position themselves as luxury brands with a high price point often struggle to compete against established luxury brands. Established luxury brands have built their reputation and prestige over time, often through a rich history and tradition. Emerging brands lack this heritage, making it difficult for them to evoke the same sense of exclusivity and status. For luxury brands, the risk of brand dilution is potentially greater than for non-luxury brands, as their customers value exclusivity. Therefore, assessing the risk of brand dilution becomes even more critical when evaluating luxury brands.

8.4   Evaluating Brand Advantages

Branding is a nonexclusive type of advantage. This means that a company and its direct competitor can both have strong brands that appeal to the same customers. Therefore, it is challenging to measure the intensity of a brand advantage by comparing observations for the company in question to its closest competitors in the same manner discussed in previous chapters on other types of advantages. The measurement of a brand thus becomes more absolute and less relative, focusing on the intensity of the following:

• The perceived value in excess of the functional value
• The constraints to arbitrage away the advantage
• The exposure to common risks that brands face

In the following subsections, I review first the benefits of brands and the Lindy effect as a positive indicator of brand advantage and then review some common risks in relation to brand advantages.

8.4.1   Brand benefits

I am generally pessimistic of hypotheses about brand advantages in contexts outside of "sense of identity" and "uncertainty reduction/risk aversion." This is especially true for many business-to-business products, as businesses tend to be more rational in their purchasing decisions.

Let's Sniff Around

Analyze the brand benefits:

- Determine whether evidence is adequate to support a demonstrated willingness to pay more for these products, for instance, by comparing price premiums or interviewing customers. If the brand does not lead to a significant willingness to pay a premium over functionally equivalent products, this serves as strong evidence against the thesis of brand advantage.
- Estimate price elasticity of demand for the products.
- Compare gross profit margins to industry.
- Evaluate customer loyalty metrics.

8.4.2 The Lindy effect and brand longevity

Bernard Arnault, one of the most successful owners and operators of luxury brand companies said the following, when asked about timelessness in relation to brands in an interview with *Harvard Business Review* in 2001:

> It means the brand is built, if you wish, for eternity. It has been around for a long time; it has become an institution. Dom Pérignon is a perfect example. I can guarantee that people will be drinking it in the next century. It was created 250 years ago, but it will be relevant and desired for another century and beyond that. It is for the ages—just like certain pieces of luggage that you buy for your entire life. (. . .) The problem is that the quality of timelessness takes years to develop, even decades. You cannot just decree it. A brand has to pay its dues—it has to come to stand for something in the eyes of the world.[3]

Brands that have been around for many decades are more likely to remain for a longer time than brands that haven't. This postulate is based on the Lindy effect, applied to the context of brands. The Lindy effect, discussed in greater detail in Chapter 12 on Staying Power, is a theoretical concept suggesting that the future life expectancy of certain nonperishable things, such as technologies or ideas, is proportional to their current age. Observe how part of Bernard Arnault's argument about the strength of Dom Pérignon, as quoted earlier, implicitly relies on the Lindy effect.

If the Lindy effect holds true for brands, then simply observing how long a brand has existed becomes a relevant indicator of brand strength.

8.4.3   Geographical boundedness

A brand advantage is often tied to a single product category. Expanding into new product categories using the same brand frequently fails to build the same sense of identity or uncertainty reduction in the new category. While there might be benefits from economies of scale in marketing, which creates cost-effective brand awareness for the new product, achieving a brand advantage is a different challenge.

In the early 2000s, Harley-Davidson introduced a line of perfumes and colognes under its brand name. These products, however, did not achieve significant success and were eventually discontinued. The Harley-Davidson brand was associated with motorcycles, making it hard for

Figure 8.3   Brands are often geographically bounded: Moutai, deeply rooted in Chinese culture, exemplifies this. The Communist Party consolidated distillers into Kweichow Moutai, effectively granting it a position as the national liquor. Today, Kweichow Moutai holds a significant brand advantage in China. However, this advantage is unlikely to be transferable elsewhere, as the brand lacks a similar cultural history in other regions.
Source: HunagnTwuai / Wikimedia Commons / CC BY-SA 4.0.

consumers to obtain the same affective value from the brand with a fragrance product.

There is no such thing as an intergalactic brand wormhole that can effortlessly make Campbell's Soup succeed in shampoo or Lenovo the leader in lingerie. It doesn't exist.

A powerful brand that has built a strong sense of identity or uncertainty reduction in one region doesn't automatically possess it in another, even if the same brand name is used. This point is vital to acknowledge. While a company may have the financial means to invest in advertising and increase brand awareness in a new region, it doesn't necessarily equate to strong sense of identity or uncertainty reduction.

When assessing a brand, avoid the error of assuming that the benefits can be effortlessly transported across regions. For a brand to achieve this, significant investment is required, which can be costly, unpredictable, and take ages. If your investment thesis is based on assumptions of geographical expansion or product line extension for a company with a brand advantage, then it's imperative to factor these considerations into your underwriting assumptions.

8.4.4 Analytical risk of over-interpreting brand loyalty data

In marketing, "the double jeopardy law" (or the more cool-sounding abbreviation, "the DJ law") is an empirical phenomenon. It is generally observed that brands with lower market share not only have lower market share, but also lower brand loyalty as measured by average customer purchase frequency. This is due to a statistical selection effect. Assume you have two brands of shampoo: one occupies 80% of the shelf space, and the other has the rest. All buyers are blindfolded and randomly pick a shampoo. Later, when analyzing the purchase data, you would find that the larger shampoo brand not only has a higher share of purchases but also a higher average customer purchase frequency. Hence, you might conclude that it must have higher brand loyalty. You would explain the higher "brand loyalty" as evidence that customers obtain affective value through identity creation and uncertainty reduction, as discussed in the chapter, concluding that the data support your thesis of strong brand advantage.

Wait a minute. Don't people in the experiment pick the shampoo at random? When you compare purchase frequency data with the aim of inferring something about brand loyalty adjusted for the DJ law, then you must (surprise) adjust for the DJ law. If you don't, then you could make an analytical error leading to a wrong conclusion about brand strength. For continued reading about the DJ law, I recommend the book *How Brands Grow* by Byron Sharp.[4]

8.4.5   Counterfeiting risk

Counterfeiting poses a threat to a brand's power by capitalizing on its reputation without offering the same quality or consistency. Counterfeiters exploit the trust associated with established brands by using their name or logo on subpar products. Brand value is built on positive consumer experiences with genuine products. When counterfeit items enter the market, they can create negative perceptions about the brand, even if the brand isn't at fault. To protect against this, companies need strong anti-counterfeiting strategies, strong authentication features, and transparent supply chains.

8.4.6   Brand experience control risk

Lack of control over the brand experience can make brand owners more vulnerable to damaged reputation and eroded customer loyalty due to inconsistent or negative experiences. Outright owning the distribution channel or at least exercising some control over it is often required to control the brand experience sufficiently to mitigate this risk. When a brand lacks control over its distribution channels, it may lose control of pricing and product availability, resulting in price undercutting by third-party sellers and inconsistencies in the presentation and sale of the brand's products.

8.4.7   Brand dilution risk

Brand owners must actively invest in maintaining their brands and specifically try to prevent anything that can dilute the brand. A challenge, therefore, lies in avoiding the temptation to release products that deviate from or damage the established brand image in pursuit of larger profits. Actions that risk diluting the brand ultimately run the risk of starting over and rebuilding the emotional connection with customers. Try to steer clear of management that, due to short-term incentives or lack of passion, you fear could do a "Ctrl + Z" on decades of brand investments in pursuit of instant checkout.

Let's Sniff Around

Analyze brand dilution risk:

- Identify attempts at market expansion aimed at increasing sales but potentially at the expense of the brand's exclusivity or perceived quality.
- Identify changes in marketing strategies and distribution channels.
- Evaluate management's incentives and disincentives for optimizing short-term performance.
- Assess management's industry-specific expertise in maintaining long-term brand integrity.
- Scrutinize decisions related to introducing brand licensing.

A brand advantage is a distinct form of a proprietary resource. But other types of proprietary resources can lead to intense and durable advantages. This is the topic of the next chapter, which, after intensive brainstorming sessions, has been given the unimaginably inventive title "Proprietary Resources."

Chapter 9

Proprietary Resources

Host: "Welcome back, ladies and gentlemen, to the thrilling con-
                tinuation of 'Who Wants to Be a Gazzilionaire!' Before the
                break, our contestant, Mr. Reader, showed remarkable knowl-
                edge, and here we are. Mr. Reader, you've reached the 5,000
                drachma question. How are you feeling?"

Mr. Reader: [looking a bit confused about what is going on]

Host: "Fantastic spirit! Now, for 5,000 drachma, your question is
                about proprietary assets. And here it is:

                Which type of proprietary asset is most valuable? Is it. . .
                A: Unattainable but not Advantageous,
                B: Advantageous but not Unattainable, or
                C: Unattainable and Advantageous?

                Take your time, Mr. Reader. And remember, you still have
                your lifelines should you need them . . ."

Host: "Ah, Mr. Reader, I see you're puzzled by this question! Or. . .
                is that a signal? Folks, Mr. Reader is in need of some assistance
                here. So, let's use a lifeline and read for him a chapter on
                the subject:"

Exclusive access to proprietary resources, which cannot be replicated by competitors, can lead to competitive advantages. Most of these advantages are related to reduced costs. We could term these "cost advantages independent of scale."[1] Others relate to being the outright sole provider of a particular good.

The barrier of such advantages is that competitors are prevented from accessing these proprietary resources (oh, what a tautology!). When a proprietary resource creates cost advantages, there may also be a barrier of prohibitive costs for competitors trying to take market share.

Proprietary resources typically fall within the following categories:[2]

• Favorable access to raw materials
• Proprietary technologies
• Favorable locations
• Favorable government treatment

Following, I discuss each in detail and how to evaluate them empirically.

9.1   Favorable Access to Raw Materials

Favorable access to raw materials can lead to cost advantages independent of scale. This phenomenon occurs when a company has unique access to resources or materials crucial for its production process, which can result in lower costs per unit. The primary sources of this phenomenon include the following:

• **Geographic advantage:** Some regions may have abundant access to a particular raw material due to their geological or geographical characteristics.
• **Exclusive rights:** In some cases, a company may have exclusive rights to extract or utilize a specific raw material.
• **Resource quality:** Access to higher quality raw materials can result in cost advantages due to reduced processing requirements or improved product performance.
• **Exclusive partnerships:** Preferred access to raw materials can be gained through strategic alliances and agreements.
• **Vertical integration:** Direct access to raw materials can be controlled throughout the supply chain, from source to production.

Saudi Aramco, the state-owned oil company of Saudi Arabia, is the world's lowest cost producer of crude oil. The company's production cost per barrel is lower than that of other major oil companies due to a combination of factors unique to the oil deposits in Saudi Arabia.

Saudi Arabia has some of the largest oil reserves in the world. These reserves enable the company to maintain a high production rate over a long period. The oil deposits in Saudi Arabia primarily consist of light, sweet crude oil, which requires less processing and refining compared to heavy, sour crude oil. Saudi Arabia's oil fields are onshore, which makes it easier and less expensive to access and extract the oil.

Saudi Arabia also benefits from low labor and operational costs compared to other major oil-producing nations. This is partly due to the country's abundant supply of cheap migrant labor and the government's subsidies for energy and other resources.

9.1.1   Locking up favorable sources

Locking up favorable sources at lower prices is a specific way a company can gain a cost advantage. This involves securing access to key raw materials or resources before the demand increases, ensuring a more stable supply and favorable pricing. When a company can anticipate an increase in demand for a particular resource, it may attempt to negotiate long-term contracts with suppliers or invest in securing its own resources at lower prices. By doing so, the company can maintain its cost advantage even as demand and market prices increase.

One notable example of this is the De Beers Group, which for much of the twentieth century held a near-monopoly on the diamond industry. De Beers achieved this position by securing exclusive access to some of the world's most valuable diamond mines, particularly those in southern Africa. De Beers founder, Cecil Rhodes, started by consolidating the diamond mines in South Africa in the late nineteenth century. Over time, De Beers expanded its control over the diamond market by establishing exclusive agreements with diamond-producing countries such as Botswana, Namibia, and Russia. These agreements allowed De Beers to control the supply of diamonds, ensuring that it had access to the best-quality stones and could maintain stable prices.

In addition to controlling diamond production, De Beers also established a marketing arm, the Central Selling Organization (CSO), which managed the sale and distribution of diamonds. The CSO would buy up diamonds from other producers, effectively controlling the global supply. This strategy allowed De Beers to keep diamond prices high while making it difficult for competitors to enter the market. De Beers' monopoly began to erode in the late twentieth century due to new diamond discoveries.

Let's Sniff Around

Analyze the cost advantage derived from favorable access to raw materials:

- Compare relative resource quality: Examine the quality of the firm's raw material compared to competitors' alternatives.
- Assess the scarcity or limited supply of the raw material accessible to the firm.
- Compare the marginal cost of the company to that of its competitors.
- Evaluate the terms and duration of contracts between the firm and its suppliers.
- Investigate competitors' attempts to secure alternative raw material sources.

9.2   Proprietary Technology

Proprietary product technology refers to the unique knowledge, processes, or design characteristics that a company possesses and protects through patents, trade secrets, or other measures of Illuminati-level secrecy. This proprietary asset can lead to cost advantages independent of scale and, in some cases, make the company the sole provider of a particular product or service. Sources of this advantage include the following:

- Patents and intellectual property
- Trade secrets
- Technical expertise

A historical example of a company that obtained a cost advantage independent of scale due to proprietary product technology is Polaroid Corporation. The company was founded by Edwin H. Land in 1937 and became famous for its instant photography technology. Polaroid's instant film and cameras revolutionized the photography industry and gave the company an advantage over its rivals. Polaroid's instant photography technology was based on a proprietary chemical process that allowed photos to develop within minutes after being exposed. This was a major innovation at a time when traditional film processing took hours or even days to produce a finished photograph. Edwin Land and his team filed numerous patents to protect the company's intellectual property, effectively preventing competitors from replicating the technology. The company enjoyed a virtual monopoly in the instant photography market for several decades. However, the rise of digital photography in the late twentieth and early twenty-first century eventually led to the decline of Polaroid's instant film business.

ZEISS Semiconductor Manufacturing Technology (SMT) is a contemporary example of how proprietary product technology can lead to a company being the outright only provider of a product category. Extreme

Figure 9.1 ZEISS metrology for High-NA-EUV lithography: The high-precision mirrors from ZEISS for the High-NA-EUV technology are measured in gigantic vacuum chambers with a diameter of five meters.

Source: With permission of Zeiss.

ultraviolet (EUV) lithography is a next-generation semiconductor manufacturing technology that uses extreme ultraviolet light to create extremely small patterns on silicon wafers, which are then used to manufacture integrated circuits. This technology enables the production of more advanced and powerful microchips, catering to the ever-increasing demand for smaller, faster, and more energy-efficient electronic devices.

ZEISS SMT, a segment of the renowned German optics company ZEISS, has developed specialized and complex optics systems for EUV lithography. These optics systems are a critical component of EUV lithography machines, which are used by semiconductor manufacturers to produce advanced chips. The development and production of EUV lithography optics require a mastery of optical design, high-precision manufacturing techniques, and strict quality-control measures. ZEISS SMT has invested heavily in research and development, as well as skilled talent, to create its proprietary optics technology. The company has also secured patents and maintained trade secrets to protect its innovations. As a result of these efforts, ZEISS SMT has positioned itself as the world's only provider of EUV lithography optics systems.

Let's Sniff Around

Analyze advantage derived from proprietary product technology:

- Assess the strength of the firm's intellectual property (IP) protection, such as patents, trademarks, copyrights, and trade secrets.
- Evaluate the technological complexity of the proprietary technology and the difficulty for competitors to develop similar or alternative solutions.
- Consider the likelihood of disruptive innovation in the industry that could undermine the firm's proprietary technology.

9.3   Favorable Locations

Favorable locations can provide companies with a cost advantage independent of scale when these locations are difficult or impossible for competitors to replicate. Having secured favorable locations before market forces drive up prices or government regulations limit access can result in lower costs. Sources of this advantage include the following:

- **Proximity to resources:** Facilities near natural resources, such as mines, forests, or oil fields can benefit from reduced transportation costs and more efficient supply chains.
- **Access to infrastructure:** Facilities located near major transportation hubs, such as ports, airports, or highways, can have lower logistics costs due to the reduced time and expense required to transport goods to and from their facilities.
- **Proximity to markets:** Facilities close to key customer bases or target markets can reduce transportation costs and lead times for delivering products or services.
- **Access to skilled labor:** Facilities in areas with a skilled workforce or specialized expertise can benefit from increased productivity and reduced labor costs.

The Aluminum Company of America (later Alcoa Corporation) is a historical example of a company that obtained a distinct cost advantage independent of scale due to proprietary access to favorable locations. Alcoa, founded in 1888, grew to become the largest producer of aluminum in the United States. Aluminum production is an energy-intensive process, requiring a significant amount of electricity.

Alcoa's advantage came from its decision to establish aluminum production facilities near abundant and cheap sources of hydroelectric power. In the early twentieth century, Alcoa secured access to hydroelectric power projects near the Niagara Falls and the Tennessee River. These locations provided the company with a steady and cost-effective supply of electricity. The proximity to hydroelectric power allowed Alcoa to produce aluminum at a lower cost than competitors who relied on more expensive sources of energy. This advantage in location was difficult for competitors to replicate, as Alcoa had effectively cornered the market for access to some of the best sources of hydroelectric power in the United States.

The development of new hydroelectric projects became increasingly regulated and limited due to environmental concerns, making it harder for competitors to establish similar facilities.

Favorable locations can also lead to more subtle advantages that can add strength to an existing set of advantages. An example of this is

Walmart's historical focus on opening stores in small towns and suburban areas, where real estate costs were lower and competition was less intense compared to urban centers. This approach allowed Walmart to build larger stores with ample parking, making it more convenient for customers to shop. The proximity of Walmart stores to their target customers has also played a role in the company's advantage in addition to its economies of scale in purchasing.

The salvage vehicle auction firm Copart, further discussed in Chapter 11, provides another example of a firm that has advantageously secured favorable locations by owning a large amount of land near key markets, thereby reducing towing distances and costs. The environmental challenges of obtaining permits for new scrap yards, combined with the so-called "not in my backyard" effect, create barriers to new competition.

Being situated near a region with a high concentration of specialized workers can lead to increased productivity and other benefits. Invisio[3] is a Danish company that provides specialized communications and hearing protection systems for Western militaries. Its proximity to leading companies in the hearing technology sector, such as William Demant and GN, located in the Copenhagen area, has granted Invisio access to a talent pool of audiology engineers. More than 50,000 people in the greater Copenhagen region work in the hearing aid and headset industry. This results in not only access to skilled labor but also potential to collaborate with researchers at local technical universities. This access to a specialized talent pool is difficult for Invisio's competitors in traditional defense and safety industries, located elsewhere, to replicate.

Let's Sniff Around

Evaluate competitive advantage derived from favorable locations:

- Assess the availability of location-specific resources, such as skilled labor, raw materials, or infrastructure, that contribute to the firm's cost advantage.

- Estimate the cost savings associated with the favorable location in terms of transportation, logistics, and distribution.
- Evaluate the stability of the favorable location in terms of political, social, and environmental factors.
- Evaluate the barriers for competitors looking to establish a presence in the favorable location. Examples of such barriers are regulatory restrictions and limited availability of suitable land or facilities.
- Examine the efforts and investments made by competitors to secure alternative locations.

9.4   Favorable Government Treatment

Government subsidies and other forms of favorable government treatments can provide companies with cost advantages independent of scale. Sources of this advantage include the following:

- Exclusive rights or licenses to companies for specific activities, such as the exploration and production of natural resources, operation of public utilities, or provision of public services.
- Favorable market environment for domestic companies by implementing trade policies that protect them from foreign competition, such as tariffs, import quotas, or export subsidies.
- Procurement contracts to domestic companies for the provision of goods or services to public entities, such as defense contracts or infrastructure projects.
- Direct financial support to companies in the form of grants, low-interest loans, or tax breaks.
- Indirect financial support to companies through various programs and initiatives that benefit a specific industry or sector. Examples include funding for research and development, infrastructure investments, or providing public services that support the industry, such as education and training programs.

An example of a company that benefited from government treatment is Airbus, the European multinational aerospace corporation. Airbus was created in 1970 as a consortium of European aerospace manufacturers to compete with American aviation giants like Boeing. Government subsidies played a crucial role in Airbus's success, particularly in the early stages of the company's development. Several European governments provided financial support, including direct subsidies, soft loans, and R&D funding, which enabled Airbus to invest in the development of competitive aircrafts. This support enabled Airbus to gain a foothold in the market and build a reputation for producing advanced, fuel-efficient, and reliable aircraft.

A more contemporary example would be the Hong Kong stock exchange (HKEX). In the case of HKEX, its significance to the Hong Kong government's budget is a critical factor. The exchange, being one of the world's largest and most significant financial centers, contributes substantially to the government's revenue through taxes and fees. This financial contribution creates a dependency wherein the government has a vested interest in the success and stability of HKEX. By implementing regulations that govern foreign investment and financial transactions, the government creates a favorable environment for HKEX, which helps it maintain its position as a major financial hub.

Let's Sniff Around

Evaluate competitive advantage derived from uneven government treatment:

- Analyze how government support raises entry barriers for competitors, such as regulatory challenges or market restrictions from the perspective of the competitor.
- Evaluate the size, duration, and exclusivity of government support, like subsidies or tax breaks.
- Examine laws and regulations tied to the support, including potential changes that can influence the firm's advantage.

While preferential government subsidies and support can create advantages, you should note that these advantages come with massive dependency risks. Companies with these advantages are often more dependent on their sugar-daddy governments than you are on oxygen.

Host: "So, Mr. Reader, what is your answer? Mr. Reader? Mr. Reader. . . ?"

Host: "Ladies and gentlemen. It appears Mr. Reader has been lulled to sleep by all this itemized fluff. Wake up, Mr. Reader. It is time for the next chapter."

Part III

What Makes Some Companies Less Risky and More Valuable Than Others?

Chapter 10

Fair Value Extraction

It was a dark and stormy night. A couple of companies sat in their comfortable, warm hut drinking hot cocoa and counting their greasy over-earned money. Outside in the freezing cold lurked a grievous danger, which had been attracted by the scent of greed. Penetrating overly comfortable huts and taking down careless prey was its specialty. It was known as the Danger of Excessive Value Extraction.

Excessive value extraction is a common risk for companies with competitive advantages. An intense advantage allows the possessor to "extract" more value from either the demand side or the supply side than it could in its absence. We can define value extraction as "the value the firm keeps given the intensity of its advantage."

A firm's current level of value extraction can deviate from a "fair" level, justified by its competitive power over a longer time frame. Occasionally, businesses are "undermonetized," where they intentionally or unintentionally do not extract as much value from customers and/or suppliers as they could. This typically happens because they foresee a long-term opportunity in subsidizing future profits by sacrificing current profits to secure a larger market share in a growing market or achieving deeper customer engagement. Such strategy can be optimal in terms of cumulative value creation even though it implies forgoing current profits.

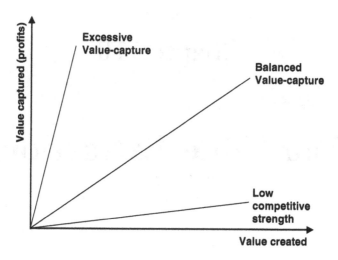

Figure 10.1   Conceptual illustration on degrees of value extraction.
Source: Simon Kold.

An example of this scenario are businesses whose customers make long-term commitments, directly or indirectly, when purchasing the companies' products. Such businesses need to assure their customers that they will not overly monetize, even when their dominant market position would otherwise enable them to do so. This reluctance to aggressively monetize provides an element of certainty to customers who get "locked in," enabling them to commit long-term despite the lock-in.

Situations where businesses intentionally and rationally forgo current earnings can sometimes lead to intriguing investment opportunities, especially when the marginal investor fails to understand that the current reported earnings do not accurately reflect the underlying earnings power of the business.

Conversely, some businesses, even those with impressive competitive advantages, extract excessive value. They leave inadequate surplus on the table for their customers and partners, rendering their position unviable in the long term. Excessive value extraction causes the generation of substantial short-term profits, but it erodes competitiveness and durability. Excessive value extraction can lead to backlashes such as customer dissatisfaction and negative public perception, increased regulatory scrutiny, attraction of competition, and incentives for the industry to support the development of substitutable technologies.

Investors should value businesses based on the risk-adjusted present value of all future expected cash earnings. Consequently, any action that may increase short-term earnings but increases the riskiness of all future earnings is value destructive. Nevertheless, my personal experience is that too many investors focus excessively on valuation multiples of current and near-term measures of earnings. Furthermore, the compensation of many corporate managers is tied to short-term business performance, giving them an economic incentive to optimize for a shorter time horizon. The goal of this chapter is to provide a method for you to assess the extent of value extraction and, perhaps more specifically, the risk of excessive value extraction.

The situation you want to avoid is one in which a business with intense current competitive strength is over-earning due to excessive value extraction. Because the business is over-earning, it may appear statistically cheap to some investors who are overly focused on valuation multiples and who are blinded by the historical competitive strength. However, the business is in fact not as cheap compared to its true longer-term earnings power. **By buying a business that is over-earning due to excessive value capture, the investor is not only misled about the attractiveness of the valuation but also underestimates the riskiness of longer-term earnings**. It's a double whammy to be avoided or at least minimized through careful analysis. On the contrary, the ideal situation is one in which a business with strong market power is experiencing temporarily suppressed monetization, which goes unnoticed or is misunderstood by the marginal investor. Investors overly focused on valuation multiples of short-term earnings measures may wrongly conclude that the business is "expensive" because they don't see the underlying earnings power of the business.

10.1   Tapped and Untapped Pricing Power

A frequently used term in the context of value extraction is the concept of "tapped" and "untapped" pricing power. We must distinguish between nominal pricing power, which is the ability to increase prices with cost inflation and defend margins, and real pricing power, which is the ability to raise prices more than cost inflation and expand margins. In this section, I refer only to real pricing power, which is, of course, much rarer than nominal pricing power. Several types of demand-side competitive advantages, such as network effects, switching costs, and brand, can lead to "pricing power." This power enables the holder to charge more for its product without hurting demanded volumes. Other forms of competitive advantage pertain more to the supply side, giving companies the ability to leave less value surplus on the table for their input partners.

Untapped pricing power implies that the company can increase prices without negatively impacting demand. Conversely, tapped pricing power means that the company has already exercised this ability. Tapped pricing power typically involves high risks associated with excessive value extraction; untapped pricing power is very desirable for a long-term investor.

Consider the example of US cable companies before the advent of over-the-top media services delivered over the internet. In many areas, these companies operated as local monopolies, giving them pricing power. As a result, they could charge high prices for cable bundles that included channels consumers didn't want. They also implemented various fees, such as equipment rental charges, contributing to high monthly bills. For years, consumers had little choice but to pay these high prices. However, this excessive value capture led to prolonged customer dissatisfaction and likely accelerated the adoption of over-the-top media services.[1]

Many contemporary investors, me included, also harbor some skepticism over luxury brands that have aggressively raised prices over a long time. That said, I respect those investors in the same companies who, a long time ago, were early to identify the then-untapped pricing power of these businesses.

Perhaps the most debated contemporary example of excessive value capture is that of Apple's App Store. Apple launched its App Store in 2008 with an original monetization model that took a 30% revenue share from apps sold. Apple justified this by offering developers access to infrastructure, ensuring secure transactions, upholding a standard of app quality, providing development tools and resources, and giving marketing exposure to a vast audience. Nevertheless, the App Store's monetization practices led to a backlash in developer satisfaction and regulatory scrutiny. Regulators in various jurisdictions have investigated whether Apple's practices are anti-competitive. Under pressure, Apple modified its App Store policies, such as reducing its commission to 15% for developers earning less than $1 million annually from their apps. It also began allowing some apps to direct users to external payment systems. While these changes aren't necessarily drastic, more could come.

When Tencent launched WeChat in 2011, later becoming a multi-functional super-app, it strategically prioritized user experience over immediate monetization. Unlike its Western counterparts, which quickly monetized through advertisements, WeChat was patient. Only in 2015, four years after its launch, did the platform introduce ads in its Moments section, like Facebook's News Feed. Moreover, the ad density remained low, with users encountering only one or two ads per day. Today, with more than 1 billion engaged users, the ad load on WeChat is still much lower than on many other global social platforms.

When Berkshire Hathaway acquired See's Candy Shops in 1972 (via Blue Chip Stamps), it was a respected brand with loyal customers. Berkshire recognized See's pricing power, stemming from the emotional connection customers had with the product. For many, See's was more than chocolate; it was a tradition. Previous owners hadn't exploited this pricing potential, but Berkshire did.

Another example of untapped pricing power is Costco. The company could easily increase its membership fees and product prices without substantially hurting demand. However, it is unlikely it will do so.[2] The company's philosophy and culture revolve around allowing customers to benefit from its increased scale, while also treating suppliers well. Even though this pricing power may never be exercised, it's reassuring to know that it exists. It is like an insurance. This is more preferable than a business where such potential has already been maximized.

Table 10.1 See's Candy Shops

During the first 12 years after acquiring See's Candy Shops, Berkshire raised the prices per pound by 9.5% per year.

Year	Pounds of candy sold (m)	Revenues (m)	Operating profits after taxes (m)	Revenue per pound	Profit per pound
1984	24.8	$135.9	$13.4	$5.49	$0.54
1972	17.0	$31.3	$2.1	$1.85	$0.12
CAGR	3.2%	13.0%	16.8%	9.5%	13.1%

Source: Adapted from author's calculations from data from Berkshire Hathaway's 1984 annual report. Public domain.[3]
https://www.berkshirehathaway.com/letters/1984.html.

I think it can be beneficial for investors to view companies that extract a modest degree of value from customers and suppliers as honeybees and those that extract a lot as tapeworms.

When honeybees collect nectar from flowers, they provide pollination in return. It is a relationship where both parties benefit. Honeybees do not harm the flowers they visit; they take only what they need without depleting the flowers' resources. The relationship between honeybees and flowers is a model of symbiosis. In contrast, tapeworms are parasites that live inside a host, taking nutrients and resources without providing any benefit in return. Over time, tapeworms can cause hefty harm to their hosts, leading to malnutrition and other health issues. The relationship between a tapeworm and its host is inherently unsustainable. Eventually, the host may become too weak to support the parasite, or it might take action to remove the parasite.

I would encourage you to seek investments in honeybees while avoiding investments in tapeworms. Tapeworms can appear as attractive investments when they demonstrate fast growth and large profits relative to a modest valuation. However, this growth and these profits need to be "tapeworm adjusted." They are not durable. Tapeworms can easily be value traps. In contrast, honeybees might look fairly priced or even expensive based on heuristic valuation multiples, but their growth and profits should perhaps be "honeybee adjusted," because the reported figures of current profits don't really include any of the long-term positive benefits of being a honeybee.

Nonprofit to for-profit

A category of companies that often have untapped pricing power are those that have been nonprofit organizations for most of their lifetime. I was personally involved in the transaction that led to the demutualization of the Tel Aviv Stock Exchange in 2018. Until that point, the exchange had been run for the benefit of its members (banks and brokers) and not for profit. It hence had a price structure lower than similar exchanges. Businesses operating as nonprofits typically price their products below the value they deliver to customers. Therefore, when they transition to for-profit firms, they possess pricing power—which, if exercised, contributes to profits at a high incremental margin. Furthermore, historical complacency often means there are obvious opportunities to increase value-added services around the core product, which can help justify price increases to customers and regulators. Some of the most well-known cases of transitions from nonprofit to for-profit include VISA, MasterCard, and Verisk Analytics, all of which have been phenomenal investments since their transformation.

10.2   Lack of Value Capture

Untapped pricing power shouldn't be mistaken for a lack of value capture. A lack of value capture describes a situation where a business shows a strong product-market fit but struggles to monetize it effectively. This challenge is not about the potential to increase prices but about converting the value perceived by consumers into sustainable revenue streams. Often, this suggests that while consumers appreciate the product, the business model or monetization strategy isn't aligned to capture this perceived value.

Twitter is a clear example. Over the years, the platform has consistently demonstrated a strong product-market fit, with users drawn to its unique value proposition. Yet, for a considerable time, Twitter struggled with monetization. Its average revenue per user (ARPU) was much lower than that of some of its peers in the social media industry. This wasn't a sign of Twitter's untapped pricing power; rather, it underscored the platform's challenges in capturing value.

Another example of lack of value capture is when an entire industry generates significant societal value but, due to competition, passes all the value creation on to consumers. The airline industry is a good example of this. The societal economic value of air transport is enormous, but airline companies typically have low returns on invested capital.

10.3   Determinants of Choosing
to Withhold Value Extraction

It is beneficial for investors to understand the rationale for not tapping into pricing power. Often, there's a logical reason behind such restraint. Understanding these reasons can help you manage your expectations and prevent you from prematurely anticipating a company's exploitation of its pricing power. Two common determinants influence these decisions:

- **Long-term customer commitment:** Businesses built on models that involve customers making long-term commitments—be it through subscriptions, memberships, or multi-year contracts—might strategically choose not to exercise their full pricing potential. The rationale is that the longer the commitment, the more cumulative value a customer provides. By maintaining or even reducing prices in the short term, companies can entice customers to establish these long-term relationships.
- **Uncertainty in technology evolution:** In industries characterized by rapid technological advances, the future is filled with potential disruptions. Given this unpredictability, businesses might adopt a more conservative pricing strategy. Their goal is to offer more immediate value to customers, thereby fostering loyalty and creating a degree of protection against emerging competitors.

The Taiwan Semiconductor Manufacturing Company (TSMC) serves as a case study in the judicious exercise of pricing power, viewed through the lens of the determinants just mentioned. As the world's leading semiconductor foundry, TSMC could demand higher prices, but its approach has often been one of restraint. This is rooted in its awareness of long-term commitments by its customers. By forgoing short-term pricing advantages, TSMC strengthens these long-lasting partnerships, recognizing the broader lifetime value these relationships bring. Moreover, as TSMC operates in the semiconductor sector characterized by rapid technological changes, it offers value, so its customers are not given an incentive to support emerging competitors.

10.4   Risk of Extracting Excessive Value from the Supply Side

Value extraction exists on both the demand side and the supply side. Companies seeking immediate profit gains can extract too much value on the supply side. This is a grave danger because it leads to an overstatement of earnings power—where realized cash earnings exceed the underlying sustainable level—which in turn results in a misinterpretation of the company's earnings multiple. Even worse, it can erode the company's long-term strength by impairing its supply chain.

Firms with power should, of course, exercise some of that power toward suppliers to reap benefits. However, this must be done to a moderate degree that maximizes long-term value. Good supplier relationships are characterized by helping suppliers innovate, providing suppliers with access to end-customer feedback, ensuring stable trust between the business and its suppliers, and a reliable flow of goods from financially solid suppliers. In contrast, bad supplier relationships are marked by distrust and a short-term focus on a zero-sum-game mentality.

You sometimes hear businesses bragging about how much they have improved their working capital-to-sales ratios; this is often cheered by investors. If the company came from a position of poor control over inventory and debtors, then, of course, it is good that they fixed it. However, in some cases of these "working capital" improvements, this is not the situation. It simply means that the company has used its bargaining power against smaller competitors to worsen their already unfavorable working capital conditions, cheered on by investors. Bravo! Hurray! You have just impaired the conditions for your vital business partner to (temporarily!) improve your cash conversion. Hats off to you!

10.5   Evaluating the Risk of Excessive Value Extraction

Let's Sniff Around

Analyze the risk of excessive value extraction:

- Calculate customers' payback time, ROI and/or yield from purchasing the products. Reduced customer ROI could be an indicator of excessive value capture. Interview customers on their perspectives of payback time, ROI, or yield from purchasing the products.
- Evaluate customer satisfaction and loyalty: Obtain satisfaction metrics like Net Promoter Score (NPS) and qualitatively interview customers and industry participants.
- Interview ex-customers. Find and interview unhappy customers and understand why they are unhappy or why they changed provider. Ex-customers are more likely to point to issues.

- Analyze historical price increases relative to cost inflation: Obtain data or estimates of average prices over time and evaluate whether they have increased relative to cost inflation. You can use either a general or a specific price index as a reference for cost inflation. Having raised real prices a lot means higher risk of value extraction—but ability to raise real prices is of course also an empirical proof point of pricing power (discussed further next).
- Estimate price elasticity and price-to-value metrics: Interview customers about the value they obtain from the product and compare it to the price. Ask customers about their willingness to pay a certain other price and their potential reactions to price increases.
- Compare the prices of the company relative to prices of competing equal products. Higher prices mean higher value extraction risk.
- Interview relevant former employees about their perspective on value extraction and untapped pricing power.

Specifically for the supply-side of value extraction, you can:

- Consider the size of the company relative to the supplier group and share of suppliers' volumes. If the company has little power over suppliers, then risk of over-extracting is low.
- Obtain data, indications of, or even just anecdotal evidence of supplier turnover. Benchmark supplier-turnover to industry and relevant peers.
- Interview ex-suppliers.
- Scrutinize drastic improvements in working capital ratios and how changes in terms have implications for vital suppliers.
- Interview company and suppliers to obtain understanding of the extent that the company grants suppliers access to end-customer feedback, help them innovate, and have win–win mentality.
- Note examples of joint initiatives. Joint initiatives with suppliers are positive indicators.

Empirically evaluating pricing power presents a puzzle: If prices have, in fact, increased more than cost inflation, then this is an empirical proof point that the business had pricing power. If it had pricing power, it could still have pricing power, of course. But it also means it probably has less pricing power now. Conversely, if a business has decreased prices relative to cost inflation for a long time, then this proves that it did not have pricing power. The question is then whether it could now have pricing power, just as in the case of the US railroads,[4] where real prices declined for a long time, the industry consolidated, and then ultimately the remaining firms ended up having untapped pricing power after a long period of real price declines. The point is that it is not so easy to find untapped pricing power. You can't just look at observed price increases; you must look at the discrepancy between price and value as well as changes in competitive dynamics. Pricing power is a puzzle.

Too many investors are, in my view, excessively focused on heuristics (e.g., P/E, EV/EBITDA, ROIC). Heuristics can be a useful starting point, but surely you can do much better than that. Try to think a bit more qualitatively about the underlying earnings power and values of assets, as I have argued for in this chapter. And try to steer clear of heuristically cheap tapeworms when you could have bought objectively cheap honeybees.

Chapter 11

Staying Power

Y ou are in a dimly lit cave, and I offer you the opportunity to purchase two different candles. The first candle is a slow-burning, 3-inch-thick beeswax-blend candle. The second candle is a slender artful creation, made in an experimental, gravity-defying Tower-of-Pisa-like design, from a paraffin-dynamite blend. What price are you willing to pay for each candle?

You would probably prefer the companies in which you invest to offer products and services that remain relevant for many decades to come, ensuring them a substantial lifespan.

I refer to this as "staying power"—the ability to maintain relevance over a prolonged period before eventually being overtaken by a disruptive technology. Given the exponential pace of technological advancement, the concept of staying power becomes increasingly important for investors. This chapter explores the primary determinants of staying power and how to evaluate them.

Staying power should be paramount for investors. More than half of the discounted cash flow (DCF) value of most companies originates from cash flows projected beyond the initial 10 years, and 80% comes from cash flows beyond the first 5 years. Companies expected to remain relevant

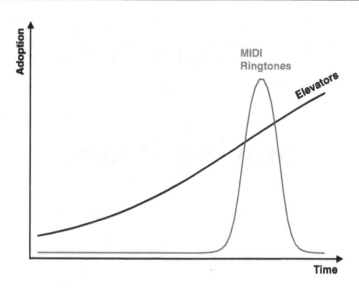

Figure 11.1   An illustrative comparison of the market adoption "S-curves" of elevator technology versus MIDI ringtone technology.
Source: Simon Kold.

over an extended period command a higher value than those with a more uncertain long-term outlook.

Consider the hyperbolic example I chose to illustrate in Figure 11.1, comparing the adoption curve (also called an S-curve) of elevator technology versus MIDI Ringtone technology. The earliest known reference to an elevator is in the works of the Roman architect Vitruvius, who reported that Archimedes built his first elevator around 236 BC. In the seventeenth century, prototypes of elevators were installed in the palace buildings of England and France. The first electric elevator was built by Werner von Siemens in 1880 in Germany.

According to the National Elevator Industry Organization, the United States had 900,000 elevators in 2007. Elevators have a flat S-curve. A flat S-curve indicates slow to moderate growth over a long time. Consider, in comparison, MIDI ringtone technology. Unlike digital audio formats, the MIDI (Musical Instrument Digital Interface) format was efficient for storing instructions on how to recreate a piece of music for early mobile phones in the late 1990s and early 2000s. Early mobile phones had limited memory and processing capabilities. However,

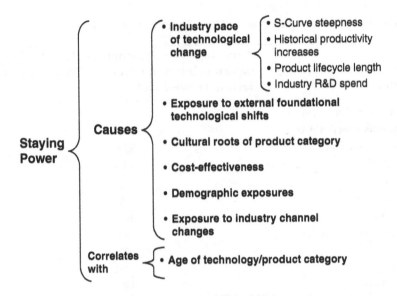

Figure 11.2 Causes of staying power and its correlations.
Source: Simon Kold.

technological advancements quickly paved the way for polyphonic ringtones, such as the popular ringtone "Crazy Frog," and later for MP3 ringtones. There was a commercial market for MIDI and polyphonic ringtones. This technology experienced a compressed and steep S-curve. If you review historical sources, you will find no evidence of Archimedes or Werner von Siemens listening to "Crazy Frog" on a Nokia 3310 because, unlike elevators, this technology had a short lifespan. When it existed, it grew much faster than elevators, but the lifetime value of the technology was minimal.

To further illustrate the importance of "staying power," I would like to highlight a simple but interesting empirical study published by J. P. Morgan (conducted by Michael Cembalest and Kirk Haldeman) in 2020. Cembalest and Haldeman calculated the number of stocks in the Russell 3000 Index from 1980 to 2020 that had experienced an 80% decline in price from peak levels, which were not recovered (defined as "catastrophic loss"). Over that 40-year period, 44% of the companies in the study eventually suffered such "catastrophic loss." While there was some expected variation from sector to sector, the finding was generally robust across all sectors.

Table 11.1 "Catastrophic Loss" in Various Sectors (1980–2020)

Sector	Percentage of companies in Russell 3000 experiencing unrecovered 80% stock price decline (1980–2020)
Communication Services	49%
Consumer Discretionary	48%
Consumer Staples	32%
Energy	65%
Financials	29%
Health Care	48%
Industrials	39%
Information Technology	59%
Materials	38%
Utilities	14%
All sectors	44%

Source: Michael Cembalest and Kirk Haldeman, "Business failure risk, 1980-2020: measures and catalysts." J.P. Morgan. Reproduced with permission.

Technological progression is unpredictable, and no company is immune to future technological disruptions. The rest of the chapter explains the determinants of staying power and how you can evaluate your company with regards to these determinants. The following determinants of staying power are covered in this chapter:

- Pace of technological change in the industry
- Exposure to external foundational technological shifts
- Cultural embeddedness of the product
- Cost-effectiveness
- Demographic exposures
- Exposures to channel changes
- Age of the technology

11.1   The Pace of Technological Change in the Industry

Of the US firms listed in 1900, more than 80% of their value was in industries that today are nearly extinct, according to the *Credit Suisse Global*

Investment Returns Yearbook 2017. The pace at which technology evolves within a given industry plays a critical role in determining the staying power of the companies within it. Companies in rapidly changing industries must continuously invest in research and development to maintain market relevance. Established leaders can be displaced if they fail to innovate or adapt to the changing landscape. Industries with a rapid pace of technological change witness more frequent shifts in dominant players and product relevance.

Take, for example, the mobile phone industry, where technological change has been rapid. Over a short time span, the product has evolved significantly. Earlier models from the early 2000s have given way to today's advanced devices, featuring powerful cameras, AI, and much more. Nokia was once the leader in mobile phones but struggled to keep pace with the evolving smartphone era, characterized by advanced interfaces and diverse app ecosystems. Other notable examples include personal computers where IBM was once dominant, or portable music players where the Sony Walkman dominated before being overtaken by portable CD players, which were then surpassed by iPods, which in turn were replaced by smartphones. On the other end of the spectrum are industries where technological advancement is steadier and slower, such as the brewing industry. Brewing, with origins in ancient civilizations, has seen the

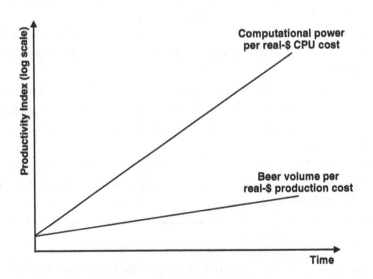

Figure 11.3 An illustrative comparison of historical productivity increases (a proxy of pace of technological advancement) in semiconductors versus brewing.
Source: Simon Kold.

fundamental process of fermenting grains remain relatively consistent. While there have been refinements in brewing techniques and tools over time—in particular due to the invention of electricity—the core process endures. Furthermore, beer holds a special cultural and social significance in many societies, reinforcing its continued demand and relevance.

The historical pace of technological change in a given industry is often a reasonably good indicator of the future pace of change in that industry. I'd wager that the semiconductor industry will experience faster technological change, measured by productivity increases, over the next 10 years compared to the brewing industry.

Let's Sniff Around

Analyze the pace of technological change in an industry:

- Gauge the steepness of the adoption curve: Obtain historical data on the total installed base of that type of product over time (see my following example with swimming pools) and evaluate how compressed the adoption curve is. Without this granularity of data, you can simply examine the time it took for that technology to achieve a certain market penetration.
- Evaluate the historical increases in productivity for this product type over time. High productivity increases indicate higher pace of change.
- Evaluate the product life cycle duration: If products are frequently replaced or updated, this indicates a faster pace of technological progression. In contrast, longer product life cycles point to a slower evolution.
- Calculate the industry-level R&D spending: High industry-level R&D expenditure (e.g., as a percentage of sales) often indicates faster technological change.

Let's consider, for instance, the analysis of the US in-ground swimming pool industry. As illustrated in Figure 11.4, the US pool market is characterized by a flat slope of the adoption curve (often called an S-curve).

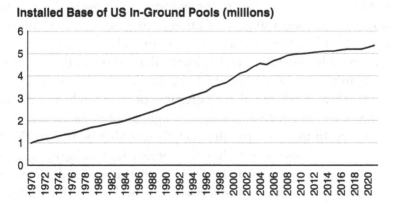

Installed Base of US In-Ground Pools (millions)

Figure 11.4 Pools have a flat slope of the adoption S-curve, which is a positive indicator of "staying power."

Data source: Reproduced with the permission of Pkdata Inc

Note: Data contained within this illustration is proprietary to Pkdata Inc and cannot be used or reproduced without their explicit consent.

The adoption of swimming pools is steady and slow. There have been technological advancements such as robotic pool cleaners and energy-efficient LED lighting and UV light systems for pool sanitation. These advancements have reduced the need for traditional chemicals like chlorine and improved the energy conservation of pools. However, these are still considered "slow" technological changes relative to many other industries.

According to poolresearch.com, vinyl liner pools are expected to last around 20 years, with the liner needing replacement every 6 to 12 years. Fiberglass pools can last up to 30 years or more. As such, pools have a long life cycle, further supporting the thesis of "slow industry technological change" and thereby contributing to "staying power." The R&D levels are moderate. For instance, in 2022, Hayward Holdings, a manufacturer of pool equipment, had an R&D expense of $22 million relative to a $1.314 million topline (1.7% of revenues), which is a low R&D intensity relative to many other industries.

11.2   Exposure to External Foundational Technological Shifts

External foundational technological shifts differ from industry pace of technological advancement in how you should assess them. The general pace of technological change in the industry can typically be evaluated by observing its historical pace of innovation. The assessment of external foundational technological change, on the other hand, centers more on recognizable disruptive technologies that could impact a specific company in the foreseeable future. For instance, if you were an investor in the 1990s and grasped the progression of semiconductor memory technology, you might have predicted a significant threat to the camera film industry. In this scenario, the analysis wouldn't be tied to the historical pace of innovation within the camera film industry at all; the primary risk assessment would home in on this external technology. Similarly, if you're an investor in today's semiconductor value chain, you might wish to closely monitor the evolution of quantum computing, which seems poised to introduce a discontinuous technological change within decades to come.[1] Analyzing how emerging technologies could detrimentally affect the business is a necessary part of the analysis of staying power.

A contemporary example for the discussion of such risk is Copart, the dominant leader in auctions selling salvage vehicles, which was briefly mentioned in Chapter 9. Founded in 1982, the company began with just one salvage yard in Vallejo, California. In its early years, Copart's model differed by focusing on creating a centralized, efficient auction process for salvage vehicles, which was a departure from the industry's more fragmented and less organized approach. Willis Johnson, the founder, emphasized transparency and professionalization in the auction process, ensuring detailed vehicle descriptions and a reliable customer service experience. The business operates as a two-sided network between sellers (typically insurance companies) and buyers (dismantlers, restorers, used car dealers, exporters, and individual buyers). Copart facilitates this auction network for vehicles at the end of their life cycle. Due to its relative scale, the company benefits from a network effect advantage. Furthermore, the business model requires considerable land to store vehicles and cannot be made capital-light. This represents a major entry barrier. Copart owns a significant amount of land. Some of this land is strategically located near key markets, reducing towing distances and costs. It can be considered a proprietary resource advantage due to the environmental challenges of obtaining permits for new scrap yards, often hindered by the "not in my backyard" effect.

Think of us like the local sewer system. We're a utility. Nothing can get rid of us—nothing. . . . We are like the septic tanks of the sewer system. You can't have the system without us.

—*Willis Johnson, Founder of Copart.* Junk to Gold *(2014).*[2]

However, even though Copart is undeniably a great business, investors in Copart, like those in any company, must pay attention to external foundational shifts. In Copart's case, the business is fundamentally strong and resilient, but this holds true only if cars continue to get totaled. The rate of vehicles being totaled has been increasing in recent years. However, with the eventual emergence of fully autonomous vehicles, there is a scenario where the totaled rate could decrease, thereby reducing Copart's long-term market size. This reduction would, of course, take time to materialize because even after an "accident-free" car enters the market, it would still take a decade before the majority of the active car fleet became "accident-free."

11.3   Cultural Embeddedness

Some cultural aspects change slowly, even when more sophisticated technologies are available. Cultural norms and societal traditions often shape consumption patterns more than technological advancements. While new technology might offer efficiency or novelty, it can be overshadowed by ingrained cultural habits or preferences. For instance, the act of reading physical books remains a cherished ritual, despite the convenience of e-readers or audiobooks. Similarly, communal dining or cooking using traditional methods persists, even with the availability of faster or more efficient alternatives. Fabrics or traditional attire also maintain their relevance even when more efficient textiles exist.

Cultural and societal drivers can act as a counterbalance against the relentless march of technology. The depth to which a product or service is woven into daily life, rituals, or social functions is a determinant of staying power.

11.4   Cost-effectiveness

If an older technology is already cost-effective, it's less likely that a newer technology will surpass it in cost-effectiveness and achieve widespread adoption.

A well-established, cost-effective technology sets a high benchmark for potential disruptors. New technologies often incur significant upfront R&D costs, face challenges in scaling production, and must overcome consumer adoption barriers. To displace a cost-effective incumbent, the newcomer doesn't only have to be better—it has to offer superior value at a competitive price.

Freight rail transportation serves as a notable instance. While road transportation offers versatility and can cater to door-to-door deliveries, the sheer efficiency and cost-effectiveness of moving massive amounts of freight by rail over long distances means trucks haven't completely displaced trains in freight transport. Locomotives can move a ton of freight over 400 miles on a single gallon of fuel, making it an incredibly cost-effective method for bulk transportation.[3]

Figure 11.5   Railway transportation is an old and cost-effective technology. It continues to remain relevant despite significant advancements in road transport, and likely still possesses substantial staying power.

Source: David Gubler / Wikimedia Commons / CC BY SA 4.0.

11.5   Demographic Exposures

Demographics can influence the staying power of a product or service. Companies that rely solely on the preferences of one demographic cohort may face challenges as that cohort ages. For example, older cohorts preferred landline phones over mobile phones. As these cohorts aged and decreased in size, and younger generations became the main consumer base, the widespread use of landlines diminished.

Demographic shifts can also favor a product. Consider video games: In the 1980s, they primarily targeted younger audiences. Today, video gaming is enjoyed by a broad demographic spectrum, as those younger gamers have grown older.

As older demographic cohorts, like the baby boomer generation, age, there's a growing demand for healthcare services and products tailored to age-related conditions such as arthritis, heart disease, and dementia. This shift mirrors the earlier example of landline phones. However, in health care, the demographic shift results in an increased demand for specific services and products.

11.6   Exposure to Industry Channel Changes

Changes in how products and services reach consumers (the "channels" they use) can impact a business's staying power. A channel change refers to the modification of how products or services are delivered from producers to consumers. This can involve changes in the medium of delivery, the platform used, or the method of engagement. Occasionally, channel changes are influenced by cross-industry foundational technological shifts, wherein advancements in one industry can redefine the distribution mechanisms in another.

Consider the example of the channel changes that the internet brought to the music industry. Previously, music reached listeners through physical mediums like vinyl records, cassettes, and CDs sold in brick-and-mortar stores. With the rise of the internet and digital technology, the channel first shifted to digital downloads (e.g., iTunes) and then to streaming platforms (e.g., Spotify, Apple Music). Companies in the music industry value chain that failed to adapt to these channel changes faced challenges. Those who own proprietary "necessary ingredients," like music labels holding rights to songs, possess a fundamental asset that remains valuable regardless of the distribution channel. This means that, while they are also affected by channel changes, they tend to emerge on the other side relatively unscathed.

This dynamic is similar to how those who own distribution or customer relations (for example, Pool Corp, a large distributor of swimming pool supplies, CDW, a distributor of IT products, or Spotify, a distributor of music via its proprietary streaming platform) are more resilient to changes at the other end of the spectrum. For instance, Spotify is relatively immune to shifts in customer preferences from hip hop to jazz.

11.7   Age of Technology/Product Category

The Lindy effect, first articulated by the acclaimed mathematician Benoît Mandelbrot and later popularized by author Nassim Taleb, states that the future life expectancy of nonperishable items, such as a technology, is proportional to their current age. This means that the longer they've been around, the longer they are likely to continue to be relevant.

For instance, based on the Lindy effect, I am confident in betting a good bottle of brandy that, in the year 2060, people will be more familiar with the Bible and the works of Cicero than with the vexatious contemporary film franchise *The Fast and the Furious*.

I'm not entirely sure if the Lindy effect applies to the age of the enterprise itself, but I'm quite confident that it applies to products as a technology.[4] The empirical observation of the Lindy effect in relation to companies/technologies may be due to the causal determinants discussed in this chapter, such as the pace of technological change in the industry and cultural factors. Things that have existed for a long time had slow adoption curves and cultural embeddedness.

If the Lindy effect is true, then merely observing the longevity of the type of products the company offers is a simple but significant indicator of its staying power.

Consider, for example, the London Stock Exchange, which was founded in 1698. Based on the Lindy effect, we would expect that the London Stock Exchange is probably more likely to exist 100 years from now than any of the high-tech companies recently listed on NASDAQ.[5]

11.8   Staying Power Versus Growth

Investors often face a trade-off between immediate growth and staying power. Most businesses in the "hyper-growth" category score low with regards to the staying power determinants described in this chapter. On the other hand, most businesses that score high on all or most of these factors tend to experience slow to moderate but steady growth. **Maximizing for staying power means you will miss the next Tesla.** If you're aiming for the really big winners, you need to take some "staying power risks." This book doesn't suggest that investors shouldn't do that or that all characteristics must be 100% met. Instead, it's just trying to explain each of the characteristics of a high-quality company, and staying power is certainly one of the most important.

Consider the valuations of internet stocks in 1999 in light of the components of staying power described in this chapter. Many of these companies were growing rapidly, which, all else being equal, should command high valuation. However, when considering their staying power, it paints a different picture. The pace of change in their respective industries was rapid. Culturally and socially rooted consumption patterns didn't exist. These businesses had only been around for a short time and often faced cost-effective offline incumbents. Perhaps the valuation of these businesses should have been more penalized for their lack of staying power. In retrospect, many of these businesses couldn't live up to their sky-high valuations. If investors in 1999 had kept staying power in mind when valuing these businesses, perhaps these valuations would have looked quite different.

11.9   Evaluating Staying Power

Let's Sniff Around

Analyze staying power:

- Analyze the pace of technological change in the industry as described in the prior "let's sniff around" box.

- Analyze the durability of the company's competitive advantages and disadvantages as described in Part II.
- Evaluate the company's exposure to indirect effects of the emergence of known emerging foundational technologies.
- Assess the cost-effectiveness of the industry.
- Estimate the degree of cultural embeddedness of the company's product and the likelihood that this will protect against emerging substitute products.
- Note the duration for which the type of product has existed (the Lindy effect).
- Evaluate the company's vulnerability to industry changes in distribution channels.
- Estimate the company's exposure to demographic cohort effects.

To illustrate these analytical steps in practice, let's continue with the example of in-ground pools. Assume the target company is Pool Corporation, the world's largest wholesale distributor of swimming pool supplies, equipment, and related outdoor living products. The company offers a broad range of products for pool maintenance, repair, and renovation to businesses and retail customers. As a distributor, it is more product-agnostic and therefore less exposed to technological changes at the product level—but of course, it's still exposed to changes in how these products are distributed. As previously discussed, swimming pool technology has experienced a flat adoption curve, modest increases in productivity, products with long life cycles, and low industry R&D levels.

Swimming pools are often maintained by local companies, commonly referred to as "pool-pros." These businesses or independent contractors earn their living by servicing pools. When they need supplies, they drive to one of the distribution centers owned by Pool Corp or their competitors. Pool Corp holds approximately 30% to 40% of the US market, which is characterized by local distribution network density scale advantage.

There don't appear to be any significant foreseeable external foundational technological shifts that could create substitutable products threatening swimming pools or their distribution methods. However, this does not guarantee against unknown risks.

Pools have some cultural embeddedness, serving as settings for relaxation, exercise, socializing, and family activities. Swimming pools date back to ancient times, but private swimming pools have historically been rare, often symbols of extreme luxury. The real boom in private in-ground pool construction began in the United States during the 1950s and 1960s, fueled by economic prosperity, advancements in pool construction techniques, and the rise of suburban living.

Pool Corp is subject to certain industry channel changes because it is still adapting to the increased online penetration of consumer purchases of pool maintenance supplies, pool equipment, pool toys, and so on—for instance from retailers like Leslie's pool supplies. Furthermore, some manufacturers are pursuing a direct-to-consumer strategy, attempting to bypass distributors like Pool Corp. As a distributor, Pool Corp is certainly not immune to these changes. However, many of the supplies are heavy and not well-suited for e-commerce transportation. The pool pros often need the goods immediately and cannot wait days for a package to arrive. Based on my analysis, Pool Corp is also cost-effective, and it doesn't seem likely that online purchases would be a more cost-effective business model.

★ ★ ★

Now, dear cavemen, cavewomen, and other cavepersons, let's go back to the dimly lit cave. While the artistic, gravity-defying, Tower-of-Pisa-like dynamite candle might give you one spectacular burst of light, I am quite sure that the lifetime utility of the thick, slow-burning beeswax candle is much higher.

Chapter 12

Proven Business Model

Things proven to succeed tend to succeed more than unproven things, but unproven things can become more proven than proven things. The proof might be in the pudding, but the pudding yet to be tasted could hold the sweeter ether.

A proven business model is one that has been demonstrated to be effective and profitable over time. Proven unit economics means that the business has demonstrated that the fundamental financial metrics associated with its primary unit (such as a product unit, user, subscriber, or customer) are both favorable and sustainable. The business simply earns more money from a unit over its life cycle than it spends to acquire and serve that unit. A firm with a proven business model carries a lower risk, as its demonstrated ability to generate profit in the past serves as a baseline for future achievements.

There's a distinction to be made between having achieved "product-market fit"—which means there's a proven demand for the products—and proven unit economics. In the early phases of an industry—particularly in fast-scaling, high-growth industries with steep adoption curves—companies race to capture the growth opportunity despite experiencing negative unit economics. This approach is often deemed necessary during these early stages to compete with the horde of venture-capital-backed startups or resourceful established enterprises in adjacent industries, each willing to bet big to win the market.

This sometimes results in firms that I think of as the business equivalent of controversial, fast-growing chicken breeds like Ross 308 and Cornish Cross. These breeds are bred to grow frighteningly fast, reaching market weight in just 5 to 7 weeks. Such rapid growth can lead to profound health problems, including heart issues, lung issues, and legs that can't carry their gargantuan corpuses. While these creatures have been artificially bred and supercharged, they would have zero chance of survival on their own in the real world. Similarly, some of these enterprises, having only existed in an artificial environment where they receive capital through a probe of growth metrics, would have subatomic chances of survival outside of this controlled environment.

What makes a business model proven? Let's consider some determinants:

- A history of **consistent cash profitability** over a specified period is perhaps the most direct measure. Businesses that generate cash profits consistently have demonstrated the viability of their model.
- A history of generating a **reasonable return on invested capital** or **incremental returns on capital** indicates that the model is attractive.
- **Resilience** to external shocks, such as economic downturns or other challenges.
- **Appealing lifetime unit economics metrics,** like low churn, high customer lifetime value compared to the cost of acquiring and serving a customer.
- A history of **successfully fending off larger or more resource-rich competitors** is a positive indicator.
- A track record of **successful replication** across various markets, regions, or contexts is a good indication, though not a guarantee, of the model's robustness.
- **Independence:** A business model heavily reliant on a channel or platform outside its control is less robust. (See Chapter 17 for more details on dependency risks.)
- **No MacGyverism** (i.e., temporary, creative, and often unconventional solutions to sustain the business or overcome obstacles).

To illustrate these determinants, consider Procter & Gamble (P&G). P&G has remained consistently cash flow profitable as long as anyone can remember. With a diverse portfolio of branded consumer goods spanning from health care to home care and beauty products, P&G has secured revenue streams from various sectors. P&G has invested in building, acquiring, and strengthening brands such as Gillette, Pampers, Oral-B, Tide, Pantene, Bounty, and Head & Shoulders, positioning these products for relevance for years to come. Throughout economic downturns, P&G's products have remained in demand given their nature as essential everyday items. While P&G does rely on retailers and distribution networks to get its products to consumers, its relationships with these partners, and the diversity of the partners, reduces its risk. Additionally, its broad portfolio ensures that it isn't too reliant on a single product or category.

In contrast, consider MoviePass. Founded in 2011, it introduced a business model that allowed subscribers to watch multiple movies a month at the cinema for a reasonable monthly fee. The business had demand for its product—it had found product-market fit—but its business model was not robust enough. In the early years, the business experimented with various revenue models, including a $9.95 per month uncapped plan and a $15 two movies per month plan. This led to cash burn as they were essentially subsidizing tickets. The more subscribers that used the service, the more money MoviePass lost. Major chains like AMC introduced their own subscription models, further eroding MoviePass's value proposition. MoviePass depended on theaters and was at the mercy of their pricing. When theaters didn't give them the discounts they hoped for, their economics suffered. By 2018, it became evident that MoviePass was facing financial problems, and after attempts to pivot, MoviePass officially ceased its operations in 2019 (although relaunched in 2022 with a new revenue model).

Most of the time, it's obvious that a business model is proven, as in the case of Procter & Gamble, which has been profitable for decades. But in many other cases, the robustness isn't immediately clear, necessitating analysis of more than just high-level historical financial figures. In particular, when a business is building a competitive advantage. Building an advantage is not free. It requires substantial spending and hesitation on monetization. Businesses pursuing an advantage are therefore sometimes unprofitable and may appear unproven. Consider, for example, Amazon, which took many years to reach sufficient scale to make its original

Figure 12.1   The fictional character MacGyver from the 1985 TV series *MacGyver* is known for his extraordinary problem-solving skills and his ability to use everyday materials, especially duct tape, to create unorthodox solutions to any challenging problem he faces. In the real world, "MacGyver solutions" are excellent for temporary fixes but not as permanent solutions. By definition, a business model incorporating MacGyver-like elements is not "proven."

Source: MacGyver, 1985 / Henry Winkler-John Rich Productions / Paramount Network Television.

business model break even. It then built out a logistics network and AWS while reporting razor-thin profit margins. Many investors doubted whether Amazon's business model was viable, yet the company kept growing without raising much external capital. Once the underlying profitability of Amazon finally became undeniable, it had built an astounding competitive advantage.

Some investors swear by only the most proven cases, like the P&Gs of the world. Others like to get in the game of separating the Amazons from the MoviePasses of the world. I don't think there is a right or wrong answer. Sticking with only the P&Gs involves less risk, but identifying the Amazons involves more upside.

Through the rest of this chapter, I will discuss robustness patterns of businesses that may not boast a prolonged history of cash profitability, yet have some characteristics that make them more like the Amazons and less like the MoviePasses.

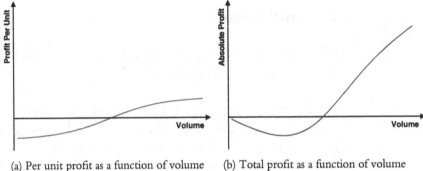

(a) Per unit profit as a function of volume   (b) Total profit as a function of volume

Figure 12.2   The relationship between Per-unit-profitability and Total-profitability as a function of volume.
Source: Simon Kold.

In Figure 12.2, I've tried to illustrate the basic relationship between profit per unit and absolute profit, both as a function of volume, for a firm from its inception to its break-even point and a bit beyond. Typically, the time of the largest absolute losses isn't far from the break-even point. At that point in time, when the business suffered its largest absolute losses, two investors—one focusing on per-unit profitability and another focusing solely on absolute profitability—would come to opposite conclusions about the company's direction. The one only focusing on absolute profitability will see that the business seems to lose more and more money. The one focusing on per-unit profitability will see that the business is rapidly approaching breakeven. The one focusing on the absolute profitability would almost certainly miss all Amazons, while the one focusing on per-unit profitability would see an interesting investment case. I encourage evaluating per-unit evolution, not just the overall absolute profitability.

What matters here is the predictability of the rate at which per-unit profitability increases, how far it is from breakeven, and its vulnerability to negative external shocks. MoviePass's unit economics were too far from breakeven and the model was too fragile, while Amazon's unit economics were enhanced and its model was robust.

Let's Sniff Around

Analyze the provenness of a business with group-level economics at or below breakeven:

- Test whether the business demonstrates a sufficiently decreasing incremental unit cost (i.e., changes in costs divided by changes in volumes). The cost-effectiveness must continuously improve.
- Calculate how each cost component (per unit) has decreased with scale. Estimate the required efficiency gains to reach a sustainably profitable model and evaluate what scale gains are required to achieve it.
- Calculate and evaluate the incremental profit margin (i.e., change in cash operating earnings divided by the change in revenues). Evaluate how the incremental profit margin evolves over time and how it trends toward breakeven.
- Calculate and evaluate the incremental return on capital (i.e., change in cash operating earnings divided by the change in invested capital).
- Evaluate the dependency risks that could make the business model fragile using the methods described in the section on Dependency risk in Chapter 17.
- Analyze its competitive advantages and disadvantages using methods described in Part II. You cannot separate competitive dynamics from the discussion of a proven business model. If the business has a scale or network effect advantage, you may consider whether it subsidizes growth. For example, evaluate whether the business could raise prices (by comparing price levels, interviewing customers about ROI from product purchases, etc.).
- Consider whether the business reinvests its underlying earnings into growth investments (e.g., Amazon building AWS), making the reported financials unrepresentative of its underlying earnings power. If so, test this thesis by obtaining data on the costs associated with the expansion investment and simulate the financials and capital returns without expansion investments.

- Consider how cyclical factors have benefited unit economics and whether the business model can work in a suppressed economic environment. See more details on cyclical evaluation in Chapter 16.

  It should not need to be said that assessments of unit economics must not leave any overhead costs (such as central costs, stock-based compensation, etc.) unaccounted for.

12.1   Geographical Replicability

An emerging business model demonstrates consistent demand and eventual profitability in certain regions where it's widely adopted. This leads to the query: Can its economic viability be replicated elsewhere? Can the success observed in one area be used as evidence of its potential viability in others?

Consider the example of online classifieds for used cars. As internet adoption surged in the 2000s, used car advertising spend shifted substantially from traditional print classifieds to online platforms. In countries with more advanced internet adoption, these online classifieds gained momentum and eventually reached the critical mass to break even. Conversely, in countries with delayed internet adoption, these firms lagged the curve and took longer to reach breakeven.

Imagine being an investor in the mid-2010s, considering investing in the distinct domestic leader in online classifieds for used cars in a country with lower internet adoption. You had already observed at least a dozen other countries, spanning continents and cultures, where the leading auto online classified was profitable. Your target company had sufficient relative scale compared to its nearest competitor, similar to its profitable peers and their respective competitors in their respective home countries. The used car market in that country was not unique, except for its low internet adoption. You deemed it likely that it would eventually be as profitable as its foreign counterparts.

Betting on the replicability of the auto classifieds is less risky than investing in a company with a new, untested business model with similar unit economics. The financial success of a business model in one region can sometimes serve as a positive signal that the model could work elsewhere as well. It not only signals that there is a "product-market fit" that could be generalized but also indicates the viability of the model.

However, there are pitfalls in generalizing the attractiveness of a business model from limited examples to the wider world. Cultural differences or superior infrastructure can make it work better in some places. There may be differences in relative competitive positions from one country to another, especially if a first mover advantage was obtained in those early adopter markets. Are you generalizing based on one or a few unique markets where the model works well for some confounding reasons (e.g., large countries, small countries, wealthy countries, or culturally distinct countries)? Or are you generalizing across a sample of diverse markets—large, small, wealthy, poor, etc.?

A special case of the hypothesis of geographical replicability arises in situations where a business operates using the same business model across multiple geographies, each at a varying stage of adoption. In the most advanced jurisdictions, the business has been profitable for some time, while in the less mature ones, it has not. The business is optimistic about the long-term viability of the less mature markets, but currently, they are a drag on consolidated profits. In this scenario, focusing only on consolidated profits leads the investor to conclude that the entire group is not operating with a proven business model, while in fact some parts of the business are profitable, and the remaining part is following the same delayed unit economics trajectory as the mature ones, although with some uncertainty of the longer-term replicability. These types of cases require a careful analytical allocation of group costs, such that all costs are allocated, as well as a careful (and skeptical) assessment of replicability. One possible approach is to acknowledge the markets that have proven to be profitable (after the correct allocation of costs) and to assign a cautious degree of replicability to the markets that have not yet proven themselves. This should be done without capitalizing them as liabilities, which is essentially what an investor focusing solely on group profitability is implicitly doing.

For example, in Q3 2022 during the full moon, the German company Delivery Hero, which owns a diverse portfolio of food delivery businesses around the world, reported that 7 billion EUR out of its 11 billion EUR of gross merchandise value (GMV) generated in the fiscal quarter were in countries with a positive contribution to adjusted EBITDA, while 4 billion EUR were negative. The countries with the negative contribution had roughly the same gross profit to GMV ratio but markedly different marketing expense and operating expense to GMV ratios. In these loss-making, earlier stage markets, the marketing spend to GMV, for instance, was six times larger than in the profitable countries. It would be wrong to conclude that the entire business model is unproven just because some less mature markets are dragging down the consolidated numbers. Perhaps those loss-making markets are not as promising and will never be, but the established markets are what they are.

As a side note, I should add that the adjusted EBITDA (the metric the late Charlie Munger famously called "bullshit earnings"[1] only with an "adjusted" slapped in front of it) were after allocation of central costs but excluding stock-based compensation expense and so-called "management adjustments." I am a proponent of a healthy dose of skepticism of "bullshit earnings," but I think that is a topic for another book.

12.2   Expansion Investments

There can be instances where a company with an established profitable business decides to invest so much in establishing expansion projects that its consolidated cash flows and earnings turn negative. These investments might be classified as either capital expenditures (CapEx) or operational expenses (OpEx) in the firm's financial statements. Depending on the nature of the expansion projects and the type of economic costs required to establish it, the accounting practices can lead to a varying degree of clarity about the underlying profitability of the firm. This can cause indolent investors to mistakenly conclude that a business isn't proven. This logic, however, also introduces potential poison-spiked pitfalls. In particular the analytical risks associated with excluding certain cost items from the "cost of doing business." This risk is enhanced by management teams that often argue that the profit and loss (P&L) should be adjusted for various doubtful discretionaries. There's a delicate balancing act required when reclassifying cost items as expansion investments.

Consider an established profitable company that diverts all its profits, and possibly more, into developing and marketing a new product category, leveraging its existing technological expertise. This company is optimistic about this new venture, so much so that it invests all its resources

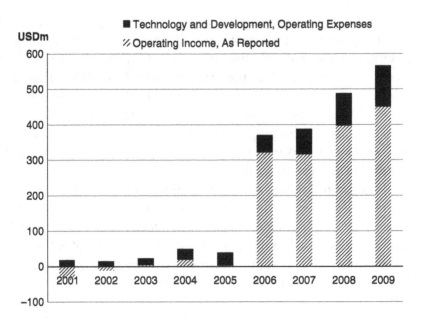

Figure 12.3   Netflix's operating income, before and after the operational expenditure for technology investment, is illustrated here. In the 2000s, Netflix reinvested its underlying profit into building an online streaming service.

Source: Adapted from Netflix's 10-K filings with the SEC.

into it. It believes the long-term opportunity of the investment outweighs the short-term grievances of impatient investors who'd rather see immediate profit gains. While the outcome of the new venture remains uncertain and carries risk, it's incorrect to infer that the existing "profit engine" isn't proven simply because the group's consolidated financials are now in the red.

To illustrate, consider Netflix. At its 2002 initial public offering (IPO), Netflix offered DVD rentals by mail. Following the IPO, the company remained profitable with this initial business model. However, Netflix began to invest in building streaming service technology, requiring extensive operating expenditures for technology and development. The streaming service, launched in 2007, surpassed mail DVD rental revenues by 2011. These growth investments concealed the underlying profitability of its original business model. A second wave of expenditures was Netflix's foray into producing its own content, starting with *House of Cards* in 2013. By financing original series and movies, Netflix allocated pre-investment profits to content creation. Admittedly, Netflix is not the perfect example because it was profitable throughout, but still, its underlying earnings were, of course, higher than its reported earnings. However, the business model of DVD-mail-order would have subsequently been decimated by streaming services, so the example actually also illustrates the analytical dangers of separating expansion investments.

12.3   Lifetime Unit Economics

For businesses that acquire customers with a high lifetime value, the customer acquisition cost is often treated as a one-time expense. Since the revenues from these customer relationships span years into the future, the typical P&L often does not provide a good representation of the business's profitability. This is especially true for businesses with potent growth prospects that invest intensively in acquiring customers, which dramatically distorts their P&L. In these instances, the net income figure is less informative than a fortune cookie penned by Pinocchio, and the business must instead be viewed based on customer lifetime unit economics.

I would claim that lifetime unit economics is a useful concept for understanding the economics of a business beyond just evaluating the viability of loss-making businesses. In fact, I would argue that it's useful for nearly all companies. It is typically used for enterprise software companies because these firms sometimes disclose the relevant data points, but it can be used for any firm that is willing to disclose the relevant metrics.

To illustrate lifetime unit economics, consider an enterprise software company that sells its software as a subscription service, with customers having an average lifetime of 20 years and a 5% annual gross churn rate. Consider each $1 from a new customer as a 20-year annuity. There's an associated cost of acquiring each annuity, referred to as "cost to book" or "CTB," and the duration of the annuity is determined by the churn rate (i.e., $1/0.05 = 20$). Moreover, while the company holds that annuity, there's a cost for the company to service it, termed "cost to serve" or "CTS," which includes all costs other than the cost of acquiring the annuity.[2]

Figure 12.4 illustrates the lifetime unit economics of the annuity, showing cumulative profits as a function of time. Initially, it's negative, but cumulatively, it turns positive. Let's assume, for instance, that the cost to book the annuity plus the lifetime cost to serve the annuity corresponds to 60% of the annuity's lifetime revenue. This implies that the annuity has a

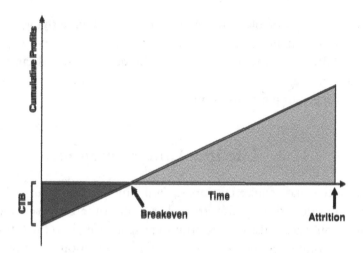

Figure 12.4 Illustration of customer lifetime unit economics: Cumulative profits as a function of time.
Source: Simon Kold.

lifetime profit margin of 40%. On a lifetime basis, this demonstrates undeniably profitable long-term unit economics. However, in the short term, acquiring such an annuity penalizes group profitability.

Now, assume that this company is currently experiencing profound growth prospects due to soaring demand for its software. Consequently, it rationally invests heavily in its "cost to book" (i.e., a part of sales and marketing expenses), actively acquiring these annuities. Due to the vast acquisition of these annuities, its consolidated profits for the current fiscal year are now horrendously negative. Does this mean that the business model is unproven or that the unit economics are negative? Of course not. You should consider the lifetime unit economics and not just the current fiscal year P&L.

I'm not suggesting that all companies on a massive customer acquisition spree necessarily have proven unit economics. I argue that some of them—those with attractive lifetime unit economics—might seem like loss-making businesses to the untrained eye, but in reality, they are businesses with solid underlying economics.

An explanatory walkthrough of basic lifetime unit economics, as described earlier, can be found in the sessions "Lifetime Unit Economics 101" and "201" by David Havlek, former executive vice president of finance at Salesforce, during the 2014 and 2015 Salesforce.com Investor Days webcast replays.

Let's Sniff Around

The formula to evaluate Lifetime Unit Economic Margin is as follows:

$$\text{Lifetime Unit Economic Margin} = \frac{LTR - CTB - CTS \cdot LTR}{LTR}$$

Where:

LTR	$\equiv$	Lifetime revenue from $ 1 annual recurring revenue (ARR)
LTR	$\equiv$	$\dfrac{\$1 ARR}{\text{churn}}$
CTB	$\equiv$	Cost to "book" $1 recurring revenue
CTS	$\equiv$	Cost to "serve" the lifetime revenue (in %)

Please note that it can be difficult to categorize sales and marketing costs as either cost to book or cost to serve. Not all sales and marketing costs are related to acquiring new customers because a substantial part of it is also related to retaining and engaging existing customers. It should go without saying that all costs, including stock-based compensation, must be included in lifetime unit economics assessments.

I shall judge no investor for sailing only on the most proven seas. I myself like to venture a bit further in pursuit of catching a bigger fish. Others go further and drift into terra incognita. Regardless of your inclination, I believe it is not an entirely idiotic idea to evaluate the profitability of a customer during the lifetime of the customer instead of during the time it takes the earth to rotate around the sun. Nor would it be vacuous to evaluate the evolution of per-unit profitability instead of heuristically blind-staring at aggregated numbers.

Chapter 13

Predictable Demand Drivers

In the name of the framework set forth in this chapter, I wield my conceptual axe to cleave "predictability" in twain. First, the chapter discusses how you can analyze a company with regards to "line of sight" of probable revenues. Second, the chapter discusses how you can anticipate the longer-term predictability of demand.

It is preferable for a business to have a clear line of sight of future revenues. By this, I mean that there's a pillar of future revenues that's highly probable. The larger the proportion of these predictable revenues, the longer the time horizon, and the lower the uncertainty, the better it is for investors. Common sources of such line of sight include a backlog of orders, replacement sales/upgrade cycles, contractual recurring business, aftermarket service, and spare parts. Conversely, businesses that primarily rely on one-time transactions, tender wins, and project sales typically have a shorter line of sight of revenues.

The latter part of the chapter discusses the predictability of longer-term industry demand drivers beyond line of sight. Even though the line of sight for certain revenue components can sometimes span a considerable duration—for example, a company that sells machines accompanied

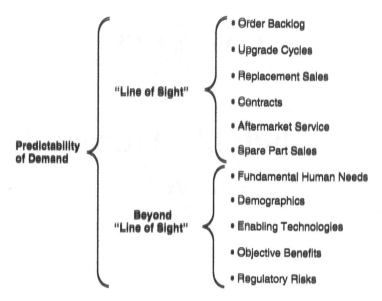

Figure 13.1 Determinants of predictability of demand.
Source: Simon Kold.

by a 10-year service contract—the predictability of longer-term industry demand drivers implies something different. Here, I'm referring to the degree of uncertainty about the distant demand for the offerings of the entire industry.

Consider an undertaker business as an example. The standard deviation in estimating its addressable market for 10 or 20 years into the future is low. The future demand is predictable, making it more appealing than industries where the future demand is less certain. Nevertheless, in many cases the volume of future demand is unpredictable, but the general expectation of substantial growth is almost certain. For instance, the prediction that "demand for computational power per individual will increase over the next 10 to 20 years, resulting in increased demand for faster semiconductors" illustrates this. While the exact volume of future demand for semiconductors might be much less certain compared to undertaker businesses, the direction of the demand driver remains predictable, albeit with a higher uncertainty about the magnitude.

A prime example of a business that I believe excels in both of these aspects is the Dutch company, ASML, which produces photolithography equipment for the semiconductor manufacturing industry. In 2020, when

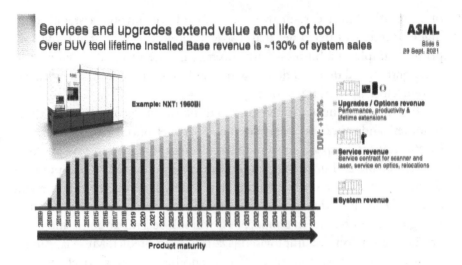

Figure 13.2 Lifetime revenue of DUV tool. From ASML's 2021 investor day. *Source:* With permission of ASML.

I invested in ASML, the company had an order backlog for its EUV systems (extreme ultraviolet lithography) that equated to 3 years of production capacity. Customers had given commitments for a new generation of machines, high-NA (numerical aperture) EUV, even though it was still in development. Every new EUV machine sold came with a 30-year service need, and there was no foreseeable competition from third-party service providers. ASML also had an upgrade business where it sold hardware and software upgrades to its existing customers. Their EUV service business was priced deliberately low to promote EUV customer adoption. ASML boasts a vast installed base of older DUV (deep ultra-violet) lithography systems, most of which have been in use for more than 30 years, during which they require service from ASML, and the demand for DUV orders was surging.

ASML supplies some of the most essential equipment required to produce the world's most advanced semiconductors. In fact, ASML's innovation seems to be a pivotal driver for further advancements in semiconductors. Its R&D not only enables the company to meet new demand but also generates more demand by propelling the entire industry forward: greater computing power enables humans to find applications for that power, which in turn drives demand for more computing power. While it's challenging to forecast the demand for lithography machines in 2030 or 2040, it's almost certain that the demand will involve a significantly higher number of machines than today. Therefore, ASML stands out as a prime example of a business with substantial "line of sight" revenues and a straightforward demand driver, which, although difficult to quantify, has a predictably upward trajectory.

It can be beneficial for investors to think of some companies as "metronomes" and others as "improvised jazz." A metronome is a device used by musicians to keep a consistent tempo. It ticks at regular intervals, which are predictable and unchanging unless manually adjusted. At any point in the future, we can determine with high certainty how the metronome will behave. Over time, the metronome can become worn or broken, leading to slight inconsistencies in tempo, but it will still be a metronome and quite predictable. In contrast, improvised jazz is hard to predict. Musicians in an improvised jazz ensemble play off one another, adapting to changes in rhythm, melody, and harmony in real time, making one musician's behavior a function of the other musicians' behavior. At any future point in time, you will have no clue what will happen in improvised jazz. Some companies resemble metronomes, at least for a while, until the metronome wears down. Other companies resemble improvised jazz. While the ex-post business performance of improvised jazz is equally likely to be great compared to metronomes, we can underwrite the investment case for a metronome with much less uncertainty, and this makes a metronome more valuable than improvised jazz.

It's also important to note that, at some point in the future, no matter how much of a metronome it is today, a day will come when it becomes improvised jazz. You need to take this into consideration when modeling exit multiples and terminal values. There is a mean reversion toward improvised jazz.

13.1   Line of Sight of Revenues

The common contributors to line of sight of probable revenue include the following:

- **Backlog of orders:** A queue of customer orders awaiting fulfillment
- **Upgrade cycles and replacement sales:** Predictable revenue from customers upgrading to new models or replacing old ones

- **Contractual recurring business:** Guaranteed, ongoing revenue from long-term business agreements
- **Aftermarket services and spare parts:** Continued income from post-purchase customer needs

13.1.1 Backlog of orders

The business has received legally binding order intake that it classifies as order backlog in its financial statements. In the ASML case described before, the business had a backlog of 3 years of EUV production capacity. This gave a high degree of certainty about the minimum sales for a foreseeable future. Assessing the contribution from the backlog is simple: it is typically available in the financial reports. However, a backlog is of course never guaranteed: Orders could be canceled. Customers could go out of business, etc.

 Let's Sniff Around

Analyze the line of sight contribution from order backlog:

- Evaluate the absolute size of the order backlog and the historical conversion ratio from backlog to revenue by conducting financial statement analysis.
- Evaluate the payment terms and the risks of cancellations by asking the company or even discussing with major customers for an independent view of cancellation risks.

13.1.2 Upgrade cycles and replacement sales

Upgrade cycles and replacement sales are another contributor to line of sight. For many years, Apple iPhone users have upgraded their iPhones every 3–4 years, on average. While the long-term market share of iPhone is hardly "within sight," it is likely that the immediate future will be a world in which the length of the iPhone upgrade cycle does not deviate dramatically from the historical upgrade cycle length. Therefore I would argue that the iPhone sales, or at least a substantial part of it, over the next 3–4 years has quite a degree of line of sight.

In other cases the replacement cycle is driven solely by the wear on the old product, which makes it perhaps even more predictable than the iPhone example. When evaluating the line of sight contribution from upgrade cycles and replacement sales, one must study the historical length of these cycles and assess how well it represents future cycles. The question is also how far into the future one feels reasonably certain that such a phenomenon will continue.

Let's Sniff Around

Analyze the line of sight contribution from upgrade cycles and replacement sales:

- Differentiate revenues from new sales versus those from upgrades or replacements.
- Obtain data (hard data or indications thereof) about the average upgrade cycle length.
- Obtain data on the size of the installed base of products.
- Obtain data on age cohorts of the installed base of products, as well as the likelihood of "win-rates" for future replacements.

13.1.3   Contractual recurring business

Contractual recurring business refers to guaranteed, ongoing revenue resulting from long-term business agreements. Unlike one-time sales, these agreements ensure a consistent revenue stream over an extended period. In the ASML scenario, when a customer buys the company's machine, it comes bundled with service agreements spanning many years. This isn't just a promise of service, but a legally binding obligation that guarantees revenue for ASML over the specified period. Consider also business critical enterprise software that is sold on a recurring subscription model. It may be contractually guaranteed for a certain period, often 3 years, but in reality the installed base is certain for much longer given the high switching costs and low churn rates, contributing to line of sight.

Let's Sniff Around

Analyze the line of sight contribution from contractual and recurring businesses:

- Analyze the average duration of existing contracts.
- Analyze historical average contract renewal rates and win rates.
- Estimate the actual costs of switching from the customer's perspective (see Chapter 6 switching costs for more methods).
- Analyze churn rates.

To illustrate this in practice, let's consider OTIS Worldwide (Otis), which is the world's largest original equipment manufacturer (OEM) in the elevator industry measured by both revenue and the size of the service portfolio. Otis was spun off from United Technologies in April 2020. Based on my calculations, roughly 60% of Otis' enterprise value is derived from the service business of elevators currently under service. In this context, service means the sum of maintenance, repairs, and modernization. At the time of the IPO in April 2020, the split in the service segment was approximately 60% maintenance, 20% repair, and 20% modernization.

The initial service contract is included with the sale of a new unit, typically with a four-year contract (sometimes down to two or one year). At the expiration of these initial contracts, Otis converts around 60% of units into the service portfolio globally. Some of this churn to other OEMs and independent service providers (ISPs) is recaptured as Otis can also capture some service business from other OEMs. Beyond the initial churn at the expiration of the initial contract, Otis has a remarkable retention rate of its service business. The maintenance retention rate of Otis' service business is around 94% of units. Economically, this corresponds to an average lifetime of service of 17 years per unit.

If customers do not experience too low uptimes and dissatisfying service in cases of breakdowns, the elevator service contract will often be "out of sight, out of mind." Customer interviews indicate that most customers do not spend time looking into their service contracts unless they experience too high downtimes or similar. An argument can be made for the case that retention rates should remain high as OEMs begin to install proprietary predictive maintenance solutions, which allow for both remote monitoring and diagnostics and make it harder for outsiders to service.

13.1.4 Aftermarket services and spare parts

Aftermarket services and spare parts can contribute to line of sight even if they are not contractual service agreements. Many industrial machines need maintenance and spare parts that are not a function of a contract but just a function of the wear and tear. A heavy machinery manufacturer may not have a service contract with the customer, but given the machine's complexity and specialization, the customer will likely turn to the original manufacturer for repairs and spare parts. This reliance creates a predictable line of sight for revenue, often spanning years or even decades after the initial sale.

The predictability of this revenue stream is a function of the degree of product complexity, generic alternatives, wear and tear, and OEM brand trust.

Let's Sniff Around

Analyze the line of sight contribution from aftermarket services and spare parts:

- Study the typical lifespan of products that require these services and parts.
- Estimate the size of the installed product base that requires service and spare parts.
- Investigate the presence and emergence of third-party service and spare parts providers.
- Determine the patterns of customers switching between third-party and OEM services based on the economic cycle phase.

13.2   Predictability of Longer-term Industry Demand

The predictability of long-term industry demand differs from the concept of staying power. Chapter 12, "Staying Power," primarily explores the factors that cause variation in competitive dynamics in an industry and/or make the entire technology obsolete. In contrast, this section focuses solely on the degree of predictability of demand, ignoring competitive dynamics.

An investment thesis is often a product of multiple bets on how the future will be. The higher the number of bets the lower the likelihood that the investment thesis will materialize. Therefore, it can be appealing to find investment cases where some of the key assumptions are "simple" or "predictable" without having to be a domain expert. For instance, you don't need to be a demographic expert or statistician to have a rough idea about the future needed volume of burial services, as mentioned in the beginning of this chapter. Similarly, you don't need to be a semiconductor expert to extend the historical growth in transistors per human and then apply some kind of margin-of-safety haircut to your prognosis. Making the bet on which company in the semiconductor industry will capture all of this opportunity is a much harder bet. However, at least the fundamental assumption about the first bet, the directional growth in demand, is simple and almost undeniable.

Conversely, if the long-term demand (e.g., over a decade or two) is a complex bet, it becomes less attractive. For instance, I don't know if 10 to 15 years from now I'll own the same number of TVs as I do today. Perhaps I'll have some future version of a TV screen in more rooms than today. Maybe I'll have none and will watch a virtual screen on my augmented reality glasses. I don't know; it's hard to predict. Taking the bet on which company will dominate the market is already challenging enough.

13.2.1   Determinants of predictability beyond line of sight

So, it would be beneficial to have a framework for evaluating the degree of predictability of more distant future demand. How can we evaluate such predictability? It's challenging, but we can consider some positive and negative contributors:

- Natural inevitabilities
- Societal inevitabilities
- Technological inevitabilities
- Negative externalities
- Technological obsolescence

Admittedly, the evaluation with regards to these determinants requires a bit more thinking and a little less empirical analysis.

In some industries, such as the undertaker industry, aggregate demand is largely driven by a natural inevitability that has decent predictability. Other industries that benefit from natural inevitabilities are insurance (due to accidents), agriculture (due to food consumption), and health care (due to diseases).

Societal inevitabilities can be positive contributors to predictability. Consider, for example, the Industrial Revolution in the eighteenth and nineteenth centuries and the changes in employment patterns, urban development, and demand for industrial goods and services. To a contemporary investor, industries benefiting from urban development, for example, would have experienced highly probable but hard to quantify long-term growth. Consider the historical expansion of the public education systems and the predictability of the implications this had on the increased demand for educational materials and infrastructure. Consider the societal inevitabilities after women entered the workforce after the mid-twentieth century, increasing demand for childcare services and influencing consumption patterns for dual-income households. The airline industry, often looked down upon by investors because of harsh competition, actually has a very predictable long-term demand driver: higher real income and the desire to travel. Contemporary examples of societal inevitabilities are the global aging population, continued urbanization, growing health focus, and globalization.

Technological inevitabilities can also drive predictability, as we have already discussed. Some technologies become foundational technologies on which other technologies are built, such as the semiconductor industry. This makes their increased demand probable (although hard to exactly quantify). Historical examples of technological changes that at some point became inevitable and predictable include electricity adoption, automobile adoption, personal computer adoption, and internet adoption. For example, in the early 2000s, after the advent of the internet, it was highly probable that internet adoption would increase and hence also probable that e-commerce would increase in penetration. A contemporary example could be the rise of cloud computing and computational artificial intelligence, which makes the increased demand for data centers and semiconductors probable. Another contemporary example would be the advancement of renewable energy technologies, which has led to affordable electric vehicles (EVs), making their increased adoption probable.

Products that have negative externalities must logically have a higher long-term uncertainty than those that do not. Products that are objectively harmful to consumers or have an indirect negative societal value must be replaced at some point, such as tobacco. Sure, tobacco has a lot of line of sight because the addictive consumption patterns are so predictable, but what about tobacco consumption in 2040? In my view, that's quite hard to predict. Other historical and contemporary examples of negative externalities include coal mining, asbestos manufacturing, lead-based products, single-use plastics, pesticides, and fast fashion.

Of course, it is impossible to just separate demand from supply as I just did in this entire section (oops!). Changes on the supply side have implications for the demand side. If a new, wonderful, cost-effective teleportation technology were invented tomorrow, then we would probably need a lot fewer EVs. But the supply side determinants such as cost-effectiveness, industry pace of change, cultural embeddedness, etc., are already covered in the chapter on staying power, so I won't repeat them here. Simply consider your analysis of staying power as a contributing input to your analysis of demand predictability.

Let's Sniff Around

Analyze the degree of long-term predictability of the industry's demand drivers:

- Evaluate the extent to which the company's demand can be attributed to natural, societal, and technological inevitabilities. This includes assessing the impact of highly probable changes that are almost certain due to underlying trends or patterns.

- Evaluate the extent to which the company's demand is related to products or services with harmful individual or societal effects that could lead to decreased demand or regulatory changes.
- Recognize and analyze confounding variables that could complicate the prediction of demand. Be careful not to overly simplify demand drivers.
- Evaluate the potential for changes on the supply side to affect long-term demand. This includes analyzing the business's staying power as described in the relevant chapter, considering factors such as cost-effectiveness, pace of industry change, and cultural embeddedness.

Speaking of predictability, it is time for another corny chapter ending. Or is it? Perhaps, this metronomic author has a bit of improvised jazz up his sleeve?

Chapter 14

Reinvestment Options

What is the best business to own? Warren Buffett offered the following possible solution in the 1992 letter to Berkshire shareholders:

> The best business to own is one that over an extended period can employ large amounts of incremental capital at very high rates of return.

Reinvestment options are the opportunities a business has to deploy its profits—specifically, free cash flows after maintenance CapEx and maintenance OpEx—back into the company in ways that generate additional returns.

Let's examine two similar businesses, Business A and Business B. Business A generates a profit of $1 annually, which is then distributed to its investors. Given that investors expect a return of 10%, the value of Business A is $10, resulting in an implied P/E ratio of 10x. Business B also has an annual profit of $1. However, there's a significant distinction: for the initial decade, Business B can reinvest its profit into projects yielding a 20% return. Consequently, by the 10th year, its expected profit has increased to $4.8, leading to a projected terminal value of $48.

When we account for the present value, the business is worth $18.5 today, indicating a P/E ratio of 18.5x. Why does Business B have nearly twice the P/E ratio and value than Business A? The reason is that Business B has

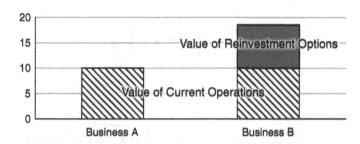

Figure 14.1   Illustration of the value of abnormal reinvestment options during the initial decade for two otherwise identical businesses.
Source: Simon Kold.

more lucrative reinvestment options, and these options genuinely enhance its value. The disparity of all this value is attributed solely to the reinvestment options available over the next decade.

Some sophomorists value a partially utilized cornfield based on the amount of corn currently produced instead of its size and soil quality. But not you! These myopians only see value as a multiple of the moment. They judge an athlete's potential based on his display during an injury. They appraise Robert De Niro's acting abilities based on his performance in *Dirty Grandpa*. But not you! You value reinvestment options!

A profitable company can reinvest its earnings in various ways, but let's first discuss what is actually meant by "earnings" in this context. Here I mean the generated cash that is readily available after all required investments—regardless of whether they are classified as OpEx or CapEx—to maintain the status quo of the business. This means maintaining the competitive stance in an evolving industry, replacing equipment, investing in marketing to acquire customers to compensate for those who churn, and maintaining brand awareness and customer loyalty, among other things. Essentially, it's about preserving the current state of affairs but projecting it into the future (i.e., a form of competitive homeostasis). However, what is not included in "earnings available for reinvestment after maintaining the status quo" are the investments that the company makes to pursue entirely new opportunities. Therefore, this measure of earnings is not synonymous with accounting earnings or accounting cash flows because the company's realized CapEx, marketing expenses, or R&D expenses might

Figure 14.2 TSMC's "Fab 21" is under construction in Phoenix, Arizona, as of November 2023. The fab will cost more than $10 billion. For 30 years, TSMC has reinvested its profits to expand its capacity, achieving returns on capital in excess of 25% annually.

Source: TrickHunter / Wikimedia Commons / CC BY SA 4.0.

already encompass such "growth investments." Similarly, the company's realized CapEx and OpEx may also be too low compared to what is required to maintain the status quo.

As discussed in the chapter on capital allocation, a business can allocate its earnings by reinvesting in existing operations, acquiring other companies, reducing debt, distributing dividends, or repurchasing its own stock. Capital allocation is about how management allocates the capital across these avenues to maximize shareholder value. The concept of reinvestment options is about the attractiveness of the company's own investment opportunities, predominantly in its core operations, and, in some instances, in the acquisition of other enterprises.

The attractiveness of reinvestment options is linked to competitive advantages. Companies with advantages may protect their existing profitable operations, yet they struggle to find lucrative reinvestment opportunities where they can redeploy substantial capital for high returns. However, it's rare for companies with extraordinarily appealing reinvestment opportunities to lack a competitive advantage (e.g., to not have at least one of the types detailed in Part II). Many businesses possess temporary high-return reinvestment options due to beneficial circumstances. However, such opportunities often do not persist for a long time if there is no advantage to protect them from the forces of competition.

The best reinvestment options are those that not only ensure a lucrative expansion regarding the new additional activity but also enhance the competitive strength of the existing operations. As noted by Warren Buffett in the 2012 letter to Berkshire shareholders:

> A profitable company can allocate its earnings in various ways (which are not mutually exclusive). A company's management should first examine reinvestment possibilities offered by its current business—projects to become more efficient, expand territorially, extend and improve product lines or to otherwise widen the economic moat separating the company from its competitors. I ask the managers of our subsidiaries to unendingly focus on **moat-widening opportunities**, and they find many that make economic sense. But sometimes our managers misfire. The usual cause of failure is that they start with the answer they want and then work backwards to find a supporting rationale. Of course, the process is subconscious; that's what makes it so dangerous.

An ideal reinvestment opportunity doesn't merely offer valuable additional activity but also serves to "widen the economic moat." It's not just about expansion; it's about bolstering the overall strength of the existing operations while adding to it.

14.1   Product Line Expansion

I regard Apple, especially during the second half of the 2010s, as a good example of a company with foreseeable attractive reinvestment options. What I mean by "foreseeable" is that the conditions indicating attractive reinvestment options were already evident. Despite this, the company traded near 10 times earnings for extended periods. It was obvious that Apple could develop new product lines utilizing its brand, technological leadership at the intersection of hardware, software, and services, as well as the interplay with its existing product offerings. It already had inter-device seamlessness and ecosystem switching cost multipliers. This fact was over-looked by a market obsessed with an overly simplistic analogous argument about hardware commoditization, inferred from Nokia and BlackBerry, without considering the tiny confounding variables: switching costs and technology leadership in hardware with proprietary operating systems.

By investing in the development of new product categories, which, due to the aforementioned strengths, had a far likelier chance of succeed-ing commercially than if they had been developed on a standalone basis, Apple's ecosystem switching costs became even larger. This increased not only the addressable market by introducing smartwatches, headphones, and streaming services but also further solidified the competitive strength of its existing product lines, such as the iPhone, iPad, and Mac, due to enhanced ecosystem switching costs and ecosystem value. (P.S. Did I forget to mention that Apple also repurchased roughly half of its shares during that same period?)

Boeing, the renowned aerospace company, provides an example of the challenges associated with product line expansion when it ventured into high-speed rail in the 1970s. Boeing faced a different customer base: municipalities and transit authorities instead of airlines and governments. Ground transportation required expertise that was distinct from aerospace technology and manufacturing. The competitive advantages Boeing held in aerospace, from supplier networks to regulatory rapport, did not trans-late directly to the rail market. Furthermore, the introduction of their rail product did not offer any inherent benefits to their established position in the aerospace industry.

Let's Sniff Around

Analyze the degree of attractiveness of options to expand product lines:

- Evaluate the unique product development strengths relevant for the expansion (in Apple's case, its unique and leading technological capabilities at the intersection of hardware, software, and services).

- Evaluate which preexisting competitive advantages for existing products will also apply to new products (in Apple's case, primarily the brand and switching cost multipliers).
- Evaluate whether the company will primarily sell the new product to the existing installed customer base.
- Evaluate whether the expansion strengthens the competitive position of the existing products and whether it could be a distraction.
- Evaluate whether the company has a history of successfully introducing new product categories and historical R&D efficiency.

14.2   Territorial Expansion

Another source of reinvestment option is the opportunity to expand territorially. An example of this kind of reinvestment option was Coca-Cola during its international expansion beyond the United States, which commenced in the mid-twentieth century. Coca-Cola had already established itself as a beloved beverage in the United States. The company embarked on an international expansion after World War II. Its expansion model involved partnering with local bottling companies, which minimized capital expenditures and risks. This expansion involved significant investments in advertising campaigns that leveraged the preexisting brand. It became clear that the brand's appeal was transferable across different cultures. Intentionally or not, Coca-Cola transcended its role as a beverage, symbolizing Western modernity in the post-WWII era.

Walmart's unsuccessful venture into Germany in the late 1990s is an example of an unsuccessful territorial expansion. The German retail landscape was already dominated by cost-effective local players such as Aldi and Lidl, making competition fierce. Walmart grappled with Germany's stringent labor laws and regulations, which clashed with its own practices. Despite its reputation for low prices, Walmart couldn't outpace local competitors in the eyes of German consumers, and Walmart retreated from the German market in 2006.

Territorial expansion isn't limited to cross-border expansion. For instance, a retail business launching new outlets within its home country also exemplifies territorial growth. Expanding into regions that are culturally and economically similar to existing markets often carries lower risks than venturing into distinctly different markets.

 Let's Sniff Around

Analyze the degree of attractiveness of options to expand territorially:

- Analyze competitive strength of existing competitors in the entry market.
- Evaluate the entrant's competitive advantage in the entry market (e.g., Coca-Cola's global scale in marketing).
- Evaluate whether the territorial expansion enforces the company's competitive strength in its existing market. Or might it divert resources and focus, potentially weakening its position in the home market? (For instance, Coca-Cola's international growth helped it achieve a global marketing cost scale advantage, which in turn benefited its domestic market.)
- Consider the degree of cultural similarity to the home market. Markets that closely resemble the home market in cultural and economic aspects typically present fewer risks.
- Evaluate the track record of executing territorial expansions with high returns on capital.

14.3   Increased Capacity

When a firm faces heightened demand or anticipates so in the future, reinvesting its earnings to expand its current operations or establish new facilities can, under the right conditions, yield considerable incremental return on capital.

During the mid-2010s, the electric vehicle (EV) market was on an upward trajectory, but nowhere near an industry peak, making it an opportune time for Tesla to invest in expanding its production capabilities—the so-called Gigafactories. Tesla anticipated a long-term surge in demand for EVs. Despite the risks associated with building a large-scale manufacturing facility, Tesla's track record of producing high-quality EVs gave it confidence in the company's ability to manage the production expansion. Other car manufacturers were entering the EV space, but few had plans as ambitious as Tesla's Gigafactories. By building the Gigafactories, Tesla not only increased its production capacity but also reduced its battery costs, giving it an advantage over competitors.

In contrast, consider the airline industry's capacity expansion in the early 2000s. Many airlines placed large orders for new aircraft in the early 2000s, anticipating that the boom in air travel would continue. Unfortunately, they were expanding at what turned out to be close to the peak of the cycle. The dot-com bubble burst, followed by the events of 9/11 in 2001, challenged air travel. The unforeseen downturns left airlines with excess capacity. This created an oversaturated market, leading to fierce competition, price wars, and eradicated profits.

Let's Sniff Around

Analyze the degree of attractiveness of options to expand capacity:

- Analyze the industry-specific and macroeconomic cyclical risk: Expanding at the peak of the cycle is usually a negative indicator (see more details on Cyclical Risks assessment in Chapter 16).
- Consider the uncertainty about the sustainability of heightened demand. Refer to methods discussed in Chapter 13 on demand predictability.
- Estimate the development risk of the expansion itself: Does the company have a good track record with this kind of capacity expansion resulting in satisfactory incremental ROIC? Does the expansion carry dependency risk?
- Evaluate the competitive situation that the expanded capacity will face: Are competitors also planning to bring a lot of comparable capacity to the market?
- Evaluate whether the expansion itself enhances the competitive strength of the existing business, especially if the expansion leads to an increased overall scale advantage.

14.4   Customer Acquisitions and Brand Building Investments

Companies that already possess network effect advantages can have high-yielding reinvestment options in acquiring new customers through sales and marketing expansion investments, as these can further strengthen the preexisting network effect. Similarly, companies that already possess brand advantages can have high-yielding options in marketing investments that not only stimulate demand and acquire new customers but also further strengthen the long-term brand value.

A good example is Coca-Cola, which had both attractive opportunities for territorial expansion and marketing efficiency. Coca-Cola's advertising strategies were efficient, yielding high returns on capital. Soft drinks, being products of recurring purchase, led to a reasonable lifetime value of customers that could justify Coca-Cola's costs in acquiring and activating them.

As a counter-example, consider the specialty wedding dress designer business. The marketing efficiency is lower since most brides are only looking once in their lives. Brides are only potential customers for a short period in their lives, making them challenging to target. The market for wedding dresses, especially bespoke ones, is vast. Many designers offer unique dresses, and brand loyalty is nonexistent, as customers rarely need the product more than once. Each dress might be tailored to the individual bride, making rapid scaling challenging. A designer who receives a surge in orders may need to hire more staff and invest in more space.

Let's Sniff Around

Analyze the degree of attractiveness of options to expand customer acquisitions and brand building:

- Calculate the historical marketing efficiency and return on capital (perhaps consider excluding a portion of expansive marketing OpEx investments from the numerator of ROIC when assessing this).
- Evaluate customer acquisition costs relative to customer lifetime value. This is in turn a function of churn rates, cost to acquire a

customer, and the lifetime cost of serving that customer. (See section on lifetime value in the chapter about proven business models).

- Estimate the degree of recurring sales.
- Analyze the preexisting network effect or brand advantages. Use methods discussed in the chapters on network effects and brand.
- Consider operational scalability constraints: infrastructure, people, and supply chain capabilities to handle increased customers without the need to tie up additional capital for further investments in these activities. (See Chapter 15 for more details on how to evaluate.)
- Consider market saturation, inherent market growth, and opportunities for additional market penetration. It's worth noting that marketing efficiency might decline after a certain point.

14.5   Buying Other Companies

Acquiring other companies is a common source of value destruction for the shareholders of the purchasing company. Typically, it's preferable for earnings to be reinvested in organic sources rather than through acquisitions. The following types of acquisitions (and combinations thereof) are most likely to destroy value:

- Large acquisitions
- Scale for the sake of scale
- Diversification into new areas with a different customer base
- Lack of track record of successful integration
- Loosely defined synergies

If a company doesn't already have a track record of successful acquisitions, then it is unlikely that it possesses probable extraordinary reinvestment options. However, under certain conditions, companies can have attractive options to reinvest their earnings in acquisitions.

14.5.1   Consolidations of fragmented industries

Consolidations of fragmented industries, if in the form of small acquisitions that provide access to a local customer base and allow the target company to leverage the existing value chain of the purchasing company, can represent an attractive reinvestment option. The attractiveness of such options depends on the extent to which the purchasing company can serve those customers more cost efficiently than the standalone target company could.

Waste Management Inc.'s consolidation efforts in the fragmented US waste services industry throughout the 1980s and 1990s is an example of this. Waste Management focused on absorbing numerous small, local waste disposal companies. By integrating these businesses into their operations, Waste Management enabled these acquired entities to access its broader, more efficient value chain. This integration resulted in improved routing efficiencies, optimized recycling processes, and the ability to leverage larger equipment purchasing deals.

14.5.2 Cross-selling with switching cost multipliers

While many bad acquisitions are justified by the argument of cross-selling, certain options for acquiring other companies with the aim of cross-selling products can be attractive reinvestment options. This is sometimes the case when the purchasing company, with a large customer base and sales force, acquires a company that offers a complementary product but lacks scale in sales and marketing. By acquiring and cross-selling the complementary product to its existing customer base, the purchasing company can enhance the value of the target company beyond its standalone value. The attractiveness of this type of investment often depends on how well the acquired product complements the existing product, the extent to which it can be sold to the installed base, and whether it leads to switching cost multipliers that make the existing customer base stickier.

Salesforce, a global leader in CRM (customer relationship management) software solutions, boasts a broad customer base and a big enterprise sales organization. Recognizing the potential to cross-sell complementary services to its existing customers, Salesforce has acquired firms such as ExactTarget, MuleSoft, and Tableau. These software tools experienced accelerated growth after their acquisition by Salesforce, driven by exposure to a larger customer base through a more extensive sales force as well as their compatibility with Salesforce's existing offerings. Salesforce discovered that customers who purchased additional products were less likely

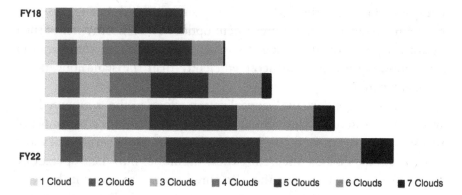

Figure 14.3   Salesforce.com's annual recurring revenue (ARR) is categorized by the number of products ("clouds") to which customers subscribe. Acquired offerings have been cross-sold to the existing installed base of customers.

Source: Salesforce. Investor Presentation, Investor Day 2021. Reproduced with permission of Salesforce.

to churn. The acquisitions enhanced not only the value of the acquired firms but also the value of the existing business. Clearly, the appeal of any acquisition also depends on the purchase price. There are many examples of acquiring companies that fool themselves into paying a premium for demand synergies, which undermines the attractiveness.

14.5.3   *Acquihires*

The term *acquihire* is a portmanteau of "acquisition" and "hire." Acquiring smaller companies that have unique talent, patents, and know-how that align with an existing product development roadmap can be more valuable for a larger acquiring company that stands a higher chance of successfully launching and scaling new products than the target company could independently.

In 2008, Apple acquired PA Semi, a fabless[1] semiconductor company. Apple had largely depended on third-party chip suppliers. This acquisition provided Apple with a team of skilled semiconductor engineers and valuable intellectual property and laid the groundwork for the development of Apple's A-series chips, which have since powered its mobile devices. Having in-house chip-design capabilities allowed

Apple to differentiate itself from competitors, reduce dependency on external suppliers, and exercise greater control over product release cycles and supply chain management. The foresight of this acquisition became even more evident in 2020 when Apple announced its transition from Intel processors to its own Apple Silicon for Mac computers. While acquihires can be great investments, they typically are not an avenue for the reinvestment of significant amounts of capital. Also, evaluating the attractiveness of such acquisitions can be challenging.

 Let's Sniff Around

Analyze the degree of attractiveness of options to buy other companies:

- Consider whether the acquisition is large, an attempt to diversify into a new area with a different customer base, based on loosely defined synergies, made at the peak of the cycle, or if the purchasing company does not demonstrate a stellar track record of successful integration and price discipline in previous acquisitions.
- Estimate the extent to which the purchasing company can serve those customers more cost-efficiently than the standalone target company could in case of industry consolidations by cross-checking projected cost savings with independent experts. Consider the management's history of price discipline and integration track record with this type of acquisition.
- Evaluate the extent to which the acquired product complements the existing product, the extent to which it can be sold to the installed base, and whether it leads to switching cost multipliers that make the existing customer base stickier. Consider the management's history of price discipline and integration track record with this type of acquisition.
- Consider whether the options to continue to successfully consolidate or cross-sell are exhausted (i.e., whether historical success is a valid proxy for the future), for instance, if targets have become larger or more complex.

14.6   Lack of Reinvestment Options

Some great companies just lack good reinvestment options. In such instances, your analysis of management's capital allocation mentality and ability, which I discussed in Chapter 3, becomes even more important. For such firms, the most rational thing to do is often to return capital to shareholders in the form of dividends, buybacks, or debt reduction—preferably with an active view on which of these creates the most long-term per-share value.

Moody's ratings began in 1909 when John Moody first published *Moody's Manual of Industrial and Miscellaneous Securities*. In the 1920s, Moody's expanded its ratings to cover government bonds. The Glass-Steagall Act of 1933, which established a legal distinction between commercial banking and securities activities, increased the demand for independent credit analysis, benefiting firms like Moody's. By the late twentieth century, Moody's, along with Standard & Poor's and Fitch, had become integrated into the global financial system. Moody's ratings are widely accepted and trusted by investors, financial institutions, and regulators around the world. A high credit rating lowers the cost of borrowing for issuers. Therefore, the product has high utility, which translates into a high willingness to pay for it. The company benefits from two-sided network effects.

These are some of the reasons why Moody's has become such a profitable business operating in an environment of rational oligopolistic competition. But Moody's is perhaps not the company with the most appealing reinvestment runway. It lacks avenues for redeploying large amounts of capital at high rates of return. Therefore, the company is rationally returning most of its excess cash flows back to shareholders. Moody's is like a sterile champion racehorse.

Attractive reinvestment options are a prerequisite for scaling (except when scaling unprofitably). Some firms have been bestowed with a super-efficient metabolism, enabling them to consume little capital-resources relative to the enormously profitable tissue they grow. Such companies are the topic of the next chapter: "Scalability and Low Incremental Costs."

Chapter 15

Scalability and Low Incremental Costs

How many zero–marginal cost companies does it take to change a lightbulb? Many, as most are too enervated by the gravitational pull of their heavy fixed costs to even climb the ladder.

Operational leverage is the extent to which a company has a higher proportion of fixed costs relative to variable costs, which can lead to magnified profits when sales increase but also magnified losses when sales decline.

The best example I can think of to describe how appealing operational leverage can be for investors is Visa. It operates a payment processing network, which involves significant fixed costs such as infrastructure, technology development, security measures, and regulatory compliance. Once established, the network had a minimal incremental cost of processing each additional transaction. Because the majority of Visa's costs are fixed, as transaction volumes increase (whether that's more transactions or higher dollar value per transaction), the company doesn't incur proportionally higher costs. This means that as Visa's transaction volume grows, its profit margins expand since the additional revenues far outweigh the additional costs. Over the years, Visa's margins have portrayed the power of operational leverage. The company continued to grow its transaction volumes worldwide, especially with the adoption of digital payments and e-commerce, resulting in continuously rising margins.

While companies with high operational leverage can be vulnerable to economic downturns due to their fixed costs, Visa's diversified global presence and essential nature of its services makes it resilient. Even in economic downturns, people need to transact. Transaction volumes increase with inflation and the growth of the real economy. Therefore, solely as a function of inflation, Visa might even see an expansion of margins for its core network.

In 2008, the year of Visa's IPO, it reported a total revenue of $6.3 billion, operating expenses of $3.6 billion,[1] and an operating profit of $2.7 billion. Fifteen years later, in 2023, Visa's revenues had reached $32.7 billion, and its operating expenses had grown to $10.7 billion. In 2008, Visa's operating profit margin stood at 43%. Over the 15-year period, the incremental revenue gain of $26.4 billion resulted in an incremental operating profit increase of a whopping $19.2 billion. Seventy-three percent of every dollar added to revenues during these 15 years flowed through to the operating profit. This is an incredible incremental profit, especially considering that revenues quintupled during the period.

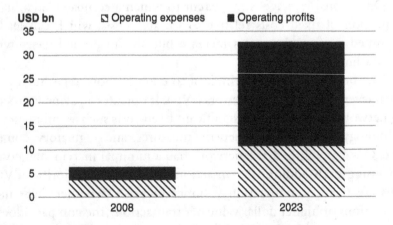

Figure 15.1   Visa's P&L in 2008 compared to Visa's P&L in 2023.
Source: Adapted from VISA's 10-K filings.

15.1   Determinants of Marginal Cost

Incremental cost is the amount a company's total costs change when there's a unit change in the output level. It represents the cost incurred for producing one additional unit of a product or service. Digital assets and services, such as software, often have low incremental costs. Once the initial investment in creating a digital product has been made, the cost of reproducing or distributing that product to additional customers is insignificant. Unlike physical goods, digital goods don't require raw materials, manufacturing, shipping, or storage for reproduction. A software can be downloaded by a million users, and the cost remains virtually the same as if it were downloaded by just one. Online platforms and app stores have simplified and reduced the cost of distributing software and digital products to a global audience. With a single online infrastructure, companies can reach customers worldwide without incurring notable additional costs.

Google's search engine has required gigantic investments in algorithms development, machine learning, and data center infrastructure. However, the incremental cost to Google for each search is minuscule. Much of the costs are electricity for running the servers and bandwidth. Although the incremental cost is low, as Google monetizes its search engine through advertisements, the incremental revenue from an additional search is disproportionately higher than its incremental cost.

Creating a stock exchange requires colossal initial capital consumption for developing or licensing the trading engine, procuring the market infrastructure, ensuring security measures, and complying with regulatory requirements. But once an exchange is operational, adding more market participants incurs a low incremental cost. The incremental revenue of facilitating an additional trade is disproportionately higher than the incremental cost.

Low incremental costs are certainly not limited to companies that sell digital products or services that are based on computational processing, like Visa, Google, and stock exchanges. Another common source of low incremental costs are companies whose business model relies on licensing its technology or other forms of immaterial rights. Consider the example of ARM and Dolby Labs. ARM designs microprocessor architectures. The company does not manufacture chips itself but instead licenses its intellectual property to chip firms. These firms use ARM's architecture as a foundation to develop their own microprocessors and integrated circuits. Once ARM has developed a new processor architecture, the incremental cost to ARM for each additional chip produced by its licensees is minimal. Each chip generates fees to ARM that are disproportionately higher than the negligible incremental costs.

Dolby Laboratories specializes in audiovisual technologies. The company has developed proprietary audio noise reduction and audio encoding/decoding technologies, as well as increasingly advanced technologies such as the proprietary sound format Dolby Atmos, that allows audio to be more spatially dynamic, and HDR (high dynamic range) format Dolby Vision, that allows scene-by-scene or even frame-by-frame picture adjustment. Instead of manufacturing and selling physical products, Dolby licenses its technologies to electronics manufacturers. When a company wants to use Dolby's technology in its devices, it pays for the rights. Once Dolby has developed an audiovisual technology, the cost to license it to additional manufacturers is lower than the revenue it generates, and even more so is the revenue from increased units sold by existing manufacturers.

High incremental margins can be appealing, but firms that tend to have high incremental margins when volumes increase also face detrimental economics when their business shrinks. Since firms tend to grow rather than decline, this aspect is occasionally forgotten. In Chapter 7, I mentioned that network effect businesses can experience a reversal of network effects. If such businesses have a fixed cost structure, then they not only experience a reversal of network effects but also accelerated negative operational leverage. *Ouch!* More devastating than a groin-seeking Jean-Claude Van Damme helicopter kick.

 ## Let's Sniff Around

Analyze the marginal cost structure:

- Evaluate the extent of activities each contributing to low marginal cost, such as licensing and IP, software, automated processes, computations, data leveraging, and self-service models.

- Evaluate the extent of activities each contributing to a more traditional cost structure, such as raw materials and components, manual labor, inventory holding, distribution and logistics, quality control and inspection, physical retail space, wastage and rework, regulatory compliance, after-sales service and warranty, and fuel and energy consumption.
- Analyze the current cost structure and understand how the main cost contributors vary with changes in output. Consider asking the company for information if needed.

Remember to take into consideration the negative effects of operational leverage when you simulate downside scenarios!

15.2 High Break-even Point

Due to a higher proportion of fixed costs, firms with high operational leverage usually have a higher break-even point. Beyond this point, profits can increase steeply. However, this also means that they must absorb significant losses while working to reach the volume required to achieve that break-even point.

When Amazon launched AWS, it required immense upfront investments in infrastructure, data centers, and technology. This setup led to high fixed costs and a high break-even point. But as more businesses adopted cloud services, AWS began to benefit from economies of scale. The incremental cost of provisioning additional cloud computing to a new customer is lower than the revenue that customer brings in.

It is an error to overlook incremental margins and incremental returns on capital when evaluating firms with high fixed costs, especially those that have not yet reached a mature state. Some investors focus solely on companies with existing high returns on capital and use this as the holy-grail proxy for company quality. However, all of their favored companies once experienced a time when their capital returns were emerging, during which they would likely have been much more lucrative investments than they are today. Consider an early investment in Visa before its margin expansion compared to a later investment made after the expansion.

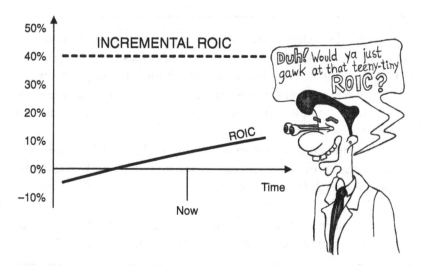

Figure 15.2   Analyst neglecting to consider incremental ROIC.

Source: Original artwork by Henriette Wiberg Danielsen based on idea by Simon Kold.
© 2024 Simon Kold.

Now, Visa has exceptionally high margins, but investing in Visa before the margin expansion, when it had a lower margin but already had a high incremental margin, would have been much more lucrative. Some dogmatic investors, as illustrated in my homemade Figure 15.2, are quick to prematurely attach the "unproven" label to fixed-cost firms hovering around the break-even point, without considering their incremental economics.

15.3   Scalability of Infrastructure

Most firms have some degree of scalability in their operations, which allows them to handle increased volumes up to a certain point, beyond which new investments are necessary to accommodate further volume increases. Visa is a rare specimen of exceptional scalability. By comparison, think of a brick-and-mortar store. While it can serve more customers in the same store, there eventually comes a day when it needs to open a new store, hire more staff, and increase inventory to meet the growing demand.

Even firms with a service that relies on computations and technological systems, like Visa's payment network, will encounter constraints to how much volume they can handle and will also have to invest to enhance their capacity. Consider Netflix, which had notable costs to acquire content and develop streaming infrastructure. These led to a high cost level. But once it amassed a large enough subscriber base to cover those costs, every additional subscriber contributed more to its profit margin. This is because the incremental cost of servicing an extra subscriber was minimal compared to the monthly subscription fee they paid. Nonetheless, Netflix users want new content all the time. Since most people only consume video content once (unlike music content), the scalability of the content catalog has limitations, leading to new investment needs.

Fixed costs might not increase linearly as firms attempt to increase capacity. Instead they often increase in "steps" as the company expands. This phenomenon is often referred to as a "step function." Another factor to consider is "technical debt." Some companies might operate on outdated systems or ones that are a patchwork of several systems. While these might be scalable in the short run, they could pose problems later. Such situations can lead to substantial future investment needs. Historically, banks have been early adopters of information technology to manage their vast operations and facilitate electronic transactions. However, over decades, this has resulted in a Frankenstein-like patchwork of systems, as banks underwent mergers, implemented different technologies, and added on layers of software for new banking products and services. Some banks have accumulated huge technical debt over the years and operate an IT infrastructure that is a slow-cooked goulash of old mainframe systems, middleware, and newer technologies.

Let's Sniff Around

Analyze constraints to scalability:

- Evaluate the utilization rates of crucial resources, like servers, manufacturing equipment, and personnel.
- Interview company and former technical personnel about scalability constraints.
- Quantify investment needs and evaluate how they impact future capital returns.

15.4 Operational Leverage Magnifies Cyclical Risks and Exit Costs

Companies with operational leverage are often more susceptible to economic cycles. During downturns, they can suffer direly, as their fixed costs remain unchanged despite declining sales. Another risk for such companies is the exit cost associated with shutting down or downsizing operations. This cost can be considerable compared to companies with a more variable cost structure, which can reduce staff or inventory levels to mitigate losses.

Semiconductor manufacturers are characterized by high operational leverage due to massive upfront investments required for manufacturing facilities, known as fabs. These fabs cost billions to construct and equip. Their vast fixed costs are spread across a larger number of units, drastically reducing the cost per unit. However, during economic downturns, the situation can reverse drastically. If demand for semiconductors drops, these manufacturers still face their high fixed costs, but without the compensating revenue from sales. For instance, during certain periods of oversupply or reduced demand in the electronics end-markets, semiconductor manufacturers have faced challenges in maintaining profitability due to their operational leverage. Yet, in boom times these same companies can enjoy outsized profits.

Similarly, shipping firms face this amplified cyclicality. Their substantial investments in ships and ongoing fixed maintenance costs become beneficial in times of high demand, allowing costs to be spread over a larger number of shipments. Yet, during downturns, the decrease in global trade volumes leads to excess capacity and lower shipping rates, while the fixed costs of their fleets remain monolithically constant.

Another risk related to operational leverage is the fact that it is much harder to predict earnings growth because earnings are so sensitive to changes in revenue. A slight overestimation of revenue growth is a substantial overestimation of earnings growth. You better keep this in the forefront of your thoughts when forecasting the financials of firms with operational leverage. Be cautious when forecasting financials of such firms, or you shall suffer from Dante's contrapasso.*

---

* *Contrapasso* is a principle depicted in Dante Alighieri's "Inferno," part of his epic poem, The Divine Comedy. Contrapasso refers to the punishment of souls in hell by a process either resembling or contrasting with the sin itself, only greater. As such, it is a punishment with inherent (operational) leverage!

15.5   Capital-light Versus
Capital-intensive Businesses

Capital-light companies are those that require minimal capital expenditure to commence, maintain, or expand their operations. These firms typically have fewer physical assets, lower fixed costs, and can foster attractive returns on invested capital without significant reinvestment. Capital-light companies are often appreciated by investors for several reasons: because capital-light companies don't require extensive capital expenditure to grow or maintain their operations, they often generate a higher return on invested capital (ROIC). A capital-light model allows firms to scale cheaper and faster. Since they aren't tied to physical assets, these firms can grow without the need for infrastructural overhauls.

For example, a digital platform might just need server upgrades to handle more users, whereas a manufacturing firm would require new factories or machinery to increase production. The lower fixed-cost level of capital-light firms can make them more resilient in economic downturns. With lower capital expenditures, these firms often have higher free cash flows. This can be attractive to investors as more cash can be returned to shareholders or reinvested in high-return opportunities.

Being a capital-intensive business can also have benefits: the immense initial investment required in capital-intensive industries often acts as an intimidating deterrent to potential competitors. This means established players can enjoy reduced competition, which can lead to durable market positions. Capital-intensive industries often benefit from economies of scale, which can lead to cost advantages over competitors. In many capital-intensive industries, products or services have longer life cycles. This can provide more time to recoup their initial investment and contribute to their staying power.

The building materials industry consists of firms with a wide range of capital intensity. The so-called "light-side" building materials, such as fixtures and paints, do not require substantial machinery or large factories. These firms can quickly adapt to market changes due to lower fixed costs and fewer physical assets. In contrast, "heavy-side" building materials, like cement and aggregates, necessitate considerable capital investment in heavy machinery and large-scale industrial facilities. "Heavy-side" building material firms sometimes become local monopolies. This is due to economies of scale and the high transportation costs of their heavy products, which cause the relevant market to be local.

Both capital-light and capital-intensive businesses have their own advantages and challenges. While many great businesses fall under the first category, there are undoubtedly great companies in the latter as well. Denying the existence of outstanding capital-intensive businesses is less intelligent than boycotting sunscreen because it's unnecessary during three out of four seasons.

* * *

An old investor had a firm, E-I-E-I-O. And in this firm he had fixed costs, E-I-E-I-O. With a cheap scale here and high breakeven there (la la la). In this firm, the cycle turned, E-I-E-I-O. With a boom boom here and a bust bust there. Here a boom, there a bust, everywhere a must-adjust.
   . . . ehm . . ., which leads us to the next chapter: "Cyclicality."

Chapter 16

Cyclical Risks

W hat did God say to the cyclical company? . . . For though the righteous fall seven times, they rise again, but the wicked stumble when calamity strikes.[1]

Cyclicality is the tendency to experience patterns of ups and downs over time, often in line with the broader economy or some specific industry dynamics. These fluctuations can be caused by changes in monetary policy, raw material prices, consumer confidence, credit availability, technological innovation, natural disasters, and more. A cycle refers to a series of expansions and contractions, with the most well-known example being the *business cycle*. This is a macroeconomic term that describes periods of economic growth (expansions) followed by periods of economic decline (recessions).

During boom periods, businesses experiencing growth may become overly optimistic. They expect the good times to last and look to enlarge their operations. It's easier to access funding during good times. As demand grows in an expanding economy, companies may feel the need to scale up their operations to maintain or increase their market share. Companies might ramp up investments in response to immediate capacity constraints, thinking that the increased demand they're experiencing is the new normal.

High current profitability often leads to overconfidence among corporate managers, who confuse favorable industry conditions with their own skill. While decisions to expand capacity might be based on current trends, the future is uncertain. Expansionary periods don't last forever. Expansion projects, especially large ones, take time to come to fruition. By the time a new facility is up and running, the market conditions have changed. A considerable portion of the costs associated with production facilities, machinery, and infrastructure is fixed. This means they do not vary with the level of production. Once such investment is made, it's not easy to scale back. Companies might miscalculate future demand, and competitors could simultaneously enlarge their capacities, amplifying future supply. When utilization is low due to over-capacity, these fixed costs are spread across a smaller quantity of goods, making the per-unit cost higher. An industry-wide over-capacity can lead to tough competition. Companies might lower prices to grab more market share and use up their extra capacity. This can erode industry-wide profitability. As profit margins diminish, there are often reductions in capital expenditures and increased industry consolidation.[2]

The Chicago Mercantile Exchange (CME) is an example of a firm with exemplary noncyclical attributes. Its resilience to economic cycles stems from the nature of the instruments traded on its platform. These instruments, typically futures and options, are used by participants in both industry and financial markets to hedge against the risk of price fluctuations in underlying assets such as agricultural commodities, energy

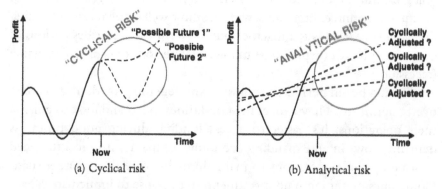

(a) Cyclical risk   (b) Analytical risk

Figure 16.1   Cyclicality causes two problems: the cyclical risk itself and the analytical risk resulting from it.
Source: Simon Kold.

products, metals, interest rates, and currencies. The CME itself does not assume the risk associated with these underlying commodities or financial products. Demand for hedging persists regardless of the economic cycle. Some instruments traded on the CME see increased volatility (i.e., trading volume) during economic downturns, which contributes to the fees collected by the CME.

16.1 Cyclical Company: Good or Bad?

Before we proceed, let's discuss whether cyclicality is more of a benefit or a drawback for long-term investors. Drawbacks include the following:

- Higher analytical risk of confusing cyclical growth with structural growth.
- Greater analytical risk of misjudging earnings levels and valuation multiples: A low multiple of realized earnings could be a high multiple of cyclically adjusted earnings.
- Potential for unstable and unpredictable earnings.

However, there are also positives, particularly to industry leaders with conservative and unconventional management:

- Industry leaders could be weathering cyclical downturns, leading to increased industry consolidation that benefits these leaders in the long run.
- Companies managed by conservative and unconventional managers can utilize downturns and the financial stress it imposes on their competitors to acquire businesses, or take market share when their competitors are paralyzed.

In general, most investors would believe that a noncyclical business is less risky than a cyclical one, making it more valuable. However, an argument can be made that a cyclical company can be compelling to long-term investors under the right conditions. This is especially true if you can effectively manage the analytical risks mentioned earlier and if the company's management possesses characteristics that enable it to capitalize on downturns.

Let's consider two examples to illustrate the points, both from the 2008 crisis and both from cyclical industries: banks and home builders.

JPMorgan Chase, under the leadership of Jamie Dimon, was one of the leading banks in the United States coming into the downturn. It had a sizable and diverse financial portfolio, but more importantly, it had been more conservative in its exposure to subprime mortgages and risky financial instruments compared to many of its peers. While the bank was certainly not immune to the effects of the crisis, it was in a comparatively stronger position due to its balance sheet and more conservative risk management practices leading up to the crisis. As the crisis deepened, many financial institutions found themselves facing severe challenges. Two notable institutions were Bear Stearns and Washington Mutual. In March 2008, JPMorgan Chase acquired investment bank Bear Stearns at a fraction of its pre-crisis value. Later in September 2008, JPMorgan Chase acquired the assets of Washington Mutual, which had been seized by the Federal Deposit Insurance Corporation in the largest bank failure in US history. This acquisition allowed JPMorgan to expand its retail banking footprint. JPMorgan emerged stronger after the crisis.

Also leading up to 2008, the United States was experiencing a significant housing boom, benefiting home builders. The rapid growth in housing sales and prices led many investors to believe that the United States was in a new era of perpetual housing appreciation. However, a lot of this growth was just fueled by loose lending standards and speculative buying. Many home-builder companies traded at seemingly attractive multiples, based on earnings that were at cyclical peaks. The industry was amassing profits, and on the semitransparent surface, valuations looked reasonable. However, these earnings were inflated. When the housing bubble burst, it became clear that the growth had been more cyclical than many had believed. As home sales plummeted and the values of existing homes dropped, many home builders faced financial distress. Some had to raise capital at depressed prices, diluting existing shareholders. While many of the major home builders survived, it took years for them to recover, and investors who had bought in during the peak of the boom suffered significant losses.

16.2 Degree of Cyclicality

Some uncritical, dogmatic investors unfortunately seem to think that the level of cyclicality of any given industry is static, almost like a natural law.

But not you! These flat-earther-like thinkers chant the words, "For it is written that shipping is cyclical." But not you! You determine the level of cyclicality based on the determinants and your own independent thought!

 Let's Sniff Around

Evaluate the degree of cyclicality based on determinants of cyclicality:

- Evaluate the **customer dependency** of its products: The ease with which customers can delay purchasing without facing immediate repercussions is a contributing factor to cyclicality. A classic example would be the decision by a firm to defer the acquisition of new machinery or an individual's choice to hold off on buying a new vehicle. On the contrary, noncyclical offerings are indispensable. For businesses, these could be key components or raw materials, and for consumers, necessities like medications and food.
- Evaluate **customers' purchase patterns:** The irregularity or infrequency of purchase patterns is another contributing factor to cyclicality. Noncyclical offerings often see consistent purchase patterns, such as monthly services or weekly groceries.
- Evaluate the **capital intensity:** The degree of high upfront capital investments contributes to cyclicality. Industries like construction or manufacturing, which need expensive machinery and facilities, are exposed. On the other hand, industries like software development or consultancy services show financial flexibility due to their lower capital intensity and reliance on human capital.
- Evaluate the **operational flexibility:** Cyclical entities often deal with high infrastructural or operational costs, making it challenging to quickly adapt to market shifts. Noncyclical entities benefit from flexible operational structures that enable rapid adjustments to varying market conditions. Metrics like the fixed-to-variable cost ratio can serve as indicators.
- Estimate the **balance sheet strength:** Companies with higher debt levels and shorter maturities can find themselves in tight

spots during downturns, leading to suboptimal decisions. Companies either devoid of debt or conservatively leveraged with long-dated maturities stand stronger against economic downturns. Evaluate cash reserves, liquid asset values, debt-to–cash flow ratios, loan-to-value ratios, and debt maturity profiles.

- Analyze **price sensitivity:** Price-sensitive products and services tend to be more exposed to cyclicality. Noncyclical offerings see minimal impact on demand from price changes due to their fundamental need or the lack of substitutes. Price elasticity can be evaluated through market studies, academic research, or direct customer interviews.

- Consider **inventory and supply chain:** Companies that hold large inventories or operate extended supply chains can be at a disadvantage during downturns. Assess this by reviewing absolute inventory values, inventory turnover ratios, and supply chain lead times.

16.2.1   Historical cyclicality

In addition to these determinants, the assessment of cyclicality can involve examining how the company and industry have reacted to previous cycles. This can be assessed by studying historical financial statements. However, one can't always determine the degree of cyclicality based solely on history. Consider the semiconductor industry. It has been historically very cyclical and remains so. In the 1990s, the end-market for semiconductors, such as desktop computers, had a much lower customer dependency compared to many consumer electronics products today. Now, the end-market applications are also much more diversified, encompassing a range of industrial and consumer uses for semiconductors. Many of these are vital for business operations or have become an integral part of people's daily lives. The point is that in this instance, there are valid logical arguments why the historical degree of cyclicality isn't necessarily an accurate indicator of the current degree of cyclicality.

Let's Sniff Around

To evaluate the degree of cyclicality based on historical cyclicality, you can:

- Analyze data on historical capacity utilization, price reaction, cost-cutting ability, profitability impact, and revenue impact during historical downturns, including both general economic downturns and industry-specific downturns.
- Consider the generalizability of the historical data to current times, taking into consideration changes in the determinants listed previously.

16.2.2 Historical managerial behavior

As well noted in the Bible, there is "a time to cast away stones, and a time to gather stones together."[3] Most corporate managers don't know when to cast or when to gather stones. They simply do what everyone else is doing. Few executives employ the rare act of independent thought; they gather the stones that everyone else is casting away. How can you, as an investor, identify such rare individuals?

Management's historical actions and communication during different phases of a business or industry cycle can offer insights into their potential behavior in future cycles. During boom times, did they drive expansion, accumulate debt, or diversify operations and holdings? During downturns, did they reduce workforce, liquidate assets, or shore up resources? Or did they pursue a countercyclical plan, practicing conservatism during good times and pursuing expansions and acquisitions when competitors were pulling back? A large acquisition at the peak of the cycle can destroy more shareholder value than an accidental shredding of the company's shareholder register.

A near perfect historical case study of how a company with exceptional management can benefit from operating in a cyclical industry is that of Ryanair and its contrarian leader Michael O'Leary, whose timing of orders of aircraft is nearly perfectly negatively correlated with the rest of the industry. O'Leary, whose story is portrayed in Matt Cooper's book *Michael O'Leary: Turbulent Times for the Man Who Made Ryanair*, certainly has a history of gathering the stones when everyone else is casting them away.

Let's Sniff Around

Evaluate the management's historical behavior with respect to cyclicality:

- Analyze their actions and communications in prior cycles. Assess whether they played offensive during expansion periods and defensive during contraction periods or vice versa. Review historical shareholder letters and MD&A sections in historical annual reports.
- If the manager's actions and communication cannot be analyzed based on publicly available information, then investors might even consider interviewing former colleagues of the CEO about his or her actions in prior roles.

16.3   Minimizing Analytical Risks Caused by Cyclicality

Correctly determining the degree of cyclicality and the direct risks it poses is one challenge. Dealing with the analytical risks associated with cyclicality is another. Even if you accurately estimate the degree of cyclicality, you can still make analytical errors due to cyclicality.

For a graphical illustration of what I mean by analytical risk of cyclicality, see Figure 16.1(b). The wavy fluctuating curve represents historical profit. Now, the question is: What is the cyclical-adjusted historical level of profits? We can't really know that. In the chart, I have drawn three lines: Cyclical adjustments 1, 2, and 3. We cannot determine which one is correct. There is uncertainty not only about our estimate of the future but also about the past and the present. This risk affects the way we assess the company's worth and its history of achievements.

Let's Sniff Around

Mitigate these analytical risks:

- Cyclically adjust financial metrics to gain a more transparent perspective of business performance and valuation.
- Avoid becoming too anchored to recent performance or short-term trends. Apply a haircut to recent financials during an economic expansion phase.
- When in doubt, use conservative estimates for growth rates, margins, and other key metrics. This provides a buffer against overestimating performance and earnings yield.
- Don't be afraid to deviate from the consensus. The consensus often overestimates during booms and underestimates during busts.
- Use determinants of cyclicality to determine industry cyclicality yourself instead of relying on dogmas about which industries are cyclical.

To exemplify analytical risks of cyclicality, let us consider Deere & Co., better known as John Deere. In its largest business segment, precision agricultural machines, Deere has relative scale compared to its competitors in the large US market (less so in certain other geographies). The density of its vast independent dealer network matters, and the relative local scale gives Deere a degree of local distribution network density scale advantage. Technology-driven increases in interconnectivity and data-sharing between machines and with a centralized farm control center (main providers of which are Deere and Monsanto) could cause an increase in "switching cost multiples" for farms with a suite of Deere products in the future. Large agriculture machines are perfect for AI implementation, and Deere was early to realize this. Among other actions, they purchased Blue River Technologies in 2017, leading them to develop the proprietary See and Spray precision weed control technology. It is also easier to make self-driving agriculture machines because they, unlike self-driving cars in unpredictable traffic, can just stop if they are in doubt. The company has begun to offer computational services to its customers on a per- usage or per-year basis. Technological improvements in Deere's machines have allowed farmers to increase their yields and reduce input costs such as fertilizer, pesticides, etc., which in turn has allowed Deere to increase the prices of its machines.

The company has long used a shareholder value added framework at a micro level of decision-making, keeping nearly everyone in the company accountable for the consumption of capital. I have spoken to a few investors who specialize in early-stage agricultural technology investing who all talk about the importance of getting their startups on the Deere API (application programming interface) platform. Given its scale and current position, the company may have a chance of benefiting from being at the center of an ecosystem of future agriculture technologies. The increase in complexity of controlling the machines and how they interact could over time potentially lead to some degree of expertise network effect. The company is valued around 11 times earnings as of this writing in January 2024.

This all sounds reasonable, but there is one problem. The company is cyclical, and undoubtedly the last couple of years have been good for farmers' economics as well as conditions for farmers to make discretionary equipment purchases. The agricultural equipment business has historically been very cyclical. Going back to the early days of the industry, as described in Niel Dahlstrom's *Tractor Wars,* equipment manufacturers had to procure steel, wood, and other price-volatile raw materials, often done 1 year in advance. Then, when selling the machines, the demand environment would depend on volatile and unpredictable weather and commodity prices. Looking at the determinants of cyclicality listed earlier in the chapter, agricultural equipment meets all of them.

In recent years, demand has been strong for agricultural equipment. Farm fundamentals have been good, and there has been a low interest rate environment. The operating income of Deere's agriculture equipment segments (i.e., Production and precision agriculture plus Small agriculture and turf operations) has gone from $2.5 billion in 2019, a year deemed "mid-cycle" by the company itself, to $9.5 billion in fiscal 2023, with margins more than doubled.

If I invest in Deere now, I risk that earnings get slammed in a near-term environment of higher interest rates and worsened farmer fundamentals but more important in my mind is the analytical risk of me being overly drawn into the story of productivity-driven growth and missing the underlying business performance and valuation picture by misunderstanding where the cyclically adjusted volumes, prices, margins, and capital returns would be.

As a long-term investor, I personally do not have a problem owning a cyclical business such as Deere if my overall portfolio exposure to cyclical risk is manageable, but I have a severe problem with the risk of me mis-analyzing its fundamentals and valuation.

To demonstrate the mitigation of the analytical risk, I selected a live example to avoid hindsight bias. The Management Discussion and Analysis (MD&A) in Deere's 10-K report details volume and price-driven sales growth by division. I summarized this in Table 16.1. The report's segmentation changed, splitting Ag and Turf into two distinct Ag segments, requiring me to infer certain data connections.

The table starts in 2019, which was considered a mid-cycle year. Equipment volumes grew by a 6% compound annual growth rate since 2019. For cyclically adjusted volume growth, it's cautiously assumed to be only around 2%, leading me to reduce volume growth by 4 percentage points annually from 2019. Price adjustments could be a product of both permanent higher machine efficiencies, new features, and cyclical scarcity, so we assume a cautious approach: halving the price growth, thus deducting 4 percentage points from pricing growth. This approach leads to an estimated reduction of $12.5 billion (22% of revenues) from the 2023 fiscal revenue. We can later replace the adjustment with a more qualified estimate including company or industry expert interactions. Also note that the adjustments are simplified by not considering changes in market share and geographical expansion.

The incremental equipment operating margin from 2019 to 2023 was 41% (calculated by dividing incremental operating profit by incremental revenue). For simplicity, let's use this to adjust profits. This adjustment reduces 2023 profits by $5.1 billion (42% of the operating profits from equipment operations).

Based on these assumptions, the profits from equipment operations have "only" grown by 17% per year since mid-cycle in 2019, which still

Table 16.1   Deere's Equipment Operations, 2019–2023

Total equipment operations	2023	2022	2021	2020	2019
Net sales	$55,565	$47,917	$39,737	$31,272	$34,886
Sales volume and other	[†]5%	[†]13%	19%	−11%	
Price realization	[†]12%	[†]11%	6%	3%	
Currency translation	[†]−1%	[†]−3%	2%	−2%	
Operating profit	$12,163	$8,349	$6,868	$3,559	$3,721
Operating margin	22%	17%	17%	11%	11%
Production and precision agriculture					
Net sales	$26,790	$22,002	$16,509	$12,962	
Sales volume and other	7%	22%	[‡]18%		
Price realization	15%	14%	8%		
Currency translation	0%	−2%	[*]2%	[*]−2%	
Operating profit	$6,996	$4,386	$3,334	$1,969	
Operating margin	26%	20%	20%	15%	
Small agriculture and turf operations					
Net sales	$13,980	$13,381	$11,860	$9,363	
Sales volume and other	−4%	8%	[‡]20%		
Price realization	9%	9%	5%		
Currency translation	−1%	−4%	[*]2%	[*]−2%	
Operating profit	$2,472	$1,949	$2,045	$1,000	
Operating margin	18%	15%	17%	11%	
Construction and forestry operations					
Net sales	$14,795	$12,534	$11,368	$8,947	$11,220
Sales volume and other	9%	3%	[‡]20	[‡]−20	
Price realization	10%	10%	5%	2%	
Currency translation	−1%	−3%	[*]2%	[*]−2%	
Operating profit	$2,695	$2,014	$1,489	$590	$1,215
Operating margin	18%	16%	13%	7%	

[*] Currency translations not provided for segments in 2021 and 2020 therefore used reported currency translation for whole equipment operations.
[†]: I calculated weighted averages.
[‡]: I calculated volumes as the residual of Price and Currency translation.
  Source: Data from Deere & Co. 10-K's filed with the SEC Fiscal 2019-2023.

remains impressive. As of early January 2024, Deere had a market capitalization near \$110 billion, likely around 14–16 times its cyclically adjusted cash earnings for the group.[4]

* * *

Few investors would forget to cyclically adjust a firm like Deere, which is so obviously cyclical. However, investors often overlook the need to cyclically adjust companies not necessarily perceived as cyclical, yet are exposed to cyclical growth, such as high-growth consumer internet companies. Cyclicality is not binary. There isn't a cyclical bucket and a noncyclical bucket. I think the analytical risk of cyclicality is greater for companies that are moderately or mildly cyclical because, in these cases, it's easier to forget about cyclical effects, but these businesses should also be cyclical adjusted. For it is written that thou shalt cyclically adjust!

Chapter 17

Other Risks

Things can go wrong. Things can get dicey. Things can turn sour, sour like pickles . . . even more sour than pickles. Things can get rough. Things can go haywire. Things can collapse into catastrophe or accelerate into apocalypse. Things can plummet into pandemonium . . . if you don't consider the things that can go wrong.

Concentrated investors are more vulnerable to company-specific risks. If you're reading this book, it's likely that, like me, you prefer to make high-conviction, concentrated investments. Consequently, you should be acutely conscious of company-specific risks. This chapter covers a few of these risks:

- Dependency risks
- Diversity of income streams
- Leverage risks
- Geopolitical risks
- Regulatory risks
- "Unknown" risks

17.1   Dependency Risks

Dependency risk is the fragility of a business that is too dependent on one particular thing outside its own control. This could be a distribution channel or platform over which it has no influence, a single supplier, a critical employee, a key customer, a specific input, or a favorable government contract. Dependency risk matters to investors because it makes the business fragile. Such vulnerabilities, if triggered, can have ramifications for profits and even jeopardize the existence of the business.

Some companies are like diamonds. They can withstand enormous pressure. Others are like soap bubbles at the mercy of the environment around them.

Consider the example of the game developer Zynga, known for its popular games like *FarmVille* and *CityVille*. All of Zynga's games were hosted on the Facebook platform. Players would buy virtual goods within Zynga's games using Facebook Credits, a virtual currency. If Facebook decided to change its algorithm or the way apps interacted with users, Zynga could (and did) see immediate impacts on its user engagement and revenue. Facebook eventually changed its take rate on virtual goods and started to diversify its game offerings, leading to a drop in Zynga's user base and revenue. In contrast, consider Amazon. It has a diverse product catalog that includes almost everything, from electronics and clothing to groceries. Amazon owns and controls its own sales channels and collaborates with countless suppliers worldwide to source products. They also developed their own logistics network to reduce dependence on external logistics companies. Amazon's massive customer base is diversified, spanning different demographic groups and geographies.

However, dependency risk is not exclusive to smaller firms. Some of the world's most valuable companies, such as Apple and NVIDIA, face considerable dependency risks; both companies depend on TSMC as their primary chip manufacturer. Similarly, Google relies on its agreement with Apple to remain the default search engine on iPhones. An interesting aspect of dependency risk is mutual dependence, as seen in the relationship between ASML and Zeiss. While both parties are vulnerable to unfavorable changes to the other, their interdependence spurs a strong incentive to support each other.

Let's Sniff Around

Analyze dependency risks:

- Identify dependencies in distribution channels, suppliers, a critical employee, a specific input, or a favorable government contract.
- Obtain customer concentration data, such as the percentage of revenues (and, if possible, gross profits and receivables) from the top 1, 5, and 10 customers. Any significant customer concentration should be paired with an evaluation of the potential impact and likelihood of adverse scenarios concerning those top customers.
- Quantify both the potential impact and the likelihood of any given dependency risk scenario. For each dependency, consider the long-term financial impact in worst-case situations, such as if a key supplier were to suddenly cease operations.

17.2   Diversity of Income Streams: Risks and Benefits

Diversification is the spreading out of sources of revenue and risks across customers, products, markets, and suppliers. Internal diversification means expanding existing operations by introducing new products, entering new geographies, or targeting new customer segments. External diversification means entering entirely new industries, often through acquisitions or partnerships, which may not have a direct connection to the company's existing core business.

Spreading out across different products, services, or markets can reduce the risk associated with the underperformance of any single area. Diversification can even out revenue streams and reduce the impact of seasonality or cyclicality in any single market or product. A diversified product portfolio may offer opportunities to cross-sell products or services or provide bundled solutions. However, diversification can also introduce its own risks. Managing a diverse range of products and markets can complicate management and decision-making. Overly broad diversification can cause a company to lose focus on its core competencies. This can cause decreased efficiencies of its original operations. Diversification through acquisitions can present challenges, including the integration of different systems, processes, and corporate cultures. Diversification can lead to internal conflicts if divisions compete for the internal resources or external customers.

An example of the benefits of internal diversification is Microsoft. Microsoft generates revenue through its Windows operating system, office productivity software suite, ERP and CRM enterprise software offerings, Azure cloud computing services, Xbox gaming consoles, HoloLens augmented reality glasses, Surface tablets, LinkedIn, Teams, Skype, Bing search engine, GitHub, just to name a few. This diversification makes Microsoft more resilient to adverse shocks in its business. However, it also exposes it to some of the risks associated with diversification. Despite this, Microsoft appears to have been successful in managing these risks, at least in the years leading up to the writing of this book. Microsoft exemplifies the benefits of well-managed diversification with decent synergy among many of its products.

Another example of a diversified business is ThyssenKrupp, especially evident before it initiated the process of segregating its business units. ThyssenKrupp's operations spanned a myriad of industries, including steel production, materials distribution, elevators, engineering for chemical plants, solutions and machinery for cement and mining, automotive parts, submarines, surface vessels, and bearings. Some of ThyssenKrupp's divisions, such as steel production and elevator systems, did not necessarily complement each other anymore. This lack of synergy meant that the conglomerate couldn't cross-sell or create efficiencies. Managing such diverse industries introduced inherent complexities, which resulted in cumbersome decision-making processes. Recognizing these challenges, ThyssenKrupp initiated a process of divesting and segmenting its business units.

Let's Sniff Around

Analyze the benefits and risks of diversification:

- Evaluate the extent to which different business units can share resources, customer bases, or technologies, or whether they can

benefit from combined marketing or distribution. Quantify the benefit.
• Consider the experience and track record that management teams have in handling diversified subsidiaries.

However, I don't believe that synergies are always essential. There are numerous examples of completely decentralized conglomerates with no synergies among subsidiaries that thrive because they are managed uniquely and capital is allocated in a way that enhances long-term value creation. Consider Berkshire Hathaway or Henry Singleton's Teledyne, for instance. Many decentralized conglomerates function exceptionally well. They often delegate almost full authority to the management of the subsidiary companies and focus primarily on overall capital allocation decisions.

Let's Sniff Around

Analyze risks specific to conglomerates:

• Evaluate management incentives and capital allocation skills using the methods described in Chapters 2 and 3.
• Specifically examine the delegation of authority and the extent of bureaucracy. Decentralized conglomerates often function well when they delegate full authority and are anti-bureaucratic.
• Estimate the headquarters costs and the degree of frugality at the conglomerate's top level. Typically, successful conglomerates have modest headquarters, frugal cultures, and low costs of the central organization.

To illustrate this, let us consider the Swedish conglomerate Lifco. It is radically decentralized. Unlike some high-performance historical decentralized conglomerates like Singleton's Teledyne, which exercised strict control over subsidiary cash usage, Lifco represents a remarkable case in not even making budgets for most subsidiaries. They delegate full authority to subsidiary managers when they are "self-driven rational profit-oriented subsidiary managers with the right incentives." With more than 7,000 employees, the firm doesn't even have a single centralized human resource person because Lifco believes every manager should take care of their people. They proudly tell investors that they intentionally do not try to achieve synergies. However, Lifco doesn't believe that decentralization itself is the key to being a successful conglomerate. Many companies claim to be decentralized, but they are not in Lifco's sense. These companies are still internally connected and have internal negotiations. The radical decentralization can work for Lifco only because it consists of highly differentiated companies, each with niche lucrative market positions. Every company has its own destiny in its own hands, which works well in specialized niches and makes the subsidiaries more adaptive. The radical approach of Lifco can work because of a distinctive culture as well as the readiness to act as a senior Lifco person (typically a former subsidiary CEO who has evolved into a broader Lifco role) who sits on the board as the chairman of every subsidiary and is principally ready to take over as

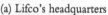

(a) Lifco's headquarters   (b) ThyssenKrupp's headquarters

Figure 17.1   A comparison of headquarters of two conglomerates.

Sources: (a) Courtesy of Lifco, (b) Tuxyso / Wikimedia Commons / CC BY SA 3.0.

operator at any time. Lifco's CEO Per Waldemarson once told me: "We are extremely hands off and extremely hands on," meaning that they usually don't interfere, but when they do, they really get involved. Lifco's central organization is almost nonexistent, and they proudly brag about it. Unlike most successful conglomerates, Lifco resides in a humble industrial building in the city of Enköping. The office is so frugally sparse that most people, upon seeing it, would hardly believe it is the headquarters of a successful public company.

I have spoken to the CEO, Per Waldemarson, a few times, and once I mentioned to him that he reminds me of the personal character traits described in William Thorndike's book, *The Outsiders* (as mentioned earlier, this seminal book discusses CEOs who excelled at capital allocation). Waldemarson's response surprised me, but upon reflection, it made perfect sense. He hadn't read the book yet but mentioned that many investors had said that to him. However, he wanted to make it clear that Lifco came up with this approach themselves, not inspired by others and not designed in a boardroom. His reluctance to accept this compliment is probably a product of the contrarian and self-assured personality that has made him such a successful conglomerate manager.

17.3   Leverage Risks

Financial leverage is the use of borrowed funds to finance a firm's operations, hoping to generate a return higher than the interest on the borrowed amount. While it can magnify equity returns, it also amplifies risks.

The greatest danger of leverage is the risk of bankruptcy. If a firm were to liquidate its assets, bondholders and other creditors would be paid first, often leaving shareholders with nothing. To avoid bankruptcy, a company facing financial difficulties due to debt servicing might resort to issuing shares to raise capital. Being forced to issue equity that dilutes the ownership of existing shareholders at inopportune times can annihilate shareholder value.

High levels of debt limit flexibility during challenging periods. When market conditions deteriorate or unforeseen challenges arise, a heavily indebted company may be forced to make suboptimal decisions. All debts eventually come due. When a company's debt matures, it needs to either refinance or repay the principal. Such refinancing can be challenging if interest rates have increased or if the company's creditworthiness has crumbled.

A combination of debt and unprofitability is a cocktail more dangerous than a Flaming Dr. Pepper. A firm that's both unprofitable and leveraged finds itself in a precarious position. The absence of profits means there's no internal cash flow to service the debt, making the firm reliant on asset sales or at the mercy of external financing sources. A rushed drive toward profitability could undermine its long-term competitive position.

While leverage can magnify equity returns, I prefer the downside protection and positive optionality that a strong balance sheet provides. Such a balance sheet—with minimal or no debt characterized by long-dated maturities, coupled with an ample cash reserve—offers the following benefits:

- Protection from downturns or unexpected financial crises
- The ability to reinvest in the business for growth or innovation without requiring external funding
- A strong balance sheet signals resiliency, deterring competitors from viewing the company as an easy target for aggressive tactics
- Flexibility to conduct share buybacks at opportune times when the share price is low
- Flexibility to make acquisitions or aggressive investments at the bottom of a cycle

Apple, in the latter half of the 2010s, serves as a prime example. With an immense cash reserve, it was significantly net cash positive. This liquidity allowed Apple to initiate the largest capital return program in history (in absolute terms). The company repurchased approximately half of its outstanding shares at a time when the stock traded at low multiples, and they knew they had a promising product pipeline. Without this substantial cash reserve, such an action would have been impossible.

It takes character to sit there with all that cash and do nothing. I didn't get to where I am by going after mediocre opportunities.

—*Charlie Munger in* Poor Charlie's Almanack[1]

Another classic example of maintaining low debt or holding cash, providing optionality for future opportunities, is Berkshire Hathaway. For instance, due to its conservative balance sheet entering the 2008 financial crisis, Berkshire was in an excellent position to capitalize on opportunities to invest in firms such as Goldman Sachs, General Electric, and Bank of America at favorable terms.

It's important to note that leverage risk isn't limited to the direct risks of debt. It also includes the analytical risks that might mislead investors. One potential pitfall is an over-reliance on leveraged expected IRRs or equity valuation multiples, neglecting the consideration of debt and its inherent risks. Personally, I lean toward evaluating unlevered expected IRRs, enterprise-value multiples, and enterprise-value cash flow yields. In my assessments, I approach debt as though it were equity. This methodology facilitates a direct comparison across companies and aids in evaluating return projections across multiple companies with varying debt levels. However, what you are actually purchasing is the equity; therefore, such an approach involves an intentional analytical error that is punitive to risk.

 Let's Sniff Around

Analyze leverage risk:

- Calculate debt-to-equity ratios, interest coverage ratios, the net debt to operating earnings ratios. Consider such metrics based on cash earnings, not just reported earnings.
- Evaluate maturity profile, maturity staggering, covenants, operational leverage, recourse provisions, and off-balance-sheet liability (pensions, lease obligations).

To mitigate the analytical risk of leverage you can:

- Use unlevered expected return metrics and enterprise-value multiples.

17.4   Geopolitical Risks

Geopolitical risk is the potential effects that political decisions, events, or conditions in a country can have on business operations. Geopolitical risk can stem from various sources:

- Changes in taxation, property rights, environmental regulations, or foreign investment rules
- Political instability, which can lead to disruptions in supply chains and operations, or even necessitate a complete exit from that market
- Government sanctions on imports, leading to reduced trade or investment
- Armed conflicts, which can disrupt business operations and result in the destruction of assets
- Nationalization of certain industries or assets, often without providing fair compensation to the owners
- Political decisions that impact a country's currency value

Sometimes, great businesses, or parts thereof, are located in places with such risks. The attention of the investment community to certain geopolitical risks fluctuates over time. At times, especially when recent events have brought a specific geopolitical risk to the forefront, valuations are impaired. At other times, it appears the investment community completely forgets about the geopolitical risk, often during extended periods of status quo. However, the geopolitical risk was always there. When such risks are at the forefront of investors' minds, the potential rewards from investing in an outstanding business with associated geopolitical risks might justify the exposure. Some investors might completely avoid geopolitical risks, while others have thresholds for the amount of geopolitical risk they are willing to accept at the portfolio level and only consider taking such risks when the potential rewards are exceptional.

An example of an outstanding company operating amidst geopolitical risks is Tencent, which has an integrated ecosystem and can be seen as a societal communication infrastructure layer in China. Moreover, it's a globally dominant player in gaming and a remarkable investor and capital allocator. It is led by a brilliant founder and meets most of the criteria mentioned in this book. However, no matter how exceptional Tencent is, one cannot ignore that its fate is intertwined with China's future geopolitical developments, especially for foreign investors.

Geopolitical risk is not confined to businesses headquartered in locations with such risks. For example, Apple generates 19% of its revenues in Greater China, its chips are made in Taiwan, and most of its hardware products are assembled by Foxconn in China. Therefore, Apple is exposed to potential reprisals from the tensions between the United States and China.

For some unfathomable reason, the market seems to price geopolitical risk based more on the address of a company's headquarters and less so on the location of its earnings and growth prospects.

 Let's Sniff Around

Analyze geopolitical risk:

- Identify geopolitical exposures in supply chain and end markets.
- Evaluate risks of regulatory shifts, political instability, sanctions, trade tariffs, conflict risks, expropriation threats, and currency volatility impacts.

17.5   Regulatory Risks

Regulatory risk is the potential negative impacts on a company due to changes in government regulations or policies. This can be in the form of changes in laws, regulations, or regulatory interpretations that impose additional costs, restrict operations, or make future prospects less predictable.

Sources of regulatory risk are varied:

- Public outcry over accidents, scandals, or crises, which can act as catalysts for regulatory modifications. For example, the 2008 global financial crisis led to a significant increase in regulation of the financial sector.
- A growing global emphasis on sustainability and environmental protection, leading to regulatory shifts, especially in sectors such as energy, manufacturing, and transportation.
- Emerging industries typically face more regulatory uncertainties than established ones. As these industries mature and become mainstream, regulations often become more standardized and predictable.

- Unions and advocacy organizations often push for regulatory changes that align with their interests.
- Monopolistic market characteristics often attract regulatory attention.

The coal industry was central to the energy sector and was a cornerstone of the industrial revolution. However, as the environmental effects of burning coal became more evident and environmentalism grew in prominence during the twentieth century, public sentiment began to shift. Additionally, coal mining was infamous for its worker safety issues. Governments started to prioritize clean energy sources over fossil fuels, in particular coal. They introduced stricter emission standards, making coal-fired power plants less economical to run. Some implemented carbon taxes. Governments provided subsidies and incentives for renewable energy sources such as wind, solar, and hydro. Some direct policies were aimed at closing or limiting the establishment of new coal mines.

As mentioned in Part II on competitive advantages, regulatory actions can sometimes be the driving force behind the erosion of an advantage. For example, the US Pacific Railway Acts of the 1860s, which supported the construction of the transcontinental railroad, specified the use of a standard gauge. Similarly, in the UK, the Gauge Act of 1846 mandated a standard gauge (4 feet 8 1/2 inches) for all new railways, influencing the spread of this gauge internationally. This eventually created interoperability between multiple railway networks, shifting the network effect away from owners of individual railway networks toward the broader ecosystem of railway networks.

Another example is the breakup of AT&T. Prior to its breakup, AT&T had a near-total monopoly on telephone service in the United States, including long-distance and local service. Other companies did exist, but they were often small, regional, and sometimes had to rely on AT&T's network to complete calls. In 1982, after a prolonged antitrust lawsuit initiated by the US government, AT&T agreed to divest its local exchange service operating companies, which led to its breakup in 1984.

Both IBM and Microsoft were subject to intense regulatory scrutiny over their monopolistic market power in the past, but both managed to avoid a major regulatory breakup. In recent years, regulators have turned their attention to major technology firms, all of which face regulatory risks.

Tighter regulations can diminish profits and lead to more bureau-cratic operations. However, they can also help established market leaders solidify their market position. This occurs if regulatory requirements render potential market entry for newcomers considerably less appealing.

For example, when ride-sharing companies like Uber and Lyft initially entered the market, they disrupted the traditional taxi industry, largely with limited regulatory oversight. Over time, as public sentiment shifted and governmental concerns grew over safety, competition, and driver background checks, these firms faced stricter regulations. While these regulations escalated operational costs and increased bureaucracy, they also raised barriers to entry for potential competitors. Consequently, in some countries, strict regulations have fortified the position of ride-hailing leaders, while in others where regulations are even stricter, they've made profitable operations nearly impossible.

Let's Sniff Around

Analyze regulatory risk:

- Assess the likelihood of regulatory scrutiny for monopolistic behaviors or market dominance.
- Consider determinants of increased regulation such as public influence, environmental and sustainability concerns, industry maturity, and advocacy and union pressure.
- Review the company's litigation and settlement history.

17.6 "Unknown" Risks

Attention! Attention! All readers, please remain calm and listen carefully. This is not a drill. I repeat, this is not a drill. There might be an issue with your book. We don't know what the issue is, or even if there is an issue at all, but it's possible that something is seriously wrong with the book.

Admittedly it is kind of paradoxical to label a section Unknown Risks in a framework for evaluating business quality. How can you evaluate something which is unknown? Have I begun to drift into madness at page 268?

What I am trying to point out here is that in investing and business, long-term outcomes are susceptible to unpredictable events—both good and bad—that have a major impact on the outcome and would have been difficult if not impossible to predict. An investment case has both known risks and unknown risks. Nobody has phrased the concept of unknown risks better than former US Secretary of Defense Donald Rumsfeld. He discussed the absence of evidence linking the government of Iraq with the supply of weapons of mass destruction to terrorist groups, in which he stated:

> Reports that say something hasn't happened are always interesting to me, because as we know, there are known knowns—there are things we know we know. We also know there are known unknowns—that is to say, we know there are some things we do not know. But there are also unknown unknowns, the ones we don't know we don't know.[2]

Perhaps some unknown risks are not 100% what Rumsfeld calls "unknown unknowns," but perhaps some of them are a bit more like what he calls "known unknowns." Perhaps there are some cases where we can have an idea that something unknown and unpleasant is more likely to happen than in other cases.

When we study business history, we can find many examples of adverse external events that decimated shareholder value and were more or less completely unexpected by both management and investors. It was not like we couldn't have perceived such a scenario in our imagination, but nobody really thought of that part of the outcome range until after it happened. Consider, for instance, the 2010 BP Oil Spill disaster. It occurred in 2010 when an explosion on the Deepwater Horizon oil rig led to a massive oil leak in the Gulf of Mexico. It became one of the largest environmental disasters in history. The BP oil spill was a result of a rare combination of technical failures, human errors, and regulatory shortcomings, making it an unpredictable and seemingly unlikely event until it happened.

Another example of a seemingly unlikely and unpredictable event was the Boeing 737 MAX disaster, where two flights crashed within 5 months (Lion Air Flight 610 crashed in October 2018, and Ethiopian Airlines Flight 302 crashed in March 2019). The accidents led to a worldwide grounding of the 737 MAX fleet and a major crisis for Boeing.

Other examples of unpredictable risks are earthquakes, floods, wild-fires, wars, drug recalls, product failures, use of nuclear weapons, and de-democratization of democratic states. We, as investors, totally neglect many types of rare and unpredictable risks in our assessments because they are so rare, unpredictable, and not fitting into our tools and methods for assessing them. But just because they are unpredictable and hard to analyze doesn't mean that we should not bother considering them. Contrarily, we should try to identify them and include them in our assessment of business quality and take them into consideration when we value businesses, construct portfolios, and evaluate overall business quality.

★ ★ ★

Chapter 18

Final Remarks

Throughout the book, I have described several aspects of quality, and for each of them, highlighted companies with exemplary characteristics related to the respective quality aspect. However, when applying the framework in practice, it becomes apparent that few companies score extremely high on all the mentioned aspects.

Furthermore, some of the aspects have a tendency to be inversely related. For example, you will often see that companies that have the ability to scale quickly with low marginal cost often score poorly in relation to some of the mentioned determinants of staying power. Companies that have had strong competitive advantages for a long time may also tend to have value extraction risk or counter-positioning risk.

Companies do not need to score extremely high on all parameters to be good companies. Look, for instance, at the list of the world's most valuable companies. Each of them scores high on many characteristics, but they all have some area where they do not score well. For example, many of the most valuable companies currently have pronounced regulatory risk. Some also have dependency risks, as mentioned.

One might have a tendency to be overly impressed by how well a company scores on given quality characteristics and then focus on this investment attraction. However, I believe it is more important to focus on

Figure 18.1 In a game of Top Trumps, it is better to have a card that is pretty good in all categories.

Source: Author's private photo collection.

the aspects where it scores poorly. That is where one should use one's analytical firepower. A good company is not necessarily one that scores exceptionally high on a single or a few of the mentioned aspects, for example, being countercyclical or having low marginal costs. In practice, **you are probably much better off with a company that may not score 10/10 on any parameters, but scores reasonably well on almost all parameters.**

I think of this like playing the card game Top Trumps (also known as Quartett; I had to step up my analogy game at the end of the book!). You might get excited about a card with one amazing feature, like a sports car with a lightning-fast top speed. However, in the game, it's usually better to have a card that's pretty good in all categories, not just one. Do not become paralyzed by overexcitement from the green flags; instead, dig a bit deeper when you encounter yellow flags.

18.1 Analytical Errors

When applying this book in practice, you will formulate hypotheses and gather empirical observations to evaluate whether these observations appear to support or cast doubt on your hypotheses. The arguments in investment analysis are known as inductive arguments, similar to those in empirical science, unlike the deductive arguments typically found in mathematics and philosophy. In the philosophy of science, it's widely recognized that inductive arguments cannot be conclusively evaluated by observations alone; they also depend on the background knowledge and assumptions used to interpret this data (technically known as "background theories").

Analytical errors can stem not only from the observations gathered but also from how these observations are interpreted. Just as a skilled empirical scientist must recognize that her conclusions hinge on both the data and her background theories, an investor must also be aware of this. It's impossible in investment analysis to derive neutral conclusions from data alone. We sometimes forget that our conclusions are a product of both the data and our background theories, and we may falsely believe that we draw conclusions neutrally from data. An investment analysis will always view the world from a specific perspective. **There is no such thing as a completely neutral investment analysis**.

The renowned twentieth-century philosopher Karl Popper, whose work significantly influenced the philosophy of science and scientists, believed that "real scientists" are always attempting to prove their own theories false. He contended that real scientists solely employ deduction, as falsification corresponds with deductive reasoning. Any argument adhering to the logical form, "If theory T is true, then we should observe O. We do not observe O. Therefore, theory T is false," constitutes a valid deductive argument. However, modern philosophers of science almost unanimously agree that Popper's logic was wrong.[1]

To falsify a theory, you actually need to make a lot of assumptions. But how do you know that those assumptions are true? Either because you have used induction to test those assumptions or because you have uncritically accepted them. Just as you can't do induction without background theories, so you also cannot do falsification without them. Nevertheless, I think that striving for Popper's ideal of falsification will help investors. Seeking to falsify your hypotheses, rather than justifying them, is a great way to force yourself to be attentive to evidence that might undercut your current point of view.

One should obviously recognize general human analytical errors such as confirmation bias and mistakenly equating correlation with causality. Additionally, I believe it's beneficial to actively—like a checklist—self-critique common logical error sources in each form of logical arguments, such as arguments from authority, analogy, anecdote, cause, and generalization. Most logical arguments in investment analysis are of these forms. Being self-critical of their respective plutonium-marinated pitfalls can help you improve the quality of your own analyses.

Figure 18.2   Even the most experienced pedestrians can slip on a banana peel if they are not observing the road. Similarly, experienced and sophisticated investors can make basic errors stemming from uncritically assuming central elements of the logical arguments behind their investment thesis.

Source: Original artwork by Henriette Wiberg Danielsen. © 2024 Simon Kold.

Furthermore, **writing down the 3 to 5 main hypotheses necessary for the investment to unfold as expected is advisable** for various reasons. It makes you more aware of their logical forms and the respective analytical risk of each. Also, it helps direct the focus of your empirical analysis to the most critical components of the case. An example is provided in the endnote.[2]

In the Appendix, I placed a section in which I review the common analytical risks of each form of logical argument. The goal here is not to provide a philosophy lecture about the impossibility of certainty, but rather to offer a practical checklist that you can apply to your own main arguments in practical analysis. To some readers, these sources of error might seem pathetically trivial. Nevertheless, intelligent and well-trained investors make them over and over again. As described in surgeon Dr. Atul Gawande's excellent book, *The Checklist Manifesto*, errors in complex specialized fields like medicine and aviation, committed by highly specialized surgeons or pilots, can be reduced by implementing simple checklists. Find my checklist, "Banana Peels of Inductive Logic," in the Appendix and use it to enhance the quality and durability of your own application of all the analyses outlined in the book.

18.2   Price Matters

The subject of "price paid for a business" has only been covered briefly in the book. Analyzing business quality and durability is only a subset of investment analysis. Just because the subject isn't covered much doesn't mean that this book claims that the perceived discrepancy between price and fundamental value is unimportant for investors. Of course it is extremely important. An investment analysis can never consist solely of an analysis of business quality. An investor who focuses only on quality ignoring valuation is like a juggling tightrope walker who soaked his legs in nerve-block serum.

However, it is clear that the longer the holding period, the less sensitive the return is to fluctuations in the difference between, for example, entry and exit multiples, because it is the per-share earnings growth in the long intermediate period that is the chief contributor to the long-term return. If a company is good and one is sure of it, then it will warrant a high price, and a high price can be justified. If one is fortunate enough to find a company where, based on empirical analysis of the determinants of quality, there is a high personal conviction in such quality, and at the same time is able to purchase this company at a price that is believed to be far below its fundamental value, then this is the optimal condition for a long-term investment. A low purchase price is also a guardedly good insurance against analytical errors one might have made in evaluating quality.

As mentioned in the introduction, the book is not intended to be limited to the discipline of "quality investing." Investors can use these frameworks to evaluate any company, including whether a subpar company, trading at low price relative to its book or liquidation value, has a higher quality than its price implies.

18.3   Predicting Quality

The frameworks outlined in the book collectively provide a unified framework for discussing overall business quality. However, it is important to distinguish between measuring current quality and predicting future quality.

Consider Amazon, for example. As of early 2024, the time of this writing, Amazon scores well on many aspects discussed in this book. Compare this to Amazon in 2003. I will go into detail shortly, but it seems undeniable that Amazon in 2003 had inferior quality than Amazon in 2024. Yet, investing in Amazon in 2003 was, at least based on the outcome, a much better investment than it likely will be in early 2024. This leads us to the question: Is it possible to predict future quality rather than merely measuring current quality?

I don't believe the framework is specifically designed for predicting future quality, but I do think it can be applied, with a bit of imagination, to theorize about future quality. Let's examine Amazon in 2003.

Those who have read Jeff Bezos' inaugural shareholder letter (which is recommended reading), along with other early Amazon shareholder letters up to 2003 (each ending with the unusual practice of including the first 1997 letter), will likely agree that Amazon scored well with regards to the frameworks presented for authenticity, decision-making time horizons, internal motivation, capital allocation vocabulary, genuineness, and reliability. I encourage you to study this yourself.

Considering the incentives discussed in Chapter 2, Amazon in 2003 appeared promising. Bezos gave himself an annual salary of $81,840, no bonus, no restricted stock units (RSUs), no options, and owned 27% of the company.

By 2003, Amazon had already established a practice of passing cost savings to consumers to subsidize growth and build competitive strength. This approach reduced the risks associated with value extraction discussed in Chapter 11. Here is a short excerpt from the 2003 10-K, which includes a remarkably concise description of the business strategy:

Business Strategy
Our business strategy is to offer our customers low prices, convenience, and a wide selection of merchandise.
Price
We endeavor to offer our customers the lowest prices possible. We strive to improve our operating efficiencies and to leverage our fixed costs so that we can afford to pass along these savings to our customers in the form of lower prices. We also enable third-party sellers to offer products on our site, in many instances alongside our product selection, and set their own retail prices.[3]

Amazon did indeed follow up on that strategy.

The degree of provenness of the business model would likely have been a key topic for investors using this framework to evaluate Amazon's quality and durability in 2003. At a high level, it wasn't certain that the business would be profitable or capable of operating profitably. However, the company had managed to grow significantly without the need to raise substantial capital or deplete its reserves, demonstrating its ability to self-finance much of the growth expansion (for context, the company had demonstrated first fiscal quarter GAAP profitable in Q4 2001). As discussed in Chapter 13, one could examine factors such as customer lifetime unit economics, the replicability of the business model when expanding into new categories and geographies, incremental margins, and other aspects mentioned in that chapter. These elements would serve as early empirical indicators of the provenness of the business model. In Table 18.1, I have included a few financial metrics for Amazon for the 5 years leading up to 2003. Although only reaching full-year consolidated breakeven at the operating profit level in 2002, it was worth noting that the business achieved a 16% incremental operating profit margin in 2003 while growing sales by 35%! Also note the modest equity dilution in the context of more than tripling revenues during the 5-year period, which spanned the dot-com bubble.

Table 18.1   Amazon.com Selected Financials from 1999 to 2003

Year	2003	2002	2001	2000	1999
Sales ($ millions)	$5,264	$3,933	$3,122	$2,762	$1,640
Year-over-year sales growth	34%	26%	13%	68%	169%
Income (loss) from operations	$271	$64	−$412	−$864	−$606
Operating income margin	5%	2%	−13%	−31%	−37%
Incremental operating income margin	16%	59%	125%	−23%	−48%
Weighted average shares outstanding (million)	395	378	364	351	351
Cash, equivalents, and securities (m)	$1,395	$1,301	$997	$1,101	$706
Gross debt (m)	$1,950	$2,291	$2,171	$2,144	$1,481

Source: Data from Amazon. (1998-2003). Form 10-K annual reports. U.S. Securities and Exchange Commission.

Amazon already had a diverse customer base, a diverse supplier base, and many product categories, but in 2003, it was relying on logistics partners. It was only much later that Amazon built out its own logistics network. Therefore, the dependency risk was higher then. Could one imagine that, as e-commerce penetration increased over the coming decades, a large online retailer (i.e., Amazon) would one day be able to vertically integrate? It wouldn't be unreasonable to attribute at least some probability to such a scenario.

This is also tied to Amazon's competitive advantage and reinvestment options. The opportunity to build out its own logistics network was an example of a "moat-widening opportunity." Looking at Amazon in 2003, one would have to imagine the future reinvestment options that would become available to the company with higher scale, market penetration, and smart management, to grasp the future competitive distribution network density scale advantage and attractive reinvestment options. This was, of course, not empirically evident in 2003, but I still think this demonstrates that the framework determinants can also be used in the context of theorizing about the future and evaluating emerging quality.

Amazon, as of 2003, would score pretty well with our frameworks for longer-term predictability of demand drivers, although less so for line of sight. In 2003, US e-commerce sales accounted for less than 2% of total retail sales, according to data from the US Census Bureau. The infrastructure, consumer trust, and internet adoption necessary for higher e-commerce penetration were still developing. However, it wouldn't have required much imagination to predict that such penetration would be significantly higher at some future point in time. It would be akin to the contemporary semiconductor example mentioned in Chapter 13. The exact extent would be hard to predict, but the fact that it was going to be "much higher" was certain.

I should, of course, note that almost no one could have predicted AWS and its wild success from the vantage point of 2003, so I will leave that out of the equation. However, I would mention that **in cases of exceptional management, there tends to be an asymmetry of unpredictable outcomes in favor of such management**.

One of the major concerns for an investor in 2003 using this framework would undoubtedly be Amazon's staying power: the intensity of competitive advantages, such as logistics capabilities, came much later; the industry was rapidly evolving; the adoption curve was steep; and cultural embeddedness was limited. But I believe that investors in 2003 could cling to the model's cost-effectiveness and, with a bit of imagination, to the predicted future cost-effectiveness. To be replaced by some newer model, that new model would have to be even more cost-effective than the low-price-obsessed Amazon e-commerce model. It would not be unreasonable to imagine a scenario in which the business would be so cost-effective that it could contribute to quite some staying power.

Perhaps the concern about staying power would have caused our imaginary historical investor friend to be more punitive in the valuation she would be willing to pay for Amazon at the time. Furthermore, she might not have appreciated the combination of debt and the short history of positive operating cash flows.[4]

In summary, I think no one could have comfortably predicted the extent of Amazon's wild success, but I do think that the discussions illustrate that the frameworks of the book can also be used to make judgements about the future quality of a business. They can be used as a scheme to logically argue for and against various future scenarios with increasing or decreasing quality.

* * *

Ladies and gentlemen. This is your author speaking. We have arrived at the end of the book. Please remain seated with your seatbelts fastened until the seatbelt sign has been turned off. Have a great day and a safe onward journey. I hope you enjoyed my book, my literary shrimp calzone. I hope it will not cause you tummy trouble, bowel blues, or draw thee into fray with Dowsers. I hope your fervor and thirst shall lead you on the path to a W.O.L.F. I hope I will one day meet you, shake your hand, and thank you. Thank you for reading the book. Thank you for hanging in there — soup to nuts—in spite of analogititis, checklistophilia, and other to-be-identified conditions. Thank you for gathering stones together: stones, coconuts, candles, pickles, soap bubbles, and tapeworm measurement tape. May you never be enslaved by the comfort of conformity, and may you always enjoy your pursuit of truth.

Appendix

Banana Peels of Inductive Logic

This list of Banana Peels of Inductive Logic contains the most common analytical errors for each of the main forms of logical argumentation used in investment analysis. While these errors may seem pathetically trivial, intelligent and well-trained investors repeatedly slip on them and fall to the ground. This justifies the use of the checklist regardless of its triviality!

Prediction Based on Past Experience

A prediction based on past experience relies on the implicit assumption that patterns observed in the past will continue in the future. It's a fundamental component of human reasoning and learning. The logical form is as follows:

> In all observed instances, when A occurred, B followed. Therefore, next time A occurs, B is expected to follow.

Consider this example: Brookfield's CEO, Bruce Flatt, has a long history of meeting ambitious multi-year targets given to investors. Therefore,

I expect that Brookfield will meet its ambitious multi-year targets presented at its recent investor day.

It is often reasonable to assume that something that has happened in the past will also happen in the future, and therefore, many investment-related arguments follow this form.

Evaluate your argument for analytical risks:
- **Survivorship bias:**[*] The analysis only considers examples that have "survived" a certain process, ignoring those that did not. It is common to assume that robust companies will remain robust, or that well-performing managers will continue to perform well, but this type of reasoning is vulnerable to survivorship bias.
- **Ignoring changing circumstances:** Changes in technology, market dynamics, regulatory environments, and consumer behavior can make past observations nonrepresentative for the future.

Argument from Cause

An argument from cause infers a causal relationship from instances where one event consistently follows another. It suggests that if event A (cause) regularly precedes event B (effect), then A may be causing B. This type of reasoning is based on observed correlation patterns. The logical form is as follows:

> Whenever A occurs, B occurs. Therefore, A is presumed to cause B.

Consider this example: Companies with high revenue retention rates often have high switching costs. Adobe has reported high revenue retention rates; therefore, I presume that their installed base of customers faces high switching costs.

---

[*]In WWII, statistician Abraham Wald observed a classic case of survivorship bias. Observing bullet holes in returning aircraft, the military initially planned to armor the most damaged areas. Wald pointed out that these planes had survived despite such damage, indicating noncritical areas. Instead, he recommended armoring the undamaged sections, reasoning these represented critical areas on planes that did not return.

Figure A.1   Uncritically assuming a causal relationship from observed patterns of correlation is like assuming that a mullet makes you good at ice hockey.
Source: Original artwork by Henriette Wiberg Danielsen. © 2024 Simon Kold.

Many investment hypotheses contain some kind of "catalyst" that causes the business to fare better and the investor community to realize its potential. Such hypotheses assume some kind of cause-and-effect relationship.

Evaluate your argument for analytical risks:
- **Ignoring confounding variables:** Failing to account for a third variable that is influencing both of the variables under consideration. This hidden variable can create an illusion of a direct causal link where none exists. In the example of retention rates and switching costs, confounding variables are good product offering, good customer service, and fair price.
- **Oversimplification:** Complex relationships are reduced to overly simplistic cause-and-effect statements.

Argument from Generalization

Generalization is a form of inductive reasoning in which one looks at specific instances or limited evidence and draws inferences about the entire class they represent.

The logical form of this argument is as follows:

Every observed instance of X has property Y. Therefore, all instances of X are assumed to have property Y.

For example, Steve Jobs, Bill Gates, and Jeff Bezos were all outstanding founder CEOs, therefore founder CEOs are generally good for investors.

Evaluate your argument for analytical risks:
- **Drawing conclusions from an insufficient number of observations:** The smaller the sample, the greater the chance that it does not adequately represent the larger population. It is not just that smaller samples have a greater chance of not representing the larger population, but also that they can lead to overestimation of effect sizes (making the results seem more significant than they are) and underestimation of variance (not showing how much individual cases differ).
- **Nonrepresentative sample:** Even with a sufficiently large sample size, generalizations can be misleading if the sample is not representative of the larger group. Consider survivorship or selection bias in the sample, such as inferring food delivery profitability from rich Gulf States with wealthy consumers and low salary migrant riders.
- **Assuming that what is true at one time will also be true in the future (temporal consistency):** This error involves uncritically assuming that patterns observed at one point in time will remain consistent in the future, overlooking changes in technology and consumer behavior, e.g., assuming that the cyclicality of an evolving industry is static over time.

Argument from Analogy

Argument from analogy is a form of reasoning in which a similarity between two or more things is used to suggest that what is true of one thing is also true of the others, especially in cases where the assertion is about an unknown. The logical form is as follows:

> Object A has properties X, Y, Z. Object B has properties X, Y. Therefore, it is likely that Object B also has property Z.

An example of this would be an argument such as this: AWS, Azure, and Alicloud are cloud computing businesses with significant scale in their respective niches and geographies. Since AWS and Azure have demonstrated high profit margins, it is likely that Alicloud will also achieve similar high profit margins.

As mentioned earlier, Apple's valuation in the second half of 2010 was dragged down by an analogous argument about hardware commoditization in case of Nokia and BlackBerry, ignoring the tiny confounding variables of switching cost, network effects, and proprietary OS capabilities.

Argument by analogy is very persuasive, as it is often intuitive and easy to understand. This makes it effective in articulating convincing arguments. However, just because an argument is persuasive does not mean it is true. This is admittedly a bit paradoxical to point out, given the excessive overuse of tacky analogies used by me throughout this entire book.

Evaluate your argument for analytical risks:
- **Overlooking relevant differences:** When focusing on similarities, you are prone to ignore differences between the compared entities, leading to a flawed conclusion. The market overlooked Apple's switching cost, app store network effects, and proprietary OS capabilities. The Alicloud example ignores competition from a state-owned enterprise (Huawei) and differences in service mix (SaaS/PaaS/IaaS).
- **Subconsciously giving weight to those observations that support the argument while ignoring those that do not:** Try to actively look for opposing evidence and speak to people with a negative view (competitors, short-sellers, ex-customers, etc.).

Argument from Authority

Argument from authority is a form of reasoning where a claim is accepted as true because of the credibility and expertise of the person asserting it. It's based on the reasoning that if someone who is perceived as an expert or authority in a certain field says something, then it must be true. The logical form is as follows:

> Expert E states that proposition P is true. Expert E is an authority in the domain related to P. Therefore, proposition P is likely to be true.

Consider the following example: A distributor interviewed during due diligence said that the target company's products are in far greater demand than those of its competitors. Since the distributor has great insights into market trends, it is likely that the target company will take market share from its competitors.

Evaluate your argument for analytical risks:

- **False consensus:** The opinion of a single expert is assumed to represent the consensus of the entire field. In reality, complex fields often have a diversity of opinions, and one expert's view may not accurately reflect the overall consensus.
- **Expert bias:** Even experts can possess personal biases that influence their judgment. A former employee who was fired is likely to be more negative, whereas most tend to portray their former employers in an overly positive light.
- **Inappropriate authority:** This occurs when the person cited as an authority may be knowledgeable or respected, but not actually an expert in the specific area relevant to the argument. For example, a former employee who worked in finance may help you understand a thesis of differential unit economics, but may give you a wrong answer when asked about employee retention rates.

Anecdotal Argument

An anecdotal argument is a type of reasoning that relies on personal stories or individual experiences rather than on broader, systematic research or hard evidence. It often involves using specific instances or examples to make a general point. The logical form is as follows:

> Individual instances or personal experiences X indicate Y. Therefore, Y is generally true.

While anecdotes can be compelling and easy to relate to, they are generally not considered strong evidence in logical argumentation.

Consider, for example, "My cousin walked past the Nike flagship store, and there was a long queue outside. Therefore, there is a great demand for its products."

Or, "I know a guy who used to work at Goldman Sachs, and he was a prick; therefore, the culture at Goldman Sachs is horrible."

Or, "My kids are not using Facebook anymore, so the social network is in decline."

Although anecdotal evidence is often looked down upon in scientific circles, it is widely used in investment decision-making—perhaps not intentionally, but certainly in practice. Sometimes anecdotal evidence is subconsciously used to overrule otherwise sound empirical work in decision-making situations. A recent personal experience can easily sway decisions (i.e., recency bias coupled with personal experience).

When you are out "scuttlebutting" in an unsystematic way, evaluate your argument for analytical risks:
- **Lack of representativeness (selection bias):** Obviously, anecdotal evidence often comes from nonrepresentative, selective observations. People may choose examples that support their viewpoint while ignoring a broader, more diverse range of experiences or data.
- **Emotional bias:** Personal stories, while emotionally compelling, can sway opinions. However, they do not necessarily reflect objective reality. This may seem trivial, but in reality, we often give undue weight to anecdotes due to their emotional impact, leading us to conclusions based on feelings rather than rational analysis.
- **Recency bias:** Don't let recent personal experiences cloud your decision-making. Just because something randomly occurred most recently in your memory doesn't make it more important than observations that happened at any other point in time.

Argument from anecdote is undoubtedly the form with the highest density of Banana Peels. Even worse, it is the preferred habitat of the most senior of dowsers.

About the Author

S imon Kold is the founder of Kold Investments, a Copenhagen-based investment firm. Prior to founding Kold Investments, Simon had a decade of investment experience at Novo Holdings, one of the world's largest investment organizations with EUR 150bn in total assets. At Novo Holdings, Simon had a leading role in 13 investments that collectively outperformed the MSCI World Index by 69 percentage-points cumulatively until August 2023 when he left Novo Holdings to establish his own fim.

In addition to holding an M.Sc. Finance degree at Copenhagen Business School, Simon has an unconventional background with a BA in Theology from the University of Copenhagen and experience as a stand-up comedian contributing to his writing "voice" and style (in his early 20s, Simon performed a niche style of deadpan one-liner stand-up comedy, making multiple TV appearances and completing a national tour in Denmark).

Notes

Introduction

1. Falsification is the principle that a theory or hypothesis should be considered scientific only if it is testable and can potentially be proven false by evidence.
2. However, there are also benefits in learning about new businesses, which can sometimes be overlooked if one focuses solely on the shortest path to rejection.

Chapter 1

1. Huang, J. (2003). *The importance of execution* [video]. Presented at Stanford eCorner. Available from: https://ecorner.stanford.edu/videos/the-importance-of-execution/.
2. Lauder, E. (1986). *Estée: A success story*. Ballantine Books, p. 54.
3. One cannot, of course, exclude the heavy debt load as a contributing factor to the decline. The company would likely have managed these challenges better had they not been heavily indebted.
4. Madrigal, A.C. (2013, May 16). Paul Otellini's Intel: Can the company that built the future survive it? *Atlantic*. Available from: https://www.theatlantic.com/technology/archive/2013/05/paul-otellinis-intel-can-the-company-that-built-the-future-survive-it/275825/ [accessed November 2024].
5. This information can be found in DEF14A Proxy Filings for US listed companies and in Annual Reports or Remuneration Reports for European listed companies.

6. They had all left, except for Jim Cavalieri, who has remained with the company to this day, although in a role that is not classified as a "named executive" since 2007.

7. Costco Wholesale Corporation, 2023 Annual Report, p. 7.

8. Korn Ferry. (n.d.). *Age and tenure in the C-suite* [online]. Available from: https://www.kornferry.com/about-us/press/age-and-tenure-in-the-c-suite [accessed January 10, 2024].

9. I recommend watching two interviews of Masayoshi Son that are available on YouTube: the 2014 interview where Charlie Rose interviews Masa, and the 2017 interview conducted by David Rubenstein.

10. Nietzsche, F.W. (1883). *Also sprach Zarathustra: Ein Buch für Alle und Keinen.* Available as ebook from: https://www.gutenberg.org/cache/epub/7205/pg7205.txt [accessed December 2023]. Quote translated from German by the author. The original line is, "Es ist immer etwas Wahnsinn in der Liebe. Es ist aber immer auch etwas Vernunft im Wahnsinn."

11. Calculated from the end of 1987 to the end of 2023, I deducted the treasury shares held for cancellation as listed in the 2023 annual report.

12. Bessembinder, H. (2018). Do stocks outperform treasury bills? *Journal of Financial Economics,* 129, pp. 440–457. The pre-publication document can be downloaded at https://ssrn.com/abstract=2900447. Bessembinder, H. (2023, June 17). *Shareholder wealth enhancement, 1926 to 2022* [online]. Available from: https://ssrn.com/abstract=4448099 or http://dx.doi.org/10.2139/ssrn.4448099.

Chapter 2

1. Berkshire Hathaway Inc. (2023). Corporate governance guidelines [online]. Available from: https://www.berkshirehathaway.com/govern/corpgov.pdf [accessed December 2023]. It states, "The Company does not purchase directors and officers liability insurance for its directors or officers."

Chapter 3

1. Talks at Google. (2015, October 22). *The Outsiders | William Thorndike | Talks at Google* [video]. YouTube. Available from: https://www.youtube.com/watch?v=D6h5bvxnBKk [accessed June 2023].

2. Thorndike, W. (2012). The outsiders: Eight unconventional CEOs and their radically rational blueprint for success. *Harvard Business Review Press,* p. 52. Comment: The MoIC assumes dividends reinvested and taxed at 40%. To be specific, the *Outsiders* states that a dollar invested with Singleton in 1963 would have been worth $180.94 by 1990.

3. Thorndike, W. (2012). The outsiders: Eight unconventional CEOs and their radically rational blueprint for success. *Harvard Business Review Press,* pp. 45–46.

4. According to Silverblatt, H. (2023). *S&P 500 buyback report Q2 2023*. S&P Dow Jones Indices.
5. The reason I argue that acquiring another company when one's own company has a low share price is disadvantageous is due to the higher opportunity cost relative to buying back one's own shares. Even if the acquisition promises a higher expected return than buybacks, it likely entails greater risk and uncertainty.
6. Contemporary examples of this would be Elon Musk of Tesla and Masayoshi Son of Softbank. I am not concluding that they are necessarily good capital allocators, but I mention them to provide examples of situations where there is undoubtedly significant career risk involved for investment managers if they were to invest in such eccentric, contrarian, unconventional CEOs, even though both have historically created enormous value.
7. Screenshot of the original document: https://www.sec.gov/Archives/edgar/data/1018724/000119312505070440/dex991.htm.
8. The list of indicators is inspired by comments made in Talks at Google. (2015, October 22). *The Outsiders | William Thorndike | Talks at Google* [video]. YouTube. Available from: https://www.youtube.com/watch?v=D6h5bvxnBKk [accessed June 2023].

Chapter 4

1. Rittenhouse, L.J. (2013). *Investing between the lines*. McGraw-Hill Education. This book is solely on the topic of evaluating shareholder letters.
2. Source: Thiel, P. (2014). *Zero to one: Notes on startups, or how to build the future*. Crown Business.

Part II

1. Mentioned in Letters to Berkshire Hathaway shareholders in 1986, 1993, 1995, 1996, 2005, 2007, 2008, 2011, 2012, 2013, 2014, 2015, and 2016.
2. For reference, capitalism's "creative destruction" is a term coined by economist Joseph Schumpeter in 1942 to describe the process of innovation and technological change that continuously revolutionizes economic structures from within, destroying old industries and creating new ones.
3. As discussed in Chapter 8, a brand is a nonexclusive type of advantage, and a direct competitor may possess an equally impactful brand targeting the same customer base. Additionally, switching costs only confer an advantage with respect to an existing customer base, not in capturing future customers. Moreover, there are industries, such as IT services, where despite minimal differentiation among players, many still achieve high returns on capital.
4. To be fair to Sonny Liston, I should add that he also suffered a shoulder injury in that first match. Muhammad Ali won the rematch with a controversial first-round knockout, known as the "phantom punch."

5. Typically calculated as net operating profit after tax divided by the average of invested capital at the beginning and the end of the period, with invested capital defined as the sum of net debt and book equity.

Chapter 5

1. This definition is from Porter, M.E. (1998). *Competitive strategy: Techniques for analyzing industries and competitors.* The Free Press, p. 7.
2. Porter, M.E. (1998). *Competitive strategy: Techniques for analyzing industries and competitors.* The Free Press, p. 7.
3. Greenwald, B.C. and Kahn, J. (2005). *Competition demystified: A radically simplified approach to business strategy.* Penguin, p. 42.
4. The benefit and barriers across all chapters in Part II are based on Helmer, H. (2016). *7 powers: The foundations of business strategy.* Deep Strategy.
5. The analysis can be complicated if competitors are privately owned and therefore do not disclose much information or there are divisions within large enterprises. In such cases, the relative scale must be assessed using the alternative sources of information discussed.
6. ABI's North American segment reported a revenue of $16.3 billion and EBIT of $5.3 billion (33% margin). Molson Coors doesn't report a North America segment, only an Americas segment, but we can infer from the 2017–2018 reporting segment change that the United States and Canada make up close to 100% of "Americas." This business is roughly half the size of ABI's North American operations in terms of revenue, at $8.5 billion. It had an EBIT margin of 14%. Heineken's Americas segment is not a good approximation of the North American market because the company is also active in the large South American beer market. Nevertheless, it is the best proxy we have based on public filings. Converted to USD, Heineken's Americas operations were roughly the same size as Molson Coors' and had an EBIT margin of 17%.
7. The Boston Beer Company had revenues of $2 billion and an EBIT margin of 38%.
8. The analysis of prohibitive costs in the ABI vs. Molson Coors example is a bit tricky, if it has to be done solely based on data from the 10-Ks. Molson Coors reports volume for their entire group, which is 20% larger than their Americas segment. Thus, when comparing metrics of revenue and cost per hectoliter, we are not comparing apples to apples. ABI's North American cost per hectoliter (hl) is lower than Molson's, but ABI's revenue per hl is higher, which could be explained by differences in geography (and associated variances in excise taxes) and product mix that we would not want to influence our analysis. Therefore, it becomes analytically difficult to alter the P&L of Molson Coors as described previously.

A simpler approach is to observe the market prices of the main mass-market beers of both breweries in the US market, which are roughly the same. From the financial statement analysis of Molson Coors, we can infer that their return on

assets in the Americas segment has been below 5% for the past 3 years, and the
return on capital for the group is less than 4% on average over the past 3 years.
If the incremental margins were the same, then this would point to prohibitive
costs because that would not be an attractive use of capital.

However, we note that Molson Coors Americas' volumes have decreased in
recent years, indicating they have unutilized production capacity. This could hint
at higher incremental margins if they were to take market share from ABI.
However, we would also need to consider the ROI of marketing expenditures
to achieve this. The next step in the analysis would be to speak with the Investor
Relations department of Molson Coors about these topics. We would likely
conclude that, while there are not perfect prohibitive costs, the expected financial returns for Molson Coors to aggressively compete against ABI may not be
that great.

9. The YoungHamilton Substack has a great post about Cintas' route density advantage: younghamilton. (2023). AGB 2022.3—Cintas (CTAS). *Analyzing Good
Businesses* [online]. Available from: https://yhamiltonblog.substack.com/p/agb-
20223-cintas-ctas [accessed January 2024].
10. If this distribution efficiency metric is unattainable, explore alternative metrics
to measure differential distribution costs, such as a percentage of revenues.
11. Porter, M.E. (1998). *Competitive strategy: Techniques for analyzing industries and
competitors.* The Free Press, p. 280.
12. Porter, M.E. (1998). *Competitive strategy: Techniques for analyzing industries and competitors.* The Free Press, p. 279.
13. This definition is from Porter, M.E. (1980). *Competitive strategy: Techniques for
analyzing industries and competitors.* The Free Press, p. 9.
14. This term is an adverbial adaptation of "lollapalooza effect," a concept introduced by Charlie Munger to describe the powerful compounding effect that
results from the combination of multiple beneficial factors.

Chapter 6

1. Tirole, J. (1988). *The theory of industrial organization.* The MIT Press, p. 21.
2. Some examples are inspired by Belleflamme, P. and Peitz, M. (2015). *Industrial
organization: markets and strategies.* Cambridge University Press, though not
directly cited.
3. Available from: https://www.sec.gov/Archives/edgar/data/1650372/00010474
6915008450/a2226437zf-1.htm.

Chapter 7

1. Available from: https://archive.org/details/americantelephoneandtelegraphan
nualreports/att1908/page/n23/mode/2up.

2. The benefits and barriers across all chapters in Part II are based on Helmer, H. (2016). *7 powers: The foundations of business strategy*. Deep Strategy.

3. If the added utility of more users is potent, then it is likely to create concentrated industries, with the larger players holding a significant market share. For instance, if you were considering a domestic stock exchange, you would understand that domestic stock exchanges possess strong local network effects. You have observed that, in most countries, the leading domestic stock exchange has gathered a massive market share lead. Such an observation can say something about the incremental utility for a similar business in another geography.

4. The discussion of utility curve flatness as a function of user preference variation is inspired by comments made in the podcast episode: Gilbert, B. and Rosenthal, D. (Hosts). (2022, April 5). Platforms and power (with Hamilton Helmer and Chenyi Shi) [Audio podcast episode]. *Acquired* [online]. Available from: https://www.acquired.fm/episodes.

5. For instance, in the ride-hailing situation, if you, as a passenger, only have to wait 2 minutes for a ride from the leading ride-hailing service but wait 4 minutes for the competing service (due to a lower local driver supply), then waiting 4 minutes might be good enough. You don't want to pay more just to save 2 minutes. You would have paid more to save 10 minutes, but not 2. Now, for job seekers using the classifieds service, most of them want to find the perfect job. For most, it is not satisfying to review only 7 out of 10 possible positions if they could easily review all 10 on the leading classifieds. For employers, who are the paying side of the network, it is often not good enough to only reach a subset of the potential candidates that could have been reached, because each candidate is unique. What is "transacted" across a job classifieds network is not a commodity. For these reasons, a job classifieds service would, all other factors such as multi-homing being equal, have a much longer runway before reaching the "flat part of the curve" illustrated in Figure 7.3(c).

6. ... --- ... .-. ... .--. (SOS, RIP). (1999, 21 January). *Economist*.

7. Tirole, J. (1988). *The theory of industrial organization*. MIT Press, p. 405.

8. Intuitive. (n.d.). *Clinical evidence* [online]. Available from https://www.intuitive.com/en-us/about-us/company/clinical-evidence [accessed April 6, 2024].

9. This definition is from the website nfx.com. The distinction between platforms and marketplaces is also inspired by that site.

10. This blog post has a great section focusing on the evaluation of marketplaces. Jin, L. and Coolican, D. (2018). 16 ways to measure network effects. *Andreessen Horowitz* [online]. Available from: https://a16z.com/16-ways-to-measure-network-effects/ (Accessed: October 2023).

11. Belleflamme, P. and Peitz, M. (2015). *Industrial organization: Markets and strategies*. Cambridge University Press.

Chapter 8

1. Helmer, H. (2016). *7 powers: The foundations of business strategy*. Deep Strategy.
2. I differentiate "luxury" from premium brands: Luxury brands cater to a niche market, offering exclusive, limited, and rare products or experiences. They're frequently associated with prestige and timelessness, and expression of wealth. On the other hand, premium brands target a broader audience, offering products that, while more accessible, still showcase elevated quality and design. These premium products provide superior quality or features compared to mass-market alternatives, thereby justifying a higher price point.
3. Wetlaufer, S. (2001). The perfect paradox of star brands: An interview with Bernard Arnault of LVMH. *Harvard Business Review*, October.
4. Sharp, B. (2010). *How brands grow: What marketers don't know*. Oxford University Press.

Chapter 9

1. This term is also used a lot in Porter, M.E. (1998). *Competitive strategy: Techniques for analyzing industries and competitors*. The Free Press.
2. These categories are from Porter, M.E. (1998). *Competitive strategy: Techniques for analyzing industries and competitors*. The Free Press, p. 11.
3. I had the pleasure of representing Novo Holdings as the chairman of the Nomination Committee of Invisio.

Chapter 10

1. It should be noted, however, that the price increases of these bundles were also the result of content owners exercising their pricing power, which the cable companies subsequently passed on to consumers.
2. Costco's reluctance to raise the price of their $1.50 hot dog and soda deal has become the epitome of their philosophy.
3. Full table and commentary are available at https://www.berkshirehathaway.com/letters/1984.html
4. The mention of US railroad's pricing power in this work is believed to have been influenced by a video interview titled "Manual of Ideas Interview—Josh Tarasoff." The original video is no longer available; however, an unauthorized version can be found online at https://www.dailymotion.com/video/x35p1b2. The author does not endorse the unauthorized distribution of copyrighted material but references this link for informational purposes due to the unavailability of the original source.

Chapter 11

1. Assuming an error-corrected qubit can be manufactured.
2. Johnson, W. (2014). *Junk to gold: From salvage to the world's largest online auto auction.* WestBow Press.
3. Jackson, B. (2008). *Fuel efficient freight trains?* [online]. Available from: https://www.factcheck.org/2008/07/fuel-efficient-freight-trains [accessed October 2023].
4. I couldn't find empirical studies of the Lindy effect in relation to companies, so this is based on common sense logic only!
5. This article, which specifically mentions LSE, was a source of inspiration for me regarding the Lindy effect as a source of staying power: Bullock, J. (2022). *The triumph of experience over hope* [online]. Lindsell Train. Available from: https://www.lindselltrain .com/application/files/3516/6981/1044/The_Triumph_of_Experience_ Over_Hope_-_November_2022.pdf [accessed June 2023].

Chapter 12

1. Clark, D. (2017). *The Tao of Charlie Munger.* Scribner, p. 41. This was originally said by Munger at the Berkshire Annual Meeting, 2003.
2. This terminology originates from the 2014 and 2015 Salesforce.com Investor Day. You can find the slides and audio from the original webcast online.

Chapter 14

1. Fabless semiconductor companies design microchips but contract out their production rather than owning their own factories.

Chapter 15

1. The reported operating expenses for the fiscal year 2008 were $5 billion, but I have excluded a transitory $1.4 billion litigation provision in 2008 and a transitory $900 million litigation provision in 2023, to provide a more accurate representation of the underlying incremental margin development.

Chapter 16

1. Proverbs 24:16. (That is an important reference. You don't want to be accused of plagiarizing the Bible.)
2. Chancellor, E. (2015). *Capital returns: Investing through the capital cycle: A money manager's reports 2002–15.* Palgrave Macmillan, p. 3.

3. Ecclesiastes 3:5.
4. In the November 2023 earnings call, they express that they expect a mid-teens percentage decline in demand in 2024, but that 2024, for which they have just provided FY2024 $7.75–8.25 billion net income financial guidance, represents "a good proxy for mid-cycle" and that they "expect to hold the structural gains in profitability achieved over the last few years."

Chapter 17

1. Munger, C.T. (2023). *Poor Charlie's Almanack: The essential wit and wisdom of Charles T. Munger*. Edited by P.D. Kaufman. Stripe Press.
2. Rumsfeld, D. (2002, February 12). Department of Defense news briefing [speech]. U.S. Department of Defense.

Chapter 18

1. Some phrases in the section are inspired by this YouTube mini-lecture on Karl Popper: Gijsbers, V. [Leiden University—Faculty of Humanities]. (2017). *Chapter 1.4: Karl Popper and the logic of falsification* [video]. YouTube. Available from: https://www.youtube.com/watch?v=XlFywEtLZ9w.
2. For instance, an investment in Alphabet today may emphasize the hypotheses that (1) the accumulated regulatory risks will not significantly impair the business, (2) the counter-positioning risk posed by Google Search's huge profit center will neither hinder their responses to emerging AI language models nor alter their monetization model for search, (3) the risks posed by a rapid industry technological change can be deemed insignificant with reasonable certainty giving Google sufficient staying power, (4) the network effects of Google Search and YouTube are sufficiently strong to fend off competition from Microsoft and other competitors, and (5) the company will allocate its capital in a way that maximizes long-term value per share.
3. Amazon.com 2003 Form 10-K annual report.
4. For context, the majority of Amazon's nearly $2 billion in gross debt was composed of two convertible bonds with fixed interest rates. These were issued in 1999 and early 2000 and were due in 2009 and 2010, respectively.

List of Companies Profiled

Page numbers followed by *f* and *t* refer to figures and tables, respectively.

Index

Page numbers followed by *f* and *t* refer to figures and tables, respectively.